ACT!® 4 For Windows® For Dummies®

Cheat Sheet

Setting ACT! Preferences

All of your default settings are selected in ACT!'s Preferences dialog box, which you open by selecting Edit⇨Preferences from the menu bar. The following are some of the selections you can make by clicking on the many tabs of the Preferences dialog box.

General tab

- ✔ Select your word processor
- ✔ Select move-between-field keys
- ✔ Select default file locations

Colors and Fonts tab

- ✔ Select ACT! windows to customize
- ✔ Select font settings
- ✔ Select text and background colors

Calendar tab

- ✔ Select the day of week to start on
- ✔ Select Day and Week calendar increments
- ✔ Select Day and Week calendar starting times

Scheduling tab

- ✔ Select automatic rollover for calls, meetings, and to-dos
- ✔ Set default priorities, alarm lead times, durations
- ✔ Set the appearance of cleared activities

E-mail tab

- ✔ Confirm when deleting messages
- ✔ Determine initial text for e-mail messages
- ✔ Create history when sending e-mail

Synchronization tab

- ✔ Set an auto-synchronization schedule
- ✔ Display a synchronization reminder
- ✔ Set modem properties

Names tab

- ✔ Select first name prefixes
- ✔ Select last name prefixes and suffixes
- ✔ Select the name that appears in the Salutation field

Startup tab

- ✔ Select default Contact and Group window layouts
- ✔ Select a startup database
- ✔ Select a macro to run on startup

Dialer tab

- ✔ Set up the dialer and select your modem
- ✔ Enable lookup with caller ID
- ✔ Set the start timer automatically on outgoing calls

...For Dummies: #1 Computer Book Series for Beginners

ACT!® 4 For Windows®
For Dummies®

Cheat Sheet

Defining ACT! Fields

In ACT!'s Define Fields dialog box (Edit⇨Define Fields), you select the attributes that apply to each field. The following are some of the many things you can do by selecting the tabs inside the Define Fields dialog box:

Fields tab

- ✔ Select the Record type — Contact or Group — that you want to modify

Attributes tab

- ✔ Change a field's name
- ✔ Set a field's default values
- ✔ Select a character type
- ✔ Set field entry rules
- ✔ Change a field's size
- ✔ Specify the appearance of data in a field
- ✔ Make a field a Primary field
- ✔ Make a field a History field
- ✔ Block synchronization for selected fields

Drop-Down tab

- ✔ Enable drop-down menus
- ✔ Add items and descriptions to drop-down menus

- ✔ Allow drop-down menu editing
- ✔ Show/hide descriptions
- ✔ Import/export drop-down lists

Triggers tab

- ✔ Select a program to launch when a field is entered
- ✔ Select a program to launch when a field is exited

Advanced tab

- ✔ Create a new index
- ✔ Select the sort order of the index
- ✔ Enable duplicate checking
- ✔ Select the criteria for duplicate checking
- ✔ Enable transaction logging
- ✔ Allow history editing

Scheduling Activities

In ACT!, you schedule activities from the Schedule Activity dialog box. To access this dialog box, do one of the following:

- ✔ Click the Call, Meeting, or To-do buttons.
- ✔ Choose Contact⇨Schedule [Call, Meeting, or To-do] from the menu bar, or choose the Schedule command after right-clicking with your mouse.
- ✔ Press Ctrl+L for a call, Ctrl+M for a meeting, or Ctrl+T for a to-do.
- ✔ Drag and drop a contact from the Contact window to the Day, Week, or Month calendar.
- ✔ Drag and drop the contact whose contact record is currently displayed in the Contact window onto the Mini calendar. You bring up the Mini calendar by pressing F4.

...For Dummies: #1 Computer Book Series for Beginners

ACT!® 4 FOR WINDOWS® FOR DUMMIES®

by Jeffrey J. Mayer

IDG Books Worldwide, Inc.
An International Data Group Company

Foster City, CA ♦ Chicago, IL ♦ Indianapolis, IN ♦ New York, NY ♦ Southlake, TX

ACT!® 4 For Windows® For Dummies®

Published by
IDG Books Worldwide, Inc.
An International Data Group Company
919 E. Hillsdale Blvd.
Suite 400
Foster City, CA 94404
www.idgbooks.com (IDG Books Worldwide Web site)
www.dummies.com (Dummies Press Web site)

Library of Congress Catalog Card No.: 98-84964

ISBN: 0-7645-0282-4

Printed in the United States of America

10 9 8 7 6 5 4 3 2 1

1B/RX/QU/ZY/IN

Distributed in the United States by IDG Books Worldwide, Inc.

Distributed by Macmillan Canada for Canada; by Transworld Publishers Limited in the United Kingdom; by IDG Norge Books for Norway; by IDG Sweden Books for Sweden; by Woodslane Pty. Ltd. for Australia; by Woodslane Enterprises Ltd. for New Zealand; by Longman Singapore Publishers Ltd. for Singapore, Malaysia, Thailand, and Indonesia; by Simron Pty. Ltd. for South Africa; by Toppan Company Ltd. for Japan; by Distribuidora Cuspide for Argentina; by Livraria Cultura for Brazil; by Ediciencia S.A. for Ecuador; by Addison-Wesley Publishing Company for Korea; by Ediciones ZETA S.C.R. Ltda. for Peru; by WS Computer Publishing Corporation, Inc., for the Philippines; by Unalis Corporation for Taiwan; by Contemporanea de Ediciones for Venezuela; by Computer Book & Magazine Store for Puerto Rico; by Express Computer Distributors for the Caribbean and West Indies. Authorized Sales Agent: Anthony Rudkin Associates for the Middle East and North Africa.

For general information on IDG Books Worldwide's books in the U.S., please call our Consumer Customer Service department at 800-762-2974. For reseller information, including discounts and premium sales, please call our Reseller Customer Service department at 800-434-3422.

For information on where to purchase IDG Books Worldwide's books outside the U.S., please contact our International Sales department at 650-655-3200 or fax 650-655-3295.

For information on foreign language translations, please contact our Foreign & Subsidiary Rights department at 650-655-3021 or fax 650-655-3281.

For sales inquiries and special prices for bulk quantities, please contact our Sales department at 650-655-3200 or write to the address above.

For information on using IDG Books Worldwide's books in the classroom or for ordering examination copies, please contact our Educational Sales department at 800-434-2086 or fax 817-251-8174.

For press review copies, author interviews, or other publicity information, please contact our Public Relations department at 650-655-3000 or fax 650-655-3299.

For authorization to photocopy items for corporate, personal, or educational use, please contact Copyright Clearance Center, 222 Rosewood Drive, Danvers, MA 01923, or fax 978-750-4470.

is a trademark under exclusive license to IDG Books Worldwide, Inc., from International Data Group, Inc.

About the Author

Jeffrey Mayer is one of the country's foremost authorities on time management and a heavy-duty ACT! user. For a living, he helps busy people get organized, save time, and become more productive. Jeff's claim to fame is his "clean desk" approach to time management. *USA Today* dubbed him "Mr. Neat, the Clutterbuster."

He walks into an office that looks like a toxic waste dump — with piles of paper strewn all over the place — and in two hours the desktop looks like the flight-deck of an aircraft carrier. He throws so much away that the wastebasket is overflowing and spilling onto the floor. All that remains are a handful of file folders, a pad of paper, and a telephone. Everything else is neatly filed away.

Long ago, Jeff realized that if everybody were better organized, they could take more control over their day and would have more time to focus on their most important work. At the end of the work day, then they could leave the office, go home, and spend more time with their family and friends.

Jeff's clients realize that time is money, and Jeff's able to help them convert wasted time into time that can be used more efficiently, effectively, and profitably. Jeff's specialty is in teaching people how to improve their follow-up systems, and there's no better program than ACT!. With a good follow-up system, a person is able to spend more time working on the things that are important, instead of the things that keep him or her busy. That's why Jeff loves ACT! so much.

Since the founding of his Chicago-based consulting firm, Mayer Enterprises, he has helped more than a 1,500 men and women (many are top executives at *Fortune* 500 Companies) get organized and use their time more effectively.

Jeff's been interviewed by almost every major newspaper and magazine in the United States, including *The Wall Street Journal, The New York Times, Newsweek, People, Forbes, Business Week,* and *Fortune.* And he has been interviewed on hundreds of radio and television programs across the United States, including the *The Today Show, American Journal,* CNN, CNBC and ABC News.

Jeff is the publisher of the *ACT! in ACTion* newsletter. If you would like a free trial subscription, complete the coupon at the back of this book.

If you would like Jeff to speak at your next business meeting, conference, or convention, you can reach him at Mayer Enterprises, 50 East Bellevue Place, Suite 305, Chicago IL 60611. His e-mail address is jeff@actnews.com.

Dedication

This book is dedicated to my good friend Bill Fletcher, who passed away in the spring of 1997. Bill was the technical consultant for my *ACT! 3 For Windows For Dummies* book, and his tips, suggestions, and comments helped to make it a great book. Bill went through my manuscript with a magnifying glass, offering his insights about how a user can get more out of ACT!.

When it came to ACT! and sales force automation, Bill was a genius! He was an absolute wizard at customizing ACT!'s contact screen. He then used that information to perform custom lookups and create reports. He knew more about how to turn ACT! into a money machine than anybody I've ever met.

During the brief time I knew Bill, I learned a phenomenal amount about how to use ACT!. Bill's help and insight have been invaluable. Bill founded and ran the San Francisco Bay Area ACT! Users group.

From those of us in the ACT! family, we miss you.

Other Books by Jeffrey J. Mayer

If You Haven't Got the Time to Do It Right, When Will You Find the Time to Do It Over?

Find the Job You've Always Wanted in Half the Time with Half the Effort

Winning the Fight Between You and Your Desk

Time Management For Dummies

Time Management For Dummies Briefcase Editon

ACT! 3 For Windows For Dummies

Author's Acknowledgments

There are many people I would like to thank and acknowledge for their help and contributions for the creation of this book.

I want to congratulate Sanjiv Bhargava, Director of Development; Dale Elliot, Development Manager; Michaela Gubbels, Sr. Product Manager; and Ryan Rosenberg, Director of Product Management; for a job well done.

Ryan was responsible for creating, developing, and bringing us ACT! 3.0. ACT! 3.0, whose code name was "Picard — The Next Generation," had been Ryan's baby since the inception. He gave three years of his life to ACT! 3.0 and has spent the past 18 months working very closely with Michaela on the development of ACT! 4.0. Ryan has helped me with all of my *ACT! For Windows For Dummies* books, and is a very dear friend.

Michaela — who has become a good friend over the past few months — was responsible for creating, developing, and bringing us ACT! 4.0. She was also my contact person when I had ACT! questions. It would have been impossible for me to complete this book without her help and assistance. Thank you.

Dale was responsible for developing ACT! 4.0, and is a very dear friend. Dale was my technical liason for my *ACT! 3 For Windows For Dummies* book, and I couldn't have written that book without his help and assistance. Every time I had a question, or two, or three, about how some feature was supposed to work, I gave Dale a call. (And before we knew it, he had given me an hour of his time.) If he didn't know the answer, he always got back to me very quickly.

Sanjiv, ACT!'s Director of Development for ACT! 3.0 and ACT! 4.0, has skill-fully coordinated the creation of two great products.

Ryan, Michaela, Dale, and Sanjiv all deserve a hearty round of applause for a job well done. On behalf of all ACT! users, thank you.

I would also like to thank Minette Norman and Carla Martin for their contri-butions in the creation of this book.

I would also like to thank Linda Keating for all of her help, support, and encouragement over the past few years. Linda was the technical reviewer for this book, and her thoughts and comments have been incorporated into this book. When it comes to database marketing, Linda is brilliant. You can reach Linda at JL Technical, Palo Alto, CA. Her phone is 415-323-914, and her e-mail address is linda@jltechnical.com. You can also visit her Web site at wwwl jltechnical.com.

A number of ACT! Certified Consultants have provided me with lots of useful information. If you have some questions on ACT!, I'm sure they can answer them. These helpful people include Ken Anderson of Lakeville, MN, 612-733-7586; Steve Chipman of San Rafael, CA, 415-256-1155; Steve Del Grosso of Boston, MA, 888-848-2658; Andy Kaplan of Charlotte, NC, 704-593-1997; Lon Orenstein of Dallas, TX, 800-238-0560; Bud Rice of Byron, CA, 510-727-6366; and Rich Spitz of Mamaroneck, NY, 914-698-7410.

And I would like to thank my editor and good friend, Tim Gallan, for all of his help, assistance, encouragement, and patience during the four years we've been working together. We started working together in the fall of 1994 when I wrote my bestselling *Time Management For Dummies*. Then we did *Time Management For Dummies Briefcase Edition* and *ACT! For Windows For Dummies*. And now we've completed *ACT! 3 For Windows For Dummies* and *ACT! 4 For Windows For Dummies*. Tim, you made everything much easier for me and helped me write five great books. It's been a pleasure working with you. (I'm looking forward to working with you on the *ACT! 5 For Windows For Dummies* book.)

And finally, I would like to thank the two women in my life, my wife Mitzi and my daughter DeLaine, for their love, support, and encouragement during the four months it took me to complete this book. They left me alone on the weekends so that I could write. And they didn't ask too many questions about why I was sitting at the computer at 4:00 a.m. on a Saturday or Sunday morning. I promise to make less noise in the future.

Publisher's Acknowledgments

We're proud of this book; please register your comments through our IDG Books Worldwide Online Registration Form located at http://my2cents.dummies.com.

Some of the people who helped bring this book to market include the following:

Acquisitions, Development, and Editorial

Senior Project Editor: Tim Gallan

Acquisitions Editor: Michael Kelly, Acquisitions Manager

Copy Editors: Kathleen Dobie, Brian Kramer

Technical Editor: Linda Keating

Editorial Manager: Leah Cameron

Editorial Assistant: Donna Love

Production

Project Coordinator: Cindy L. Phipps

Layout and Graphics: Lou Boudreau, Linda M. Boyer, J. Tyler Connor, Angela F. Hunckler, Jane E. Martin, Brent Savage, Kate Snell

Proofreaders: Christine Berman, Sally Burton, Nancy Price, Rebecca Senninger, Janet M. Withers

Indexer: Lynnzee Elzee Spense

General and Administrative

IDG Books Worldwide, Inc.: John Kilcullen, CEO; Steven Berkowitz, President and Publisher

IDG Books Technology Publishing: Brenda McLaughlin, Senior Vice President and Group Publisher

Dummies Technology Press and Dummies Editorial: Diane Graves Steele, Vice President and Associate Publisher; Mary Bednarek, Director of Acquisitions and Product Development; Kristin A. Cocks, Editorial Director

Dummies Trade Press: Kathleen A. Welton, Vice President and Publisher; Kevin Thornton, Acquisitions Manager

IDG Books Production for Dummies Press: Beth Jenkins Roberts, Production Director; Cindy L. Phipps, Manager of Project Coordination, Production Proofreading, and Indexing; Kathie S. Schutte, Supervisor of Page Layout; Shelley Lea, Supervisor of Graphics and Design; Debbie J. Gates, Production Systems Specialist; Robert Springer, Supervisor of Proofreading; Debbie Stailey, Special Projects Coordinator; Tony Augsburger, Supervisor of Reprints and Bluelines; Leslie Popplewell, Media Archive Coordinator

Dummies Packaging and Book Design: Patti Crane, Packaging Specialist; Kavish + Kavish, Cover Design; Michelle Vukas, Product Packaging Coordinator

♦

The publisher would like to give special thanks to Patrick J. McGovern, without whom this book would not have been possible.

♦

Contents at a Glance

Cartoons at a Glance

By Rich Tennant

"IT'S ANOTHER DEEP SPACE PROBE FROM EARTH, SEEKING CONTACT FROM EXTRATERRESTRIALS. I WISH THEY'D JUST INCLUDE AN E-MAIL ADDRESS."

page 137

"Now, when someone rings my doorbell, the current goes to a scanner that digitizes the audio impulses and sends the image to the PC where it's converted to a Pict file. The image is then animated, compressed, and sent via high-speed modem to an automated phone service that sends an e-mail message back to tell me someone was at my door 40 minutes ago."

page 193

"NIFTY CHART, FRANK, BUT NOT ENTIRELY NECESSARY."

page 95

ANAGRAM COMMUNICATIONS

O HELL...

page 323

"The new technology has really helped me get organized. I keep my project reports under the PC, budgets under my laptop and memos under my pager."

page 7

The Perls of Pauline

Help! I'm losing depth recursion! My subroutines are confusing!! My hash tables are degrading—heeeeelp!!

page 69

"For my finale, Rollo here will flawlessly activate my voice recognition system while I empty this bag of marbles into my mouth."

page 277

Fax: 978-546-7747 • E-mail: the5wave@tiac.net

Table of Contents

· ·

Introduction

• •

*A*CT! 4 for Windows is a brand-new product. Well, it's not really a new product; it's just the next generation of ACT!. I've written *ACT! 4 For Windows For Dummies* for both experienced ACT! users — some go back to the days of ACT! for DOS — and for the people who have just purchased ACT! and installed it on their computer. This book is filled with information about how you can use the many timesaving and productivity-improving features of ACT! 4, just like my previous ACT! books — *ACT! For Windows For Dummies* (version 2) and *ACT! 3 For Windows For Dummies* — so that you can get more work done in less time and with less effort (and, with any luck, make more money).

In addition, I've included many time-management tips — since that's what I do for a living — that will make you more productive, efficient, and effective in your daily work.

Why I Love ACT!

When I began my business career almost 25 years ago, I was taught to keep track of all my calls, meetings, and to-dos in a daily-planning book. And I was also taught to keep detailed notes of all my meetings, phone conversations, and observations in manila folders. Over the years, I found this process helped to improve my productivity immeasurably.

Then I discovered ACT!. Once I started using it, I became hooked. With ACT!, I could do everything that I had been trained to do with a pencil and a piece of paper using my computer instead. Today, I have information on thousands of people in my databases, and with just a few keystrokes, all of this information is at my fingertips. Since I began using ACT!, my personal productivity has increased four or five fold. Working from my home with ACT!, a laser printer, and fax machine, I'm able to produce all by myself the work that used to take a full day for an office of six people.

In addition to writing books, I'm also a time management/business management consultant, and during the past few years, I discovered that many of my consulting clients had ACT! loaded on their computers, but they didn't really know how to use it. So I started teaching them how they could keep track of all of their activities with ACT!. Today, I'm now paid more than $300 per hour to teach people how to use ACT!.

Now why am I paid so much money to teach a person how to use a computer program? Because I'm able to eliminate the learning curve. In just a couple of hours, I can teach people how to make ACT! work for them — even if they've never used a computer before. And that's what I've done for you in *ACT! 4 For Windows For Dummies*. I'm giving you the information that you need to make ACT! work for you.

Like many of you, I'm just an everyday user who thinks ACT! is the best productivity-improving tool on the market. Read and enjoy.

And if you like this book and want more, you'll probably want to subscribe to my ACT! newsletter, *ACT! in ACTion.* The three-month trial-subscription form is at the back of this book. Or you can fill out a Web form by visiting my Web site at www.ACTnews.com. My ACT! in ACTion Online Web site has articles from previous issues and lots of other ACT! information.

How to Use This Book

Like all *...For Dummies* books, this book is a reference, which means that you don't have to read it from cover to cover. Each chapter focuses on a single topic and is meant to stand on its own; however, I've tried to organize the parts of this book in a logical manner, just in case some of you want to read it from start to finish.

To get started, look up a topic in the table of contents or index. When you see something that interests you, flip to that section of the book. If I've done my job, you'll find out how to use ACT! in a new and interesting way, and you'll want to read more chapters. Fortunately, I've sprinkled cross-references throughout the book to help you find information on topics related to whatever you happen to be reading.

Occasionally, I present a block of text in a gray box called a sidebar. I use these sidebars to present incidental, often nonessential information. If the title of the sidebar interests you, go ahead and read it. If not, feel free to skip it. I won't mind.

What I Assume about You

For the sake of your health and safety, I can't let you read this book unless you meet the following requirements:

✔ You have ACT! version 4 installed on a computer running Windows 95 or Windows NT.

✔ You know the basics of using whatever version of Windows you happen to be running. (You know how to click, double-click, open and close windows, select menu commands, and so on.)

✔ Your computer has enough power to run ACT!; that is, it has a 486 or Pentium processor and at least 8MB of RAM (more is better).

I also assume that you have a need to organize your contacts, efficiently schedule your activities, and keep track of your calls, meetings, and to-dos. If you don't need to do those things, why'd ya buy ACT!?

How This Book Is Organized

This book contains seven parts. Each part contains a few chapters covering related topics. Here's a brief summary of the aforementioned parts:

Part I: Getting to Know ACT!

In Part I, you get an overview of ACT! 4's new features. I explain how to get contacts into your ACT! database; how to set up your general preference settings; how to get the most out of the Contact window; how to work with the Contact window's different tabs; and how to define the fields of your ACT! database.

Part II: Using Your Database

In Part II, I guide you through the process of entering information into ACT!. I show you how to move from one field to another and how to customize your individual fields. I also show you how to view your contact information as a list. And most importantly, I help you get contacts into ACT!. After all, ACT! is almost useless unless you fill it with the information about the important people in your life.

Part III: Working with ACT! Contacts

In Part III, I show you how to find people. You've got instant lookups, standard lookups, and advanced queries. And you can even look up people over the Internet and add them to your ACT! database. Once you've created a lookup, then I show you how to *save* your lookup by creating ACT! groups.

Part IV: Scheduling: A Play in Four Acts

In Part IV, I help you use ACT! to take control of your day. I present the nitty-gritty details of scheduling activities. ACT! provides several different ways for you schedule activities, and I show how to do them all. That way, you can select the method that's best for you.

Part V: Communicating with the Outside World

ACT! makes it easy for you to keep in touch with your contacts. In Part V, I describe how to use these communications features, everything from phone and e-mail management to custom reports and letter templates.

Part VI: Advanced ACT! Stuff

ACT! is a complex program, but this part of the book should give you the courage to try some of its coolest features, which include customizing commands, managing your database, and designing your own contact screens.

Part VII: The Part of Tens

Every *...For Dummies* book is supposed to have a Part of Tens, and this book is no exception. In my Part of Tens, I offer some tips on keeping your database in shape. I also provide lists of ACT! add-on products and lists of resources that can provide more information.

Conventions Used in This Book

ACT! provides several different ways to activate the same function or feature. You can use your mouse to pull down a menu and select a command from that menu. When I want you to choose a command from a menu, I present the menu first, then an arrow, and then the command, as in, for example, File➪Save. I'm basically saying, "Select the Save command from the File menu."

You can also access commands using Ctrl key keyboard shortcuts, which I provide to you like this: Ctrl+S. This means press and hold down the Ctrl key and then press the S key. ACT! stores many commands in buttons on its Toolbar. Whenever I suggest that you click a button with the mouse, I give you a little picture of that button in the left margin.

ACT! allows you to access many commands from a menu that appears when you click the right button on your mouse (also called right-clicking). Different commands appear on this menu depending on where your pointer is when you click the right mouse button.

Icons Used in This Book

This icon indicates that I'm telling a story of some kind. These stories usually have a point, but I won't make any promises. I tend to ramble sometimes, which reminds me of something that happened to me on the way to. . . .

I use this icon to point out important conceptual information that you shouldn't forget.

As you might expect, this icon flags tips, tricks, hints, and secrets that can help you get your work done quickly and efficiently.

This icon has two purposes: It lets the technologically-inclined know that I'm about to cover something complex and exciting, and it lets technophobes know that they ought to skip over that section because the information flagged by the Technical Stuff icon will only confuse and/or frighten them.

This icon lets you know of some potential danger, like if you click the wrong button in the ACT! Self Destruct dialog box, your computer might explode. Just kidding. I do try to warn you of situations that may cause awful things to happen, like data loss, hair loss, weight gain, and insomnia. By the way, some parts of this book are a great cure for insomnia. Ask my editor.

Where to Go from Here

If you have never used ACT! before, head to Chapter 1. If you're upgrading from version 2 of ACT!, I suggest that you skim Chapter 1 and then look up whatever topic interests you from the table of contents or index.

If you're upgrading from ACT! 3, just think of this book as a reference book. When you've got a question about how to use a specific ACT! feature, just look it up in the table of contents or the index.

Make it a point to visit my ACT! in ACTion Online Web site — www.ACTnews.com — regularly because I have lots of useful and beneficial information there.

Part I
Getting to Know ACT!

The 5th Wave   By Rich Tennant

"The new technology has really helped me get organized. I keep my project reports under the PC, budgets under my laptop and memos under my pager."

In this part . . .

ACT! is a very complex tool, on par with a top-of-the-line database or spreadsheet program, and if you don't fine-tune its features to match your specific needs, you won't be using this tool to its fullest potential. Driving a Porsche is probably a great experience, but it'd be an even better experience if you adjust the seat and mirrors before hitting the road. (Lame analogy, I know, but I'm just getting warmed up.) This part helps you set up ACT! so that it meets your needs. I show you how to insert contact information into ACT! and get your preferences in order. I also explain how all of the windows and tabs work.

One last thing: Don't skip Chapter 1. It's the most important chapter in this book.

Chapter 1

ACT! 4: An Overview

• •

In This Chapter

▶ Very important ACT! information

▶ ACT! windows

▶ Help when you need it

• •

Some Very Important ACT! Information

Read the first part of this chapter before you look at any other part of this book! The stuff I talk about here will save you hours of frustration and maybe even save your life — maybe. Anyway, while you may be itching to jump ahead and learn about scheduling activities and creating custom reports or whatever, I strongly urge you to give the first part of this chapter a good once-over. You may think you know it all, or maybe you think that this section, because it comes early in the book, won't contain any real information. Well, it does, darn it, so humor me and continue reading!

End of tirade. I promise not to yell at you anymore.

ACT! is people-oriented, not task-oriented

The whole concept of ACT! is that it's people-oriented, not task-oriented. For most of us, this is a different way of approaching the subject of how to stay on top of all of our unfinished work, tasks, and projects. When you become comfortable with this concept, ACT! is a very easy program to use.

For years, we've all been keeping track of our activities by using some version of a things-to-do list — we write down all of our tasks and update the list every few days. With ACT!, you don't make a list of things to do; you associate each task with a specific person and then use ACT! to help you to keep track of all your unfinished tasks. So instead of having an item on your things-to-do list that says, "Call Jeffrey Mayer," you use ACT! to go to Jeffrey Mayer's contact record and schedule the item "Follow-up on last week's presentation" as a call.

The ACT! Task List holds information on your calls, meetings, and to-dos, and displays your schedule for any date you choose — past, present, or future. Clicking the Activities tab brings up all the activities scheduled for a specific contact. For more information on the Task List, including lots of pretty pictures, see Chapter 16. Chapter 13 covers the Activities tab.

Remember to record history items

Keeping a history of your activities and other things is a very important part of ACT!. Your history notations are automatically recorded and can be viewed by clicking a contact's Notes/History tab. History records serve several important purposes:

  ✓ First, they provide an automatic record of the date, time, and purpose for all the activities that you have *cleared* for each contact. (If you don't clear an activity, it's not recorded as a history item.)

  ✓ Second, ACT!'s history feature automatically records the date and file name of any correspondence — letters, memos, faxes, and e-mail — that you have sent to the contact.

  ✓ Third, you can automatically create a history notation that records any specific information that you enter into an ACT! field. The Last Results field, for example, is a History field.

The recording of history notations is extremely important because it gives you the capability to automatically record all the events and communications that have taken place between you and the important people in your life. After you've created this information, you can then include it in a report for your boss or supervisor. With ACT!'s Record History feature, ACT!'s reporting capabilities become huge productivity-improving and timesaving tools.

For the lowdown on the Notes/History tab, turn to Chapter 5.

Put everybody you know into ACT!

Because ACT! is contact oriented, you really need to get a substantial number of people into the database before you can use ACT! exclusively. (See Chapter 7 on how to import information from another database, word processing merge file, or contact management program into ACT!.) If you're a new ACT! user, you should plan on using it a little bit at a time while you continue using your present system (such as your daily-planning book).You do more and more things with ACT! as you become familiar with its features and you add more people to in the database. Then one day you realize that you're using ACT! all of the time.

If you're an ACT! 3 user, ACT! 4 automatically installs over it. If you're converting from ACT! 2, or an earlier version of ACT!, you may want to spend a bit of time learning its ins and outs before you convert your data and go live.

Turn ACT! into your electronic Rolodex file

Feel free to include the names, addresses, and phone numbers of your family, your friends, your doctor, your dentist, your lawyer, your auto mechanic, and the butcher, the baker, and the candlestick maker, as well as all of your business contacts. The more people you have in your ACT! database, the easier it will be for you to use the program.

Initially, your goal should be to get as many people as you can, as quickly as you can, into the program. The basic information includes each person's name, company name, and phone number. You can fill in additional pieces of information — such as address, city, zip code, and so on — as time permits.

When talking on the phone to a person you want to add to your contact list, make sure you get all of the person's important information — company name, address, phone number, and so on. You can save time by typing the information directly into ACT!. However, you *must* take a moment to read this information back to the person, especially checking the spelling of his or her name, mailing address, and phone number to ensure that you recorded it properly.

The best way to learn how to use ACT! is to play with it. Click the different icons and watch what happens. Select the different commands listed on the menus and see what each of them does.

Back up your ACT!

The more you use ACT!, the more important it becomes that you back up your database on a regular basis. Losing data or other files can be disastrous.

One of the new features of ACT! 4 is built-in backups, whereby you can backup your database, as well as your envelope, letter, and report templates — and your ACT! layouts. You can also backup your ACT! data with Connected Online's Internet Backup software. Backing up and restoring your ACT! database is covered in Chapter 26.

Practical Sales Tools has an ACT! utility, Backup Your ACT!, that has some very neat features. For more information, give them a call toll-free at 888-433-2891 or visit their Web site at www.pstools.com.

One of the easiest ways to backup your hard drives and your ACT! databases is to use an automatic backup system with a tape backup or ZIP drive.

ACT! is such an important part of my life that I back it up twice a day. Scheduled, automatic backups of my ACT! files occur every day at 12:30 p.m. and at 6:30 p.m. I back up all files that have changed on my hard drive. (I do a complete backup of my hard drive about once every week.) For years, I've been using Hewlett-Packard's Colorado Memory System's Jumbo Tape Drives, and they work just great!

If you're not backing up your computer, and your ACT! database, on a regular basis, you're taking an unnecessary risk because sooner or later, something bad is going to happen, and you're going to lose some or all of your data. It's happened to me more than once, and my tape backup system has been both a lifesaver and a huge time-saver.

Protecting access to your ACT! database with a password

You should take great care to prevent unauthorized access to your ACT! database by using a password.

If you're using ACT! on your laptop and taking it with you when you leave the office, you should definitely password-protect your ACT! database. If you're using ACT! on a stand-alone computer in a small office environment, password protecting your database *may* not be necessary.

To assign a password to a database, take the following steps:

1. **Select File⇨Administration⇨Set Password from the menu bar.**

2. **If you already have a password and want to change it, enter the current password in the Old Password field.**

   Important: If you don't have a password, leave the Old Password field blank.

3. **Enter your new password in the New Password field.**

4. **Retype your new password in the Retype New Password field to confirm the new password and click OK.**

Saving your user password

If you're using ACT! on a network or sharing a database with other users, you must enter your name and password each time you want to use ACT!; otherwise, ACT! doesn't know which user you are. When there are multiple users of an ACT! database, each user has his or her own My Record contact record, and all of that person's activities are associated with that My Record file. By entering your name and password, you're instructing ACT! to bring up your My Record contact record.

The Remember Password option in the ACT! preference settings gives you the capability to have ACT! automatically enter your name, or your name and password, in the Login To (name of database) dialog box whenever you turn ACT! on.

Warning: The Remember Password option creates the opportunity for a breach of security. If you select this option, someone else can sit down at your computer, turn on ACT!, and have complete access to your ACT! database.

Opening a password-protected database

When you open a password-protected database, the Logon To (name of database) dialog box appears. Enter your user name and password and click OK.

If you want ACT! to remember your password for use the next time you log on to this database, choose the Remember Password option. The Remember Password option can also be set by selecting it on the General tab of the Preferences dialog box, which you open by selecting Edit⇨Preferences from the menu bar.

If you forget your password, call ACT! Technical Support (541-465-8645) and ask about the Password Removal Service.

Using ACT!'s Windows

In ACT! 4 you can view the Contact Layout; Contact List; Day, Week, and Month calendars; Task List; Groups; and e-mail in separate windows. You can open all of these windows at the same time, and you can choose to have them cascaded or tiled (vertically or horizontally). You can move from one open window to another by clicking the window you want, clicking the appropriate icon at the bottom of the Contact window, or pressing Ctrl+Tab.

Here's an example of working with multiple windows: To schedule an activity, just click any portion of a contact's contact record, drag it onto an open calendar window, and drop it on the day and time you want.

Open any window

You open ACT! windows by clicking the appropriate icon. Figure 1-1 shows the icons.

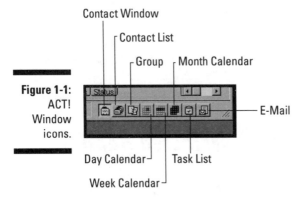

Figure 1-1:
ACT!
Window
icons.

You can also open windows by selecting the View command from the menu bar, or by using these function keys:

- ✔ F8 opens the Contact List window.
- ✔ F7 opens the Task List window.
- ✔ Shift+F5 opens the Daily calendar.
- ✔ F3 opens the Weekly calendar.
- ✔ F5 opens the Monthly calendar.

To close any window other than the Contact window, press Ctrl+F4. Pressing Ctrl+F4 in the Contact window closes the database. Pressing Alt+F4 closes ACT!.

Getting Help When You Need It

The reason you bought this book is because you wanted to learn how to use ACT! 4, and there are a number of resources available to you if you need information that is beyond the scope of this ...*For Dummies* book. Though

I've done such a thorough job of researching this book that I don't think it's possible that I didn't answer each and every question you could possibly have, just in case I missed something, I'll provide you with some other resources.

Online ACT! help

The online help feature in ACT! is very good. It's a quick and convenient way to look up information about how to use a particular feature or command. If you have a specific question about an ACT! feature or command, select Help Topics from the Help menu, and you may be able to find the answer to your question all by yourself.

Help for the currently active window

Press F1 to open the help topic for the currently active window. For example, if the Contact window is active and you press F1, the "Contact Window" help topic appears.

Click the Help icon in the Toolbar — it's the question mark — from any ACT! window. This button takes you to the main ACT! Help Topics window.

Press Shift+F1 if you want to learn about a specific ACT! command

If you have a question about a specific ACT! feature or ACT! command, press Shift+F1 from within an ACT! window, and the pointer becomes a question mark. Use the question mark to highlight any item from the pull-down menus, and ACT! Help will display a description of that specific feature or command.

From within any ACT! menu, you can get information about a command by moving the pointer over the command and pressing F1.

Right-click like a lunatic

Within any ACT! dialog box, use the right mouse button to click an option about which you'd like more information. If you click in a blank area of a dialog box, you get general help information about that dialog box.

Try ACT! training

ACT! includes multimedia training provided by ViaGrafix. To view the ViaGrafix training materials — you must insert the ACT! 4 CD-ROM into your computer — choose Help⇨Getting Started with ACT! — and choose from the displayed list of topics. This list includes Creating a Database, Using Lookups, Scheduling Activities, Using Calendars, Printing, Using Groups, Using Mail Merge, Faxing, Using E-mail, Using Reports, Customizing ACT! 4, and last but not least, Getting Help.

 You can also view training materials from any of the dialog boxes that have the Training Tool icon displayed.

View ACT!'s online manuals

The ACT! 4 CD-ROM also has online manuals. You access the online manuals by selecting Help⇨Online Manuals. (Converting from ACT! 2 to ACT! 3 and the ACT! Administrator's Guide are additional documents installed on the ACT! 4 CD-ROM. You access them by inserting the CD-ROM and opening the ACTDOCS directory.)

Visit Symantec online support

Technical support for ACT! is available online. The Internet address for the ACT! Support Center is `http://service.symantec.com/act`. (You do, of course, need an Internet browser and an Internet Service Provider (ISP).)

At the support center, you have quick access to the following services: Service File Download Area, Frequently Asked Questions (FAQs), Interactive Technical Support System, Knowledge Bases, and Online Discussion Groups.

To browse all the files in the Symantec file download section, connect to the ACT! file download area at `http://service1.symantec.com/DISCUSS/SUPPORT/files.nsf/act`.

For a complete explanation of Symantec's Online Support features, select Help⇨Symantec Online Support.

 You log on to Symantec's Web site by selecting Tool⇨Internet Links⇨ Symantec. Then choose from the list of sites that includes ACT! Small Business Resource Center, Mobile Resources, Technical Support, Try It Before You Buy It, and Symantec Corporation. Using ACT!'s Internet Tools is covered in Chapter 22.

Chapter 2
Getting Contacts into ACT!

• •

In This Chapter

▶ Creating a new ACT! database

▶ Converting a database to the ACT! 4 format

▶ Importing contacts into ACT!

▶ Managing your ACT! databases

• •

After you've installed ACT! and have it up and running, you need to create a database of contacts so that you can keep track of them. Just by coincidence, I cover that very topic in this chapter.

Creating a New ACT! Database

You create a new ACT! database by taking the following steps:

1. **Select the File⇨New command from the menu bar.**

   The New dialog box appears.

2. **Select ACT! Database in the File Type box and click OK.**

   The New Database dialog box appears.

3. **Give the new database a name and click Save.**

   The Enter "My Record" Information dialog box opens.

4. **Enter information about yourself in the Enter "My Record" Information dialog box and click OK.**

   ACT! creates the new database.

Do not use the File⇨New command to convert a previous ACT! database to the ACT! 4 format. If you do, you will overwrite the database and lose all your contact information!

If, by chance, Chris Huffman's contact information appears in the My Record contact record instead of your contact information, just enter your name, address, phone number, and so on, in the appropriate fields. This little problem sometimes occurs if you were using ACT!'s Demo database at the time you created a new database. You can find the My Record contact record by selecting Lookup⇨My Record.

Converting a Previous ACT! Database to ACT! 4

You can convert a database from a previous version of ACT! into an ACT! 4 database by taking the following steps. Just remember that an ACT! 4 database cannot be read by a previous version of ACT!.

Converting an ACT! 3 database to ACT! 4

This is how you convert an ACT! 3 database to the ACT! 4 format:

1. **Select the File⇨Open command from the menu bar.**

   The Open dialog box appears.

2. **Locate the directory containing the database, which is probably your ACT! 4 database directory.**

3. **Select ACT! 3.0 - ACT! 4.0 Database from the Files Of Type drop-down menu, if it isn't already selected.**

4. **Click Open.**

   A warning box appears with this message: `This database is in an ACT! v3.0 format. You may continue to use this format but if you do, you cannot add the Company Name or Telephone Number columns to the Task List. If you share this database with other ACT! v3.0 users, you must not convert it to v4.0 format.`

5. **Click Yes if you do or No if you don't want to convert the database to the ACT! 4 format. If you click yes, the database opens.**

Converting an ACT! 2 database to ACT! 4

This is how you convert an ACT! 2 database to the ACT! 4 format:

It's my suggestion that you copy your ACT! 2 database from your actwin2\database directory to the act4\database directory *before* you make the conversion.

1. **Select the File⇨Open command.**

   The Open dialog box appears.

2. **Locate the directory containing the ACT! 2 database. You'll probably find it in the actwin2\database directory.**

3. **Select the database and click OK.**

   The Convert Database dialog box appears, as shown in Figure 2-1. Here ACT! gives you two important options:

   - **To create a backup of your previous database.** It is my recommendation that you select the Create Backup option as protection if there is some sort of failure during the conversion process. The backup copy of your ACT! 2 database is stored in the ACT! 4's database\backup directory.

   - **To move your new database from your actwin2\database directory into ACT! 4's default directory.** I recommend selecting the Move To Default option.

4. **Make your selections and Click OK.**

   ACT! converts your database.

Figure 2-1:
The Convert
Database
dialog box.

Always backup your ACT! database before converting it! If you don't have a tape backup system, open the database directory and copy the files that makeup the database to another directory.

If you were using the Library field in ACT! 2, be aware that ACT! 4 doesn't contain a Library field. Any Library files that were part of a contact's record appear as an attachment in the contact's Notes/History tab in ACT! 4. To avoid losing data stored in the Library field, map the Library field to another ACT! 4 field.

ACT! 4 does not use description files. If you have more than one description file you use with your ACT! 2 database, make sure that your primary description file is the one that is applied at the time you convert your ACT! 2 database to the ACT! 4 format.

Importing Contacts into ACT! from Another Database

If you already have a list of names, addresses, and phone numbers in a database, a contact manager or a personal information manager (or, for that matter, just names and addresses in a word processing merge file), you can import that information directly into ACT! and spare yourself the time and effort of re-entering each individual's information, piece by piece, into your ACT! database.

This is how you import a text delimited (.TXT) file of names and addresses into ACT!:

1. **Open the database you want to import the records into.**

2. **Select File➪Data Exchange➪Import from the menu bar.**

   The Import Wizard appears.

3. **Select the type of file you want to import from the File Type drop-down list.**

   You can select from ACT! 3.0 – ACT! 4.0 (*.DBF) files, dBASE III–V files, Q&A 4.0 – 5.0 Data files, and Text-Delimited files.

   If you don't see the file type that you want, you may need to convert your existing file to a text delimited file.

4. **Use the Browse button to open the Open dialog box; then select the directory where the file's located.**

5. **Highlight the file and click the Open button.**

   The file's path is displayed in the Filename and Location field in the Import Wizard.

6. **Click the Next button.**

   The Wizard asks you what kind of records you want to import.

7. **Pick either Contact Records Only or Group Records Only.**

8. **Click the Options button.**

   The Import Options dialog box opens.

ACT! asks you to make the following choices:

- **Select the type of field separator.** It can be either a Comma or a Tab.

- **Choose the character set.** In the character set field, you tell ACT! what kind of character information you're importing. ACT! wants to know if your imported file is formatted for Windows, DOS, or Macintosh.

- **Do you wish to import the first record?** Sometimes, the first record displayed in a database file is the list of field names, such as Company, Contact, Phone, City, State, and so on. You probably don't want to import that record into ACT!. If the first record of the database you're importing is indeed a list of field names, leave the Yes Import The First Record check box empty. If the first record is a contact, you should check this box.

9. **Make your selections and click OK.**

10. **Click the Next button.**

   ACT! asks you if you want to use a predefined map file. A map file is a template that matches the database fields from other applications (ECCO, FedEx, GoldMine, Janna Contact, Maximizer Organizer, Schedule+, Sharkware, Sidekick, and Tracker) to fields in an ACT! database.

11. **Select the map you wish to use when you import your data.**

   If you wish to use a map, click the Next button, and you can view your map in the Contact Map, a feature discussed in the next section.

   The Contact Map appears, as shown in Figure 2-2.

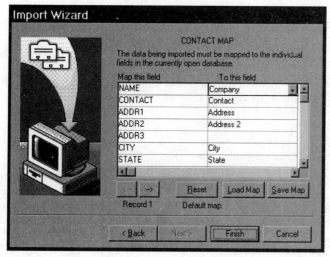

Figure 2-2: The Contact Map.

12. **If you do not wish to use a predefined map, click the Next button, and you can manually map your fields in the Contact Map.**

13. **When the fields you are importing are mapped to the correct ACT! fields, click the Finish button.**

ACT! imports your contacts into the database.

Mapping your database fields

When you import a file into ACT!, you want to make sure that everything ends up in the right place. For example, you want the company's name to appear in the Company field, the contact's name to appear in the Contact field, and so on. After all, it doesn't do you much good if the contact's phone number is in the City field, does it? So ACT! included a feature that allows you to map your fields.

Mapping is the process of matching fields from a file you want to import into ACT! with the appropriate fields on an ACT! contact layout. You can map each field from an import file to any ACT! field that you choose. You can also exclude any field you want from the importing process.

The Contact Map dialog box (see Figure 2-2) displays the contents of each field of the import file, beginning with the first record, and it enables you to map, or match, each of those fields to the appropriate ACT! field.

To match the import fields with the appropriate ACT! fields, choose a field in the Map This Field column and then select the ACT! field that you want to map it to from the drop-down list in the To This Field column.

Be careful not to corrupt your ACT! database

When you import data from another database into ACT!, you should first create a new ACT! database into which you will import these contact records. (You may want to give this new database a name like Import.) This way, as you map the fields and import the information into this new database, you can see how it actually looks.

If everything is mapped correctly, you can import the new contact records into the ACT! database of your choice. If something isn't mapped the way you want, you can delete the new database and start over again without corrupting your original ACT! database.

Tip: The Edit⇨Replace command enables you to move contact information from one field to another and to swap information between fields; that is, move the information that's in field A to field B and vice versa. ACT!'s Replace feature is covered in Chapter 7.

You then work your way through the list of fields you're importing into ACT!, one field at a time, and determine which ACT! field you want to map the import field to.

If the file you're importing lists the contact's first and last names in separate fields, select the First Name and Last Name fields (rather than the Contact field) from the To This Field column. When you import the file into ACT!, the First Name and Last Name fields automatically combine in the Contact field.

If you don't want to import a particular field into ACT!, you can exclude that field by selecting the Do Not Map selection from the drop-down menu, which leaves the field blank.

dBASE memo fields cannot be imported directly into ACT! contact notes. To import this information from the contact records of your previous database, contact manager, or personal information manager, you must use the cut-and-paste features of Windows to move each contact's notes into the ACT! notepad, one record at a time.

Viewing the contacts information

After mapping the fields of your first contact, click the View Next Record button to view the contact information of the next contact in the import file. Viewing the records of several contacts helps you determine how the imported fields should be mapped to their corresponding ACT! fields. (To view the previous contact's information, click the View Previous Record button.)

Continue this process until all the fields from the import file have been mapped to the correct ACT! fields or have been excluded from the importing process.

If the data in an import file field is larger, or longer, than the ACT! field you are mapping it to, ACT! truncates the data.

Saving your map settings

After mapping your data, you can save your map settings by clicking the Contact Map's Save Map button (see Figure 2-2) so that the settings may be used again if you need to import information from the same source into one of your ACT! databases.

Using your map settings

To apply one of your previously saved map settings, click the Contact Map's Load Map button (see Figure 2-2) and select the setting you want to use from the list that's displayed in the Open dialog box. Then click OK.

If you're importing contact information from ECCO, FedEx Ship, GoldMine, Janna Contact, Lotus Organizer, Maximizer, Microsoft Schedule+, Sidekick, Sharkware, or Tracker, ACT! has already mapped the fields for you.

Ready, click, ACT!: Importing the file

After mapping all the information in your import file to the appropriate ACT! fields and saving your map settings (if desired), it's time to begin the actual import. When you're ready, click Finish, and ACT! imports the contact information into your ACT! database. If you change your mind and don't want to import this information, click Cancel.

Importing Contact Information from Non-Electronic Sources

We've all got names, addresses, and phone numbers on pieces of paper. They're hard to keep track of, and as you may have guessed, ACT! can't work with them. This section covers ways to get contact information in paper form into ACT!.

Business card scanners

Do you have a huge stack of business cards in the bottom of your desk drawer? Put them into ACT!. I know, it's a big pain to type in all of that information. But with a business card scanner, you can eliminate the biggest hurdle to getting this important information into your computer. Seiko Instruments' Smart Business Card Reader is a very good business card scanner. Available through Seiko Instruments, 1130 Ringwood Court, San Jose, CA 95131-1726; phone 800-688-0817. Their Web site is www.seikosmart.com.

Typing services

If you've got mailing lists, business cards, or Rolodex files you want typed into your computer, get in touch with Contact Data Entry, P.O. Box 3998, Bartlesville, OK 74006; phone 918-335-0252, Web site: `www.contactentry.com`. You send them your lists they type the names into their computer, then send them back to you. Within minutes, you have your list of names inside ACT!.

Mailing lists

The following companies provide business prospect mailing lists:

- *business*USA: *business*USA is a useful tool for sales leads, tele-marketing, direct mail, business profiles, and much, much more. *business*USA is a database of 10 million businesses with access to complete and accurate business information. infoUSA is a division of American Business Information, Inc.: phone 800-624-0076, Web site `www.LookupUSA.com`.

- **List Merchant for ACT!:** List Merchant for ACT! is another source of information for sales leads, mailing lists, prospect lists and market research. It offers a way to download mailing lists and sales leads directly into ACT! over the Internet. Data Merchant is an online data-base of 12 million businesses and 95 million U.S. consumer sales leads. List Merchant for ACT! : phone 888-849-0400, Web site `www.listmerchant.com/act`.

Managing Your ACT! Database

This section covers some of the basics of working with your database.

Opening an ACT! database

Once you create an ACT! database, you'll probably want to be able to open it. To do this, you select the File⇨Open command. The Open dialog box appears, and the list of ACT! databases is displayed. Highlight the desired database, click the Open button, and voilà — your database!

In the ACT! Preference settings, you can tell ACT! what database you want it to load whenever you start the program. You do so by selecting Edit⇨Preferences from the menu bar and then clicking the Startup tab.

In the Startup database section of the Preference Startup tab, you have two choices:

- ✔ **Last opened:** Choose this option if you want ACT! to open the most recently used database every time you start ACT!.

- ✔ **Named database:** Choose this option if you want ACT! to open a specific database every time you start ACT!. To select the path for the named database, click the Browse button (it has three dots) to find the database's file location.

If you're having trouble with your database, try getting in touch with Linda Keating — an ACT! Certified Consultant in Palo Alto, California, and vice president of JL Technical Group. Linda developed a utility called TroubleSpotter that searches for invalid data within ACT! database tables. Using TroubleSpotter on many hopelessly damaged databases, Linda has seen all sorts of nasty stuff: characters in date fields, invalid pointers to note formatting records, duplicate "unique IDs," missing links in note records, and more. TroubleSpotter has been able to fix all of these problems. For more information on TroubleSpotter, you can reach Linda by phone at 415-323-9141 or e-mail at `Linda@JLTechnical.com`. You can also check out this Web site: `www.jltechnical.com`.

Closing an ACT! database

To close an ACT! database, select File➪Close from the menu bar. You can also press Ctrl+F4.

Deleting an ACT! database

To delete an ACT! database from your computer, select File➪Administration➪Delete Database. Highlight the database you want to delete, and an ACT! message box asks you, `Are you sure you want to delete this data-base? [Database Name Inserted]` Click Yes and ACT! deletes the database. Click No and ACT! cancels the deletion. (If the database has a password, you must enter the password before ACT! deletes the database.)

Deleting a database erases all the contacts in that ACT! database. When a database is deleted, all your contact information is gone for good!

Chapter 3

ACT!'s General Preferences

I know you're in a hurry to start using ACT!, but I feel that you should first set up the program so that you can use it in the most efficient and effective way. To do this, you need to access ACT!'s preference settings. Simply click the Edit menu and choose the Preferences command. The General tab of the Preferences dialog box is shown in Figure 3-1.

The Preferences dialog box contains several tabs for a number of different ACT! settings. In this chapter, I discuss only the settings that pertain to getting started: General and Startup. I cover the other tabs with their specific ACT! features in other parts of the book. (For example, I think that it makes more sense to discuss how to work with the calendar preferences in the chapter on how to use the ACT! calendars.)

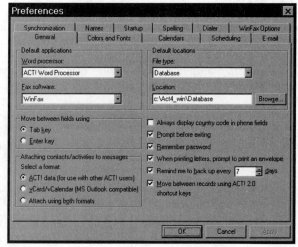

Figure 3-1:
The General tab of the Preferences dialog box.

The following tabs are in the Preferences dialog box:

- ✔ **General:** Discussed in this chapter
- ✔ **Colors and Fonts:** Discussed in Chapter 24
- ✔ **Calendar:** Discussed in Chapter 15
- ✔ **Scheduling:** Discussed in Chapter 13
- ✔ **E-mail:** Discussed in Chapter 20
- ✔ **Synchronization:** Discussed in Chapter 25
- ✔ **Names:** Discussed in Chapter 7
- ✔ **Startup:** Discussed in this chapter
- ✔ **Spelling:** Discussed in Chapter 18
- ✔ **Dialer:** Discussed in Chapter 17
- ✔ **WinFax Options:** Discussed in Chapter 19. If WinFax PRO is not installed on your computer, this tab will not be displayed. There is now complete integration between ACT! 4 and WinFax PRO 8.03 or higher. If you're using a previous version of WinFax PRO, I suggest you upgrade to WinFax PRO 8.03.

If you're not faxing from your computer, you may want to get yourself a copy of WinFax PRO, which gives you this capability. It will save you time and make you much more productive. WinFax PRO is another great Symantec product. Symantec's customer service number is 800-441-7234.

Preferences Dialog Box Basics

When you select the Preferences command, you can customize the various functions and settings for your ACT! database to your individual tastes. After you make your preference setting selections, click the OK button at the bottom of the Preferences dialog box. ACT! saves your settings and returns you to the Contact window.

If you don't want to save your changes to the preference settings, click Cancel or press the Esc key. ACT! returns you to the Contact window with your prior preferences settings still active. Here are some additional things you can do:

- ✔ To apply a setting without closing the Preferences dialog box, click the Apply button at the bottom-left corner of the box.
- ✔ To move from one field to another within the Preferences dialog box, you can use the Tab key, click with your mouse, or press the Alt key plus the underlined letter.

✔ To change tabs, click the tab with your mouse. When a tab is high-lighted — it will have a dotted box around it — use the arrow keys to move between tabs.

✔ To move backward through the dialog box, use the Shift+Tab key combination.

The General Tab

In the General tab, you select default applications, file locations, phone formats, and other default settings.

Which word processor do you want to use?

In the Default applications section of the General tab, you choose your word processor. You have three choices: You can use the ACT! word processor, Microsoft Word, or WordPerfect. Using word processors is discussed in Chapter 18.

What faxing software do you want to use?

You choose the fax software you want from those listed in the drop-down list in the Default applications section of the General tab.

ACT! 4's QuickStart Wizard makes it easy to select your word processor and faxing software, and set up your e-mail systems. It also gives you the option of converting previous ACT! databases to the ACT! 4 format. The Wizard walks you through the process. To find the QuickStart Wizard, select Help⇨ QuickStart Wizard.

Where are your ACT! files located?

The Default locations settings enable you to define the default directory for your ACT! database, as well as the default directory for your reports, documents, form letter templates, macros, queries, and so on.

If you use databases on both your own computer and on a network drive, you need to know how to change the default location of your database so that ACT! can find it. Read on.

When you select a type of file database from the drop-down menu, for example, Database in the File Type field, its path automatically displays in the Location field. If you want to change the location of a directory, click the Browse button to the right of the Location field, and the Browse For Folder dialog box appears. Use this dialog box to choose a new directory path.

Tab or Enter? Moving with keys

In the Moving Between Fields Using [Tab or Enter Key] section of the General tab, you can choose either the Tab key or Enter key as the one that moves the cursor from one field to the next.

Display country codes in phone field?

If you like the field for the country code — [1] for the United States, [33] for France, [81] for Japan, and so on — to appear in each Phone field throughout ACT!, select this option.

Prompt before exit?

Would you like ACT! to ask you if you *really* want to quit each time you exit ACT!? If so, select the Prompt Before Exiting option. (It's my suggestion that you check this box so that you can't close ACT! by accident.)

The Alt+F4 key combination automatically closes ACT!.

Need ACT! to remember your password?

If you want ACT! to remember your password each time you open an ACT! database, select the Remember Password option.

Which Shortcut keys?

If you use ACT! 2, you know Ctrl+Home moves you to the first record in a lookup, and Ctrl+End moves you to the last record in a lookup; the PageUp key moves you to the previous record, and the PageDown key moves you to the next record.

If you like to use the ACT! 2 shortcut keys, select this option on the General tab.

In ACT! 4, the key combinations are different. Alt+Home moves you to the first record in a lookup. Alt+End moves you to the last record in a lookup. Ctrl+PageUp moves you to the previous record. The Ctrl+PageDown key moves you to the next record.

The Startup Tab

The Startup tab enables you to select a default contact and a group layout, select which database you want ACT! to open each time you start ACT!, select a macro to run when you start ACT!, and more.

Contact window options

The following startup options apply to the Contact window:

- **Select a default contact layout:** You choose the contact layout ACT! uses whenever you start the program in the Default Contact Layout field. Click the Browse button to the right of the Default Contact Layout field, and select from the list of available layouts.

- **Make all new contacts public or private:** If you want all the new contacts you add to the database private — meaning that their contact information is *not* shared with ACT! users with whom you are sharing your ACT! database — check the Make New Contacts Private check box. Public activities can be viewed by everybody who is using the database.

Group window options

You choose the following startup options in the Group window:

- **Select default group layout:** The group layout is what ACT! uses when you start the program, and you get to choose the layout you want to use from the list of available layouts in the Default Group Layout field. Click the Browse button to the right of the Default Group Layout field to display the list.

- **Make all new contacts public or private:** If you would like to make all the new groups you add to the database private, check the Make New Groups Private check box. The contact information of private groups is not shared with any ACT! users with whom you are sharing your ACT! database.

✔ **Display a second column in the Group window:** In the Second Group Column field, select the second column you want to display from the drop-down list.

Database options

ACT! lets you choose which database it opens when you start it. You have two choices:

✔ **Last Opened:** Choose this option if you want ACT! to open the database you were working with when you last exited ACT!.

✔ **Named Database:** If you want a specific database to open every time you start ACT!, choose this option. To select a specific database, click the Browse button to the right of the Named Database field and select the database you want from the list of available databases.

Macro options

If you want ACT! to run a macro when you start the program, select that macro and insert its path in the Run Macro On Startup field. To select a macro, click the Browse button and select from the list of available macros.

Enable ACT! Speed Loader

If you would like ACT! to load faster, select this option. ACT! places the Speed Loader — which contains several ACT! files — in your Startup folder. When you start Windows 95, these files load into your computer's memory so, that ACT! doesn't have to load them.

If you select this option and discover your computer's performance slows down, you may want to remove the Speed Loader from the Startup folder. This is done by opening the Startup folder and deleting the shortcut icon.

Chapter 4

The Contact Window

● ●

In This Chapter

▶ Exploring the Contact window

▶ Working with the Contact layout's tabs

▶ Using the Classic Contact layouts

● ●

*1*n the ACT! Contact window, you view contact information on a contact layout. ACT! comes with a number of different contact layouts. You switch from one to another by clicking the Contact Layout button at the bottom of the Contact window. ACT! comes with the following contact layouts:

- ✔ Contact 4.0
- ✔ Contact Layout
- ✔ Classic Contact 1
- ✔ Classic Contact 2
- ✔ Alternate
- ✔ Rotary Index
- ✔ Large Font
- ✔ Contact 3.0

ACT! layouts have many fields in which to store information about your contacts. There is a simple reason why ACT! provides so many fields: The more information you're able to store and record about the important people in your business and personal life, the easier it is to develop and maintain long-term relationships.

For ACT! 2 users, the Classic Contact 1 and Classic Contact 2 layouts are the same as the Contact 1 and Contact 2 layouts in ACT! 4.

A *field* is where you enter information about a person — such as "Mayer Enterprises." The *field name* (in ACT! 2 it was called a field label) for Mayer Enterprises would be the word "Company." Every field needs to have a field name; otherwise, you wouldn't know what information to enter where.

ACT! enables you to create additional fields with the Edit⇨Define Fields command. This feature is discussed in Chapter 6. When you create a new ACT! field, you have to put it on the contact layout for it to be of any use. You do this task by using the Layout Designer. To open the Layout Designer, select Tools⇨Design Layout from the menu bar. The Layout Designer is discussed in Chapter 23.

Looking in the Contact Window

Before I describe the ins and outs of ACT!'s contact layouts, I want to first cover the other things in the Contact window, which is shown in Figure 4-1.

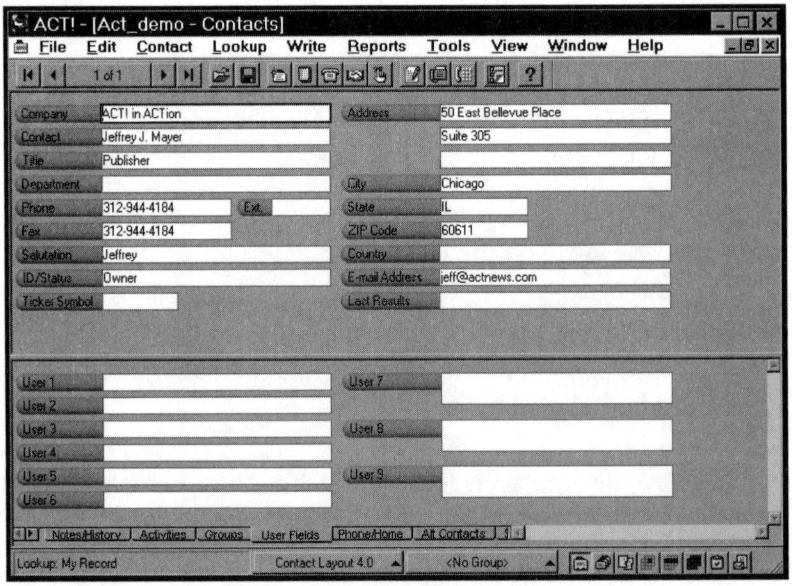

Figure 4-1:
The Contact window.

The menu bar

At the top of the ACT! Contact window, there's a menu bar with lots of menu items: File, Edit, Contact, Lookup, Write, Reports, Tools, View, Window, and Help. It is from this menu that you access all ACT! commands.

For example, clicking the Contact menu button brings you the list of the various ACT! commands having to do with managing your contacts. From the Contact menu, you can insert a new contact record; duplicate an existing contact record; delete a contact; schedule a call, meeting, or to-do; and so on.

You activate these commands by clicking the specific command with your mouse. You can also use the arrow keys to highlight the specific command, then press Enter. To the right of each command is the appropriate function key combination, if you like to use shortcut keys.

When you highlight a command either with your mouse or from the keyboard, the status bar at the bottom-left corner of the Contact window displays a description of the command.

To make changes to the commands that are displayed on the menu bar — add commands, remove commands, or change their positions — select Tools⇨Customize. Customizing ACT! is covered in Chapter 24.

The toolbar

As shown in Figure 4-2, ACT! displays and uses 16 standard buttons — ACT! calls them tools. (If you're using WinFax PRO, ACT! adds a 17th button to the toolbar. This is the Quick Fax button.) The following buttons are pre-installed on the Contact window toolbar.

Figure 4-2:
The standard toolbar icons.

✔ **First Record:** The First Record button moves you to the first record of the lookup. (To find out more about the powerful Lookup feature, see Chapter 10.)

✔ **Last Record:** The Last Record button moves you to the last record of the lookup.

To move to the first contact record in your lookup, press either Alt+Home or Ctrl+Home. To move to the last contact record in your lookup, press either Alt+End or Ctrl+End. To move between contact records, select the Move Between Records Using ACT! 2 Shortcut Keys in the General tab in ACT!'s Preferences. This option is discussed in Chapter 3.

✔ **Previous Contact:** The Previous Contact button moves you to the previous contact record.

✔ **Next Contact:** The Next Contact button moves you to the next contact record.

✔ **Contact Number:** The numbers on the Contact Number button tell you the position of the current contact record within the current lookup. It also tells you the number of contacts in the current lookup. (For example, 18 of 125 means that the current contact is the 18th record in a lookup that contains 125 records.)

✔ **Open File:** The Open File button brings up the Open File dialog box so that you can open a new file.

✔ **Save File:** The Save File button saves changes you make to the current contact record.

✔ **New Contact:** The New Contact button adds a new contact to your ACT! database.

✔ **Insert Note:** The Insert Note button lets you write a note to yourself about a contact.

✔ **Schedule Call:** The Schedule Call button schedules a new call. (Scheduling activities — calls, meetings, and to-dos — is discussed in Chapter 13.)

✔ **Schedule Meeting:** The Schedule Meeting button schedules a new meeting.

✔ **Schedule To-do:** The To-do button schedules a new to-do.

✔ **Letter:** The Letter button opens the letter template (letter.tpl). (Writing letters in ACT! is covered in Chapter 18.)

✔ **Quick Fax:** The Quick Fax button facilitates sending a fax. You do, of course, need faxing software.

 ✔ **Dial Phone:** The Dial Phone button displays the Dialer dialog box, which contains a list of all of a current contact's phone numbers. (Using ACT! to dial the phone is covered in Chapter 17.)

 ✔ **SideACT!** The SideACT! button launches a new ACT! utility that enables you to schedule activities even if ACT! isn't running. SideACT! is discussed in Chapter 14.

 ✔ **Help Topics:** The Help Topics button opens the Help Topics dialog box, which gives you access to information on the commands and features of ACT!.

The look and feel of the ACT! toolbar can be customized and modified. Here are some of the things you can do:

✔ **Change the toolbar position:** To change the position of the toolbar, click a blank portion of the toolbar — don't click a button — and drag the toolbar to another position on the window. If you want the toolbar to float as a palette, just leave it positioned anywhere you want in the Contact window.

✔ **Change the size of the buttons:** To change the size of an button (large or small), right-click a blank portion of the toolbar and make your selection from the menu that appears. From this menu, you can also choose whether buttons appear with or without text.

✔ **Add Tool Tips:** If you need help remembering what an button does, just place your mouse above the button, and a brief description of the button's function appears. This information is called a Tool Tip. To enable the Tool Tip option, right-click the toolbar, select Toolbars from the menu, and select the Tool Tips option.

✔ **Customizing the toolbar:** Right-click the toolbar and select Customize from the subsequent menu, or select Tools⇨Customize from the menu bar, and the Customize ACT! dialog box opens. Here you can add or remove buttons from the toolbar, and lots, lots more. For more information on how to customize the toolbar, menus, and keyboard, check out Chapter 24.

What is a lookup?

Throughout this book, you'll see references to ACT!'s Lookup feature. This feature makes ACT! so powerful because you use it to find people in your ACT! database.

When you do a lookup, you're searching your ACT! database for contact records with similar or identical information, such as everybody who has a last name of Smith or everybody who lives in Chicago. When ACT! finds these records, it groups them together.

For example, let's say that you are planning a business trip and you want to create a list of all the people you know in the city you're visiting so that you can schedule additional meetings or appointments while you are in town. Here's what you do:

1. **Select Lookup⇨City.**

2. **Type in the name of the city.**

3. **Click OK.**

   ACT! creates your list in a fraction of a second.

You can also use the Lookup feature to find single contacts in your database. (I use this feature all day long. ACT! has become my personal Rolodex file.) To find someone in ACT!, just select Lookup⇨First Name; Lookup⇨Last Name; or Lookup⇨Company. You then type in the first two or three letters of the name, click OK, and ACT! creates a complete list of all the people who fit that lookup criteria.

If your lookup finds more than one contact record, you can use the PageUp or PageDown keys to move through the list. Or you can view the results of your lookup as a list by opening the Contact List window (select View⇨Contact List from the menu bar, press F8, or click the Contact List button). I've devoted a whole chapter to the subject of lookups, so see Chapter 11 for more information.

The status bar

The status bar at the bottom-left of the Contact window displays information about what ACT! is doing. It also contains some useful buttons. What follows are descriptions of some of the status bar's functions.

Viewing your lookup and command descriptions

Whenever you perform a lookup, the status bar at the bottom-left corner of the Contact window displays the type of lookup.

Highlighting a command from the menu bar using either the mouse or the keyboard replaces the lookup information with a description of the command.

Changing layouts with the Layout button

Click the Layout button on the status bar, and a list of available ACT! layouts is displayed from the drop-down menu. Highlight the layout you want, and ACT! applies that layout. The name of the layout that is currently selected appears on the Layout button.

With Layout Designer, you can change and customize ACT! layouts. You open the Layout Designer by selecting Tools⇨Design Layouts. The features of the Layout Designer are discussed in Chapter 23.

Changing groups with the Group button

Click the Group button on the status bar, and the drop-down menu displays a list of available Groups. Highlight the Group you want, and ACT! brings up the members of that group. The name of the group currently selected is displayed on the Group button. (Using groups is discussed in Chapter 12.)

Opening ACT!'s windows by clicking window buttons

There are eight buttons on the status bar, as shown in Figure 4-3. Clicking a window button opens a different ACT! window. Or you can do the same thing by using the commands on the View menu.

Figure 4-3:
The eight
buttons
on the
status bar.

 ✔ **Contact window:** This button displays the contact layout. It is in this window that you enter contact information.

 ✔ **Contact List:** Clicking this button opens the Contact List window. You use this window to view the list of contacts in the current lookup. The Contact List is discussed in Chapter 8.

 ✔ **Group:** This button displays the Group window, where you create new groups, modify existing groups, and delete unused groups. Chapter 5 addresses Groups.

 ✔ **Day Calendar:** Clicking the Day Calendar button shows you all the activities scheduled for a specific day. ACT!'s calender features are covered in Chapter 15.

✔ **Week Calendar:** Clicking the Week Calendar button brings up the ACT! Week calendar, where you view all the activities scheduled for a specific week.

 ✔ **Month Calendar:** Click the Month Calendar button to bring up the Month calendar, which displays all the activities that you have scheduled for a specific month.

 ✔ **Task List:** This button opens the Task List window, where you view a list of all of your unfinished tasks — your calls, meetings, and to-dos — for past, present, or future dates. The Task List is discussed in Chapter 16.

 ✔ **E-mail:** Clicking here opens the E-mail window. In this window, you can view the e-mail messages that are in your inbox, outbox, or briefcase. You also create e-mail messages from this window. See Chapter 20 for a discussion of the ACT! e-mail features.

The Fields of the Contact Layout

Like all of ACT!'s contact layouts, the Contact Layout — the layout you'll probably use the majority of the time — is split in half. (The bar that separates the portions of the window is called the *splitter* bar.) The top half of the Contact Layout layout contains general contact information. The bottom half of the Contact Layout layout contains seven very useful tabs.

The top half of the Contact Layout layout

The top half of the Contact Layout layout contains fields for entering general contact information, such as the company, contact name, phone and fax numbers, title, mailing address, and so on.

The User Fields tab

Click the User Fields tab, located at the bottom of the Contact Layout window, and User fields 1 through 9 display. You use these fields to customize ACT! so that it best suits your needs and requirements. (For additional information about customizing your User fields, see Chapter 24.)

Here are some User field tab tips:

✔ Use the Tab key to move forward through the fields.

✔ Use the Shift+Tab key to move backward through the fields.

✔ All the User fields are designated as drop-down menu fields by default.

✔ User fields 10 through 15 are on the Status tab.

✔ To expand the size of the tab window without manually moving the splitter bar, double-click on the splitter bar.

The Phone/Home tab

The Phone/Home tab contains fields for the contact's home address and phone number, as well as fields for additional telephone numbers.

The Alt Contacts tab

The Alternate Contacts tab contains fields in which you can store information about the contact's assistant and additional contacts who work closely with the contact.

I suggest that you create a separate contact record for every person with whom you want to maintain a relationship. Use the Assistant, 2nd Contact, and 3rd Contact fields to enter basic information about people who work closely with your contact. Having these additional names and telephone numbers available is very helpful when you're unable to reach your contact.

The Status tab

The Status tab contains reference information about your phone calls, meetings, correspondence, and contact management information. It also contains User fields 10 through 15.

Following is a brief summary of the Status tab fields. Be aware that these are all system fields and cannot be modified unless otherwise noted.

✔ **Last Reach:** The Last Reach field records the date you last reached the contact by phone. This field updates automatically when you record a completed telephone call from the Record History dialog box. It is a system field and cannot be modified.

✔ **Last Meeting:** The Last Meeting field records the date you last met with the contact. This field is updated automatically when you clear a scheduled meeting. It is a system field and cannot be modified.

✔ **Last Attempt:** The Last Attempt field records the date you last attempted to phone the contact. This field is updated automatically when you record an attempted telephone call from the Record History dialog box. It is a system field and cannot be modified.

✔ **Letter Date:** The Letter Date field records the date of the last letter that you sent to the contact. It is a system field and cannot be modified.

✔ **Create Date:** The Create Date field records the date the contact record was created. It is a system field and cannot be modified.

✔ **Edit Date:** The Edit Date field records the date that the contact's record was last edited. This field is updated automatically whenever a change is made to the contact's record. It is a system field and cannot be modified.

You can use the dates displayed in the Edit Date, Last Reach, Last Attempt, Last Meeting, and Letter Date fields to do custom database queries. For example, with ACT!'s Custom Query options, you can do a search for all the contacts with whom you haven't had a meeting since April 1 or all the people you haven't reached on the phone since September 15. For more on database queries, see Chapter 11.

The edit date does not change when an activity is scheduled, a note is entered, or a history item is recorded. The edit date changes only when the contact record itself is edited, or when the Last Reach, Last Meeting, Last Attempt, or Letter Date fields change. I think this is a serious design flaw because it limits your ability to search your database.

✔ **Merge Date:** The Merge Date field records the date that the contact record was merged into this ACT! database. It is a system field and cannot be modified.

✔ **Record Creator:** The Record Creator field records the name of the person who created the record. It is a system field and cannot be modified.

✔ **Record Manager:** The Record Manager field records the name of the manager of the contact record. If the record was created in your database, the manager information is automatically inserted from the My Record contact record. If the contact record was imported from another database (yours or someone else's), the Manager field contains the information from that user's database. The information in this field can be edited manually.

✔ **Public/Private:** If you're using ACT! in a multi-user environment, other users who log on to your ACT! database will be able to see the contacts marked as public. You may, however, want to add some of your personal contacts to your ACT! database. If you do not want other users to see these records, mark them as private.

The Contact Layout's other tabs

In addition to the Contact Layout tabs that contain contact information, there are three tabs containing information about all the things that are happening, or have happened, between you and your contacts.

- ✔ **Notes/History tab:** The Notes/History tab contains the notepad, the contact history, and the names of any files attached to the contact. The features of the Notes/History tab are described in Chapter 5.

- ✔ **Activities tab:** The Activities tab contains a listing of all the activities that you have scheduled for a contact. Chapter 5 covers the features of the Activities tab.

- ✔ **Groups tab:** The Groups tab enables you to view the groups of which an individual is a member. Find out more about the features of the Groups tab, in Chapter 5.

Printing contact information

If you want a hard copy of your contact information, just print a contact report. You do this by selecting Reports⇨Contact Report. Creating ACT! reports is covered in Chapter 21.

To print your Notes, Histories, Activities, or Groups, click the respective tab, select File⇨Print⇨[Notes/Histories, Activities, or Groups] from the menu bar, and ACT! prints a custom report.

The Classic Contact Layouts for ACT! 2 Users

If you've been using ACT! 2 and would like to stay with your old familiar Contact Screen 1 and Contact Screen 2 layouts, use the Classic Contact 1 and Classic Contact 2 layouts.

Chapter 5

Notes, Histories, Activities, and Groups

. . . .

In This Chapter

▶ Using the Notes/History tab
▶ Using the Activities tab
▶ Using the Groups tab
▶ Assigning Shortcut Keys to your tabs

. . . .

*A*t the bottom of the Contact window are seven tabs containing contact information. Four of those tabs — User Fields, Phone/Home, Alt Contacts, and Status — contain contact information that is part of the person's contact record. I cover these tabs in Chapter 4.

The other three tabs — Notes/History, Activities, and Groups — contain information about recorded notes and history items, the scheduled activities, and the groups that the person is a member of. I cover these three tabs in this chapter.

An ACT! Contact window consists of two parts. The top section contains general contact information, and the bottom section has seven tabs in which you can view different information. The bar between the two is called the splitter bar. To change the size of a split window, position the cursor on the splitter bar so that it changes to the sizing tool, hold down the mouse button, move it upward or downward, and release the mouse when the window sizes are where you want them. To expand the tab portion of the split window so that it takes up the entire window, place the cursor on the splitter bar (it changes into the sizing tool) and double-click.

To scroll through the contact list while the Notes/History Tab, Activities tab, or Group tab is selected, use the Ctrl+PageUp or PageDown keys.

The Notes/History Tab

One of the reasons ACT! is such a powerful tool is that it enables you to keep a record of all of the things that have gone on between you and the important people in both your business and personal life. With more information at your fingertips, you can develop closer relationships with your customers, clients, and prospects, which ultimately means more money in your pocket.

You store this information in one of the three following ways, and access it through the Notes/History tab.

- ✔ **The Insert Note** command lets you write notes to yourself about your meetings, telephone conversations, and any other thing that may come to mind.
- ✔ **The Record History** command helps you maintain a record of all your meetings, calls, to-dos, and any other information that you want stored as a history entry.
- ✔ **The Attachments** feature enables you to attach files to contact records. With a click of your mouse you can open the attached file in the program that created it.

The Notes/History tab is shown in Figure 5-1.

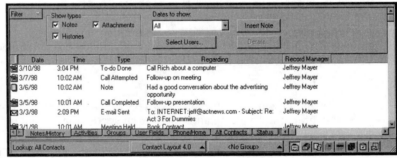

Figure 5-1:
The Notes/
History tab.

The more information you collect about your contacts, the easier it is for you to develop long-term relationships.

Entering notes

ACT! gives you lots of ways to enter notes. You can select Contact⇨ Insert Note from the menu bar, or press the F9 key, from any ACT! window. You can also click the Insert Note button on the Notes/History tab, or select the Insert Note command by right-clicking within the Contact window, the Notes/History tab, the User Field tab, the Phone/Home tab, the Alt Contacts tab, the Status tab, or any other tab you may add to the contact layout.

Every time you have a conversation with someone, write a note to yourself about the particulars of that call. The more you write down, the less you need to remember.

Writing a note

When you select the Insert Note command, ACT! automatically creates a new note and places the cursor in the Note Regarding field, where you type your note. When you're finished, just execute another ACT! command or click something else with your cursor, and your note is saved.

In addition, ACT! automatically inserts the date in the Date column, the time in the Time column, and inserts "Note" in the Type column. Now isn't that easy?

Recording your activities

The ACT! History feature serves several important purposes. First, it provides an automatic record of the date, time, and purpose for all the activities that you have cleared for each contact. (If you don't clear an activity, a history record is not created, so you won't know what you did or didn't do with that person.)

Second, the history feature also automatically stores the date and filename of any correspondence — letters, memos, faxes, and e-mail — that you have sent to the contact.

How ACT! notes can improve business relationships

One day I got a call from a client's assistant who informed me that my appointment with her boss had to be rescheduled. I asked why, and she explained that his wife wasn't feeling well and that he had to take her to the doctor.

I recorded this information as a note in ACT!. When I met with my client a week or two later,

I checked my notes in ACT! and recalled that his wife had been ill. At our meeting, I asked how his wife was feeling. "Much better," he said. He was very appreciative of the fact that I inquired about her health. I also made the sale.

Third, the history feature can hold any specific information that you entered into an ACT! user field that had been selected as a History field with the Define Fields setting. The Last Results field is a History field. Whenever information is entered in the Last Results field, it is automatically recorded as a history item.

To make a field a History field, open the Define Fields dialog box by choosing Edit➪Define Fields from the menu bar, select the desired field, and choose the Generate History option.

With all this recorded information, you can easily answer your boss's questions like: Who did you meet? When did you meet with them? What happened?

Entering history notations

You enter History notations into ACT! from the Record History dialog box, shown in Figure 5-2.

Figure 5-2:
The Record
History
dialog box.

You can open the Record History dialog box in one of three ways:

- ✔ Select Contact➪Record History from the menu bar.
- ✔ Press Ctrl+H.
- ✔ Right-click anywhere within the Contact window, the Notes/History tab, the User Field tab, the Phone/Home tab, the Alt Contacts tab, the Status tab, or any other tab you may add to the contact layout, and select Record History from the shortcut menu.

In the Record History dialog box, choose from the following history choices:

- ✓ **Contact:** Select the contact for whom you wish to record the history item. Click the down-arrow and you can assign this activity to any contact within your ACT! database. The list can be sorted alphabetically by the contact's last name or the company name.

- ✓ **Date:** Select the history item's date.

- ✓ **Time:** Select the history item's time.

- ✓ **Activity Type:** Select Call, Meeting, or To-do as the activity type and type in information about that activity in the Regarding field or enter information from the drop-down menu.

    The information on the drop-down menu changes to reflect entries in the Call, Meeting, or To-do Regarding field when Call, Meeting, or To-do is selected.

    You can select from a pop-up list by pressing F2 when your cursor is in the Regarding field.

- ✓ **Activity Results:** You have the following choices for the result of an activity:

    When a Call is selected, you have the following Call Results to choose from:

    - Call Attempted
    - Call Completed
    - Call Left Message
    - Call Received Call

    When a Meeting is selected, you have the following Meeting Results to choose from:

    - Meeting Held
    - Meeting Not Held

    When a To-do is selected, you have the following To-do Results to choose from:

    - To-do Done
    - To-do Not Done

✔ **New Contact:** Click the New Contact button and the Add Contact dialog box opens. This is where you add a new contact to your database. In Chapter 9, I give a complete dissertation on how to add contacts to ACT!.

✔ **Schedule a Follow-up Activity:** Click the Follow Up Activity button and the Schedule Activity dialog box opens. Here you can schedule an activity for this contact or any contact in your ACT! database. I have a whole chapter on how to schedule activities. It's Chapter 13.

Use the Record History dialog box to record the results of impromptu meetings and to-dos that were completed before they were ever scheduled.

Attaching files to contact records

You can attach any kind of file to a contact record. For example, you may have created a database to track sales to a specific contact. When you attach the database file to the contact's record, that file will always be part of the contact's record. Just double-click the attachment icon and ACT! opens the file in the application that created it.

When you print a letter or word processing document, ACT! enables you to automatically attach the document to the contact's contact record. Chapter 16 covers printing and attaching documents.

This is how you attach a file to a contact record:

1. **Select the contact record.**

2. **Select Contact⇨Attach File from the menu bar, press Ctrl+I, or choose the Attach File command from the menu that appears after clicking the right mouse button.**

   The Attach File dialog box appears.

3. **Select the file you want to attach and click OK.**

   The file is attached to the contact record.

You can attach any file to a contact record by dragging it from the desktop or from the Windows Explorer and dropping it onto the Notes/History tab in the Contact window.

Opening an attached file

To open an attached file, double-click on the attached file icon, and ACT! launches the program that created the file and opens the file.

To launch a program from an attached file, locate the program's executable file (programfile.exe), and make that file the attachment. To launch the program, just double-click on the attachment icon.

Viewing the details of a note, history entry, or attachment

To view the details of a note, history entry, or attachment, highlight the specific item by clicking its icon, click the Details button, and the Details dialog box appears. The Details dialog box shows the same information that displays in the Notes/History tab if all of its columns are displayed.

The Details dialog box displays the following information:

- ✔ **Type:** The Type field displays the type of the item, such as note, attachment, or completed activity.
- ✔ **Date:** The Date field shows the date of the selected item.
- ✔ **Time:** The Time field shows the time of the selected item.
- ✔ **Created by:** The Created by field shows the name of the ACT! user who created the item.
- ✔ **Attachment:** The Attachment field shows any attachments with the selected item.
- ✔ **Group Assignment:** The Group assignment field shows the group to which the selected item is assigned, if any.

Deleting a note, history, or attachment

To delete a note, history, or attachment, highlight the item(s) by clicking the desired icon. Press the Delete key or select the Delete Selected command after clicking the right mouse button. A message box appears asking, `Are you sure you want to delete the selected item(s)?` To delete the selected entry, click Yes.

Create your own reference library

You can create your own reference libraries using the ACT! attachment feature by attaching specific documents to contact records.

If you're an ACT! 2 user and have any library files in the Library field, ACT! will make them an attachment when you convert your ACT! 2 database to the ACT! 4 format.

Here are some of the things you can do with a Reference Library file:

✔ You can store information about a person's family members — such as their birth dates, anniversaries, social security numbers, and credit card numbers.

✔ You can create a list of points that you always want to discuss when you're speaking with someone on the phone — for example, a telemarketing script.

✔ You can store reference information, such as area codes or zip codes, for easy access.

✔ If you have different price lists for your customers, why not record your price lists in a file and attach the appropriate price list to each of your customers? For example, Client X gets a 20-percent discount, Client Y gets a 10-percent discount, and the rest are 100-percenters. When you're talking with a customer on the phone and you need to quote a price, just open the document, and that person's price list appears. And when your price list changes, all you have to do is make the changes to the attached file.

✔ If different product descriptions, company guidelines, parameters, statistics, or other types of information are meaningful to a group of your contacts, store that information in a file and attach it to the contact's record.

With ACT!'s attachment feature, any document, spreadsheet, or graphics file, can become part of your reference library.

To highlight two or more entries next to each other, hold down the Shift key while you click on the first and last entries. To highlight entries not next to each other, hold down the Ctrl key while you select each entry individually.

A highlighted item can be deleted by pressing the Ctrl+X key.

Cutting, copying, and pasting notes, histories, and attachments

From time to time, you may want to move or copy a note, history, or attachment from one contact to another. You do this using the Cut (Ctrl+X), Copy (Ctrl+C), and Paste (Ctrl+V) commands. Just highlight the item you want to cut or copy and select either the Cut or Copy command. Switch over to another contact record and paste the note, history, or attachment into the contact's Notes/History tab.

Modifying the particulars of a note, history item, or an attachment

In the Notes/History tab, you can display up to seven columns. (Adding and removing columns is discussed later in this chapter.) The seven columns are Date, Time, Type, Regarding, Record Manager, Group, and Attachment.

With the exception of the information that ACT! enters in the Type field when it creates a note, records a history item, or creates an attachment, all the information that's in the other ACT! columns can be modified or edited.

- ✔ To modify the Date, Time, or Group, click on the desired field and select a new date, time, or group from the drop-down menu calendar, Mini calendar, or Group drop-down menu.

- ✔ To associate a note, history item, or attachment with a specific group, select the group from the drop-down menu in the Group column.

- ✔ To edit the information in a Regarding field, simply place your cursor in the field and begin typing.

- ✔ To change an attachment, click the Attachment field, and the Browse button appears. Click the Browse button, and the Open dialog box appears, where you can select a new attachment.

When you're finished making your changes, execute another command and your modified note, history item, or attachment is saved.

If you would like to prevent history editing, just disable the Allow History Editing feature. To access the Allow History Editing feature, select the Advanced tab in the Define Fields dialog box, which you open by selecting the Edit⇨Define Fields command from the menu bar.

Sorting your notes, history, and attachments

To change the sort order of the notes, history, and attachments, just click any of the column headings — Date, Time, Type, and so on — and ACT! re-sorts the items in the Notes/History Tab.

You can also place your cursor on the Date, Time, or Type column headings and click the right mouse button. A menu appears where you can select Sort Ascending or Sort Descending. Make your selection and ACT! re-sorts the items. An upward or downward arrow shows the sorting selection.

Viewing notes, history, and attachments

With the Filtering command, you choose which information — notes, history, or attachments — you want to view for a given range of dates.

A Filter button is at the top of the Notes/History tab. This is shown way back in Figure 5-1. Click the button and you can make the same selections described in the Filter Notes/History dialog box.

To open the Filter Notes/History dialog box, select View⇨Filter Current Tab View from the menu bar, or select the Filter command from the menu that appears when you right-click in the Notes/History tab.

You can also show or hide (filter) your notes, histories, and attachments by selecting or not selecting the Notes, Histories, and Attachments check boxes located on the Notes/History tab. (If you want to see those check boxes again, find your way back to Figure 5-1 again.)

In the Filter Notes/History dialog box, you have the following options:

- ✔ **Users:** In the Users section you apply the filter options to selected users or to all users of the database.

- ✔ **Show:** Choose which information to view by selecting or not selecting the Notes, Histories, or Attachments check boxes.

- ✔ **Select Dates:** Your options for viewing dates include All dates, Today, Past dates, Future dates, or a range of dates in the Select dates section.

Working with columns

The Notes/History tab can display up to six columns: Date, Type, Time, Regarding, Group, Record Manager, and Attachment. ACT! enables you to change the look and feel of your columns. You can do the following:

- ✔ **Add columns:** Select the Add Columns command from the menu that appears when you click the right mouse button within the Notes/History Tab, and the Add Columns dialog box appears. Select the column you want to add and click OK.

- ✔ **Change the position of columns:** Click the column heading (the cursor turns into a hand) and drag it to its new position.

- ✔ **Remove a column:** Click the column heading and drag it upwards (the cursor turns into a garbage can) and off the Notes/History tab.

- ✔ **Show/Hide Column Headings:** Select the Show/Hide Column Headings command from the menu that appears when you click the right mouse button.

- ✔ **Change the width of a column heading:** Place the cursor on the line between two column headings — it turns into a sizing tool — and move the column left or right to make the column smaller or wider.

- ✔ **Show Grid Lines:** Select the Show Grid Lines option in the Notes/ History settings in the Colors and Fonts tab of the Preferences dialog box. (Did you get all that?) To open preferences, select Edit⇨Preferences from the menu bar. The Colors and Fonts tab of the ACT! Preference dialog box is explained in Chapter 24.

Changing the tab's appearance

To change the appearance — font, font size, font style, font color, and background color of the Notes/History tab — open the Preferences dialog box and select the Colors and Fonts tab. Open the Preferences dialog box by selecting Edit⇨Preferences from the menu bar. You use this ACT! feature in the same way for every ACT! window and tab — all 11 of them — so I'm only going to explain it once — in Chapter 24.

Printing your notes, histories, and/or attachments

Click the Notes/History Tab, select File⇨Print Notes/Histories from the menu bar, and ACT! prints a custom report.

The Activities Tab

The Activities tab, shown in Figure 5-3, displays the activities — calls, and to-dos — scheduled with the current contact. Click the Activities tab to display all the activities you've scheduled with a specific person.

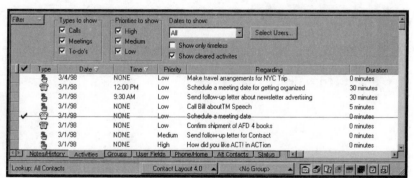

Figure 5-3:
The
Activities
tab.

Some of the things you can do from the Activities tab include

- ✔ Schedule a new activity.
- ✔ Reschedule an activity.
- ✔ Clear an activity.
- ✔ Unclear a cleared activity.
- ✔ Clear multiple activities.
- ✔ Modify a previously scheduled activity.

In addition, you can filter your activities by User, Activity, Priority, and Date.

You can change and customize the appearance of your Activities. You can add or remove the column headings; change the position of the column headings as well as their width; change the font, font size, and font color displayed in the Activities tab; you can even change the background color.

The features of the Activities tab are identical to those of the Task List with only one difference: The Task List shows a list of all your scheduled activities, and the Activities tab shows your activities for a single contact.

For this reason, I decided to explain how to use the features of the Activities tab and the Task List in the chapter on how to use the Task List, which is Chapter 16.

To schedule an activity using the Windows drag-and-drop feature, click on a blank portion of the contact layout (the cursor turns into a circle with a line through it), drag and drop the cursor onto the Task List, or any of the ACT! calendars, and the Schedule Activity dialog box appears. Scheduling activities is covered in Chapter 13.

To print your Activities, click the Activities tab, select File⇨Print Activities from the menu bar, and ACT! prints a custom report.

The Groups Tab

In the Groups tab, you can view a list of all the groups the contact is a member of. The Groups tab is shown in Figure 5-4. Creating ACT! groups is discussed in Chapter 12.

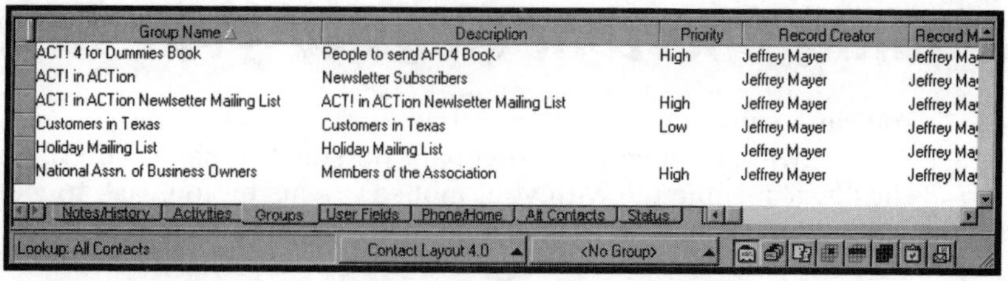

Figure 5-4:
The Groups
tab.

Changing group membership

To change the contact's group membership — you can add a person to a new group or remove a person from an existing group — select Contact⇨ Group Membership from the menu bar, or select the Group Membership command from the menu that appears when you right-click within the Groups tab, and the Groups Membership dialog box appears.

From the Group Membership dialog box, you can view and edit the groups that the selected contact belongs to. You have the following options:

- **Add:** Click the Add button to add the selected contact to the group displayed in the Edit Group field.
- **Remove:** Click the Remove button to remove the selected contact from the group displayed in the Edit Group list.
- **Select All:** With the Select All button, you can select all the listed contacts.

Changing the groups tabs

You customize the appearance of the Groups tab by changing the column headings: Any field that is in a group layout can become a column in the Groups tab. You can also change the position and width of the column headings, as well as the font, font size, font color, and background color. The use of these features is identical to what was described earlier in this chapter in the section about how to customize the Notes/History tab.

Printing group information

To print your Groups, click the Group tab, select File⇨Print Groups from the menu bar, and ACT! prints a custom report.

Assigning Shortcut Keys to Your Tabs

You can open each tab with shortcut keys — Alt+(a letter) — while in the Contact window. If you're a keyboard person, this saves you the trouble of clicking a specific tab with your mouse whenever you wish to view the contact information on a specific tab.

These shortcut keys are already assigned:

- ✔ **Alt+N:** Notes/History tab
- ✔ **Alt+A:** Activities tab
- ✔ **Alt+G:** Group tab

To assign a shortcut key to any of the other tabs in the Contact window you must edit your layout from inside the Layout Designer. This is how you do it:

1. Select Tools⇨Design Layouts.

The Layout Designer opens.

2. Select Edit⇨Tabs.

The Define Tab Layouts dialog box appears, as shown in Figure 5-5.

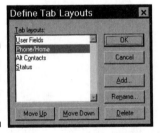

Figure 5-5:
Define Tab
Layouts
dialog box.

3. Highlight a specific tab and click the Edit button.

The Edit Tab dialog box appears. Here you enter, or modify, the tab's name and select the character you wish to use as a shortcut key. You can choose any of the letters in the name as the shortcut key.

You must assign shortcut keys to the tabs of each layout individually.

Editing ACT! layouts is discussed in detail in Chapter 23.

Chapter 6

Defining ACT! Fields

● ●

In This Chapter

▶ Selecting records to customize

▶ Customizing fields

▶ Working with default settings when adding new contacts to your database

▶ Creating drop-down menus

▶ Turning a field into a Trigger field

▶ Creating your own indexed fields

● ●

*I*n this chapter, you discover how to customize the appearance of individual fields within your ACT! database. This flexibility enables you to customize ACT! to fit your individual work habits and work style and makes entering information into ACT! much easier for you.

Once you have customized ACT! fields, you can change the layout of your ACT! fields on the contact layout. To change the layout, you use Layout Designer, which you access by selecting Tools⇨Design Layouts from the menu bar. Customizing your ACT! layouts is discussed in Chapter 24.

The Define Fields dialog box is where you set the individual characteristics, or properties, for each field in an ACT! database. To edit a field's attributes, select Edit⇨Define Fields from the menu bar. The Define Fields dialog box, shown in Figure 6-1, appears.

If you're using ACT! on a network, only the network administrator can access and change the field attributes.

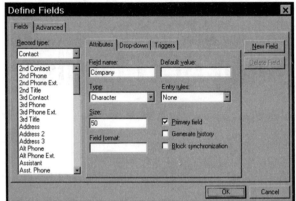

Figure 6-1:
The Define
Fields
dialog box.

Selecting a Record Type to Customize

Before you customize a specific ACT! field, you must first decide whether you want to change the contact fields or the group fields. You do this by choosing either Contact or Group in the Record type field. Next you select the field you want to define by highlighting the field in the Field list box. (The list of fields is displayed in alphabetical order.)

Any field in ACT! can be modified or changed.

To scroll through the list of ACT! fields, use your mouse, the up/down or left/right arrow keys, or the Page Up/Page Down keys. And you can press any letter of the alphabet to move to the first word in the list that begins with that letter. Ctrl+Home takes you to the first item in the list; Ctrl+End takes you to the last item in the list.

Customizing Fields

This section covers all of the different ways to customize ACT! fields.

Changing a field name

Each field has a name that is displayed in an ACT! layout. For example, if you select User 1 in the List of Fields box, the word "User 1" appears in the Field Name box. By changing the name of a field, you change the field's name on the ACT! layout.

The number of characters of a field's name that ACT! displays in a layout is limited to the size of the Field Name. If the name is too long, the text will be truncated when it appears in the layout.

Deciding what type of data to enter in a field

The Type field's drop-down menu contains different types of data you can enter into a field. This variety allows you to customize each individual field for a specific purpose.

- ✔ **Letters and Numbers:** A Character field accepts any character or number in the alphabet. The Company field is an example of a Character field.

- ✔ **Currency only:** In a Currency field, ACT! inserts a dollar sign ($) in addition to commas. Type 123456789, and it appears as $123,456,789. This field accepts only two decimal places unless you make changes to the Windows default number settings.

  To record the dollar amount of a client's most recent order, designate one of your ACT! user fields as both a Currency field and a History field. When you enter the dollar amount of the order, the date and time is automatically recorded as a history item in the contact's Notes/History tab.

- ✔ **Nothing but dates:** A Date field allows only dates. Click the field, and ACT! provides a drop-down calendar from which you select a date. If you want to enter the dates manually, ACT! already provides the slash marks (/) between the day, month, and year.

- ✔ **Initial caps only:** In an Initial Caps field, the first letter in each word is capitalized.

- ✔ **Lowercase only:** In a Lowercase field, every character you type appears as lowercase text.

- ✔ **Numbers only:** In a Numeric field, ACT! automatically inserts a comma after every third number. Type 123456789, and it appears as 123,456,789. Just type your number, and when you tab to the next field or use your mouse to move to another field, ACT! automatically inserts the commas in the proper place. This field only accepts two decimal places unless you make changes to the Windows default number settings.

- ✔ **Phone numbers only:** A Phone Number field accepts only numbers, and they appear in a phone-number format. You don't have to enter the dash between the area code or after the first three digits of the phone number. Type 3129444184, and ACT! enters it as 312-944-4184.

Any field you designate as a phone field — including a fax number, beeper number, or any other kind of phone number — appears in the list of telephone numbers in the Dialer dialog box whenever you click the Dial Phone icon or select the Contact⇨Phone Contact command from the menu bar. If you have a modem, double-click the desired number, and ACT! dials the phone number for you. (When you insert phone numbers, you should always include the area code.)

✔ **Time:** In a Time field, all numbers are changed to a time format, like this: 5:00PM.

✔ **Uppercase only:** In an Uppercase field, any character you type appears as uppercase text. For example, it makes sense to use the Uppercase data type in the State field, so that **il** is displayed as I L.

✔ **URL Address:** Specify a field as a URL (Uniform Resource Locator) Address field to record Web site addresses. With a URL entered, the field becomes an active link to the specified URL so that clicking the address in the field automatically launches your Web browser and your browser goes to the specified Web site.

You change the Windows 95 Number, Currency, Date, and Time settings by opening the Regional Settings dialog box. The Regional Settings dialog box is in the Windows Control Panel (often in the Windows Tools folder).

Sizing a field

In the Size field, you determine the number of characters that can be entered in each field.

Choosing a field format

In the Field Format field, you specify how the data in certain fields (Character, Initial Capitals, Lowercase, or Uppercase) is automatically formatted. You use the following characters as placeholders:

✔ Alphabetic Characters: @

✔ Alphanumeric Characters: %

✔ Numeric Characters: #

Use this feature to record contract or invoice numbers.

Applying rules to the field

In the Entry Rules field, you select what options are available to a user when information is entered into an ACT! field. You choose the Entry Rule options from the drop-down list. You have the following choices:

✔ **None:** Choose None if you do not want any entry rules to apply.

✔ **Protected:** Choose Protected to keep the entries in the field from being modified.

✔ **Required:** Choose Required to specify that information must be selected from the drop-down menu that appears when the user enters the field. With this selection, the field cannot be left blank.

✔ **Only From Drop-Down:** Choose Only From Drop-Down to specify that information *must* be selected from the field's drop-down list.

Working with Default Settings When Adding New Contacts to Your Database

Several settings apply specifically to what information ACT! adds to a new contact record in your database.

When you add a new contact to your ACT! database using the Contact⇨ New Contact command (or pressing the Insert key), ACT! uses the value (data) that has been entered in the Default Value field.

Many ACT! users use this feature to make their life easier when adding a new contact to their ACT! database. You can, for example, insert default values for your city, state, and so on. If the default value needs to be changed after you've created the new contact record, just delete it and enter the new contact information.

You have three ways to add a new contract to your ACT! database. They are as follows:

✔ **Blank contact record:** To insert a new contact without copying any information from the contact whose record you're presently viewing, select the Contact⇨New Contact command. Any default values are inserted into this new contact record.

✔ **Duplicate contact from primary fields:** To add a new contact to the database by copying the data from the primary fields, select the Contact⇨Duplicate Contact command and select the Duplicate Contact From Primary Fields option. This option is useful if, for example, you are adding numerous contacts to the database who all work at the same company.

Choosing the Primary Values command copies the information from the primary fields of the current contact's contact record into the new contact's contact record. (The default primary fields are the Company, Phone, Country Code, Fax Phone, Address 1, Address 2, Address 3, City, State, and Zip Code fields.)

✔ **Duplicate data from all fields:** To insert a new contact by copying all the data from the current contact record, select Contact⇨Duplicate Contact and choose the Duplicate Data From All Fields option.

If you want to designate an additional field as a Primary field — so that information in this field copies into a new contact's record — enable the Primary Field attribute for that field.

Automatically Recording Information in Fields as History Items

ACT! uses history items — part of the Notes/History tab — to maintain a record of all the things that have gone on with a particular contact. When you place a call, attend a meeting, perform a to-do, or send correspondence, including letters, memos, faxes, or e-mail messages, ACT! automatically makes a notation of this event and stores it in the contact's Notes/History tab. This notation includes the date and time the event took place, the type of event, and a brief description of the event.

You can also designate specific fields as History fields. An example of this is the Last Results field. Entering information in the Last Results field — notes of a telephone conversation, for example — automatically records that data as a history item. Another field designated as a History field is the ID/Status field.

Here's an example of how to put the history feature to use. Say you designated the User 4 field as your "Last Sale" field and made it a History field. Whenever you close a sale, just type in the dollar amount of the sale, indicate what was purchased, and the notation is automatically entered as a history item. When you open the Notes/History tab, you see a complete listing of your sales activity — what the person bought, how much was spent, and when the purchase was made.

To designate fields as History fields, enable the Generate history option for that field in the Define Fields dialog box.

I was told of one ACT! user who named a field "Enclosures." He then made a drop-down menu listing the names of everything he encloses when he sends out a letter or other correspondence. The items listed in the enclosure were automatically recorded as history items. By using this ACT! feature, he always knew what information he sent and when he sent it.

Setting Block Synchronization

If you do not want this field to be available for data synchronization, choose this option. Data synchronization is mentioned in Chapter 25.

Creating a New Field

Click the New Field button in the Define Fields dialog box, and ACT! creates a new field. Give the field a name and assign any field attributes (such as Field Name, Default Value, Type) you like to it.

Deleting Fields You Don't Use

If you find that you no longer use certain fields and want to delete them, highlight the field in the Field List box of the Define Fields dialog box and click the Delete button.

When you delete an ACT! field, you lose any information in that field.

Creating Drop-Down Menus

When you select the Drop-down tab for a particular field — the Drop-down entries for the State field are shown in Figure 6-2 — you are provided the opportunity to enter information in a field from a drop-down menu.

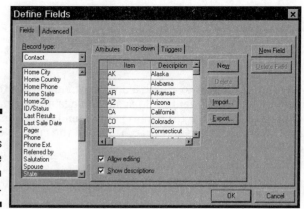

Figure 6-2: The entries of the State drop-down menu.

A drop-down menu contains lists of available entries for a specific field. Choosing an entry from a drop-down menu automatically inserts that entry into the field. This feature saves you lots of the time because you don't have to type the information for each contact. Entering information from drop-down menus is discussed in Chapter 7.

You can do the following in the Drop-down tab:

- ✔ **Name the drop-down item:** In the Drop-down item field, you enter the name of a drop-down item. This option is available by clicking the New button.

- ✔ **Provide a description:** In the Description field, you enter a description of the drop-down item. This option is available after you click the New button.

- ✔ **Add a new item:** To add a new item to the drop-down menu, click the New button.

  A new item is placed at the end of the drop-down menu. However, when it appears as a drop-down menu item in the ACT! field in the Contact window, the menu is sorted alphabetically.

- ✔ **Change an item:** To change an item, click the item and type your changes.

- ✔ **Delete an item:** Highlight the item by clicking the button on the left-hand side of the item, then click the Delete button.

- ✔ **Allow editing:** If you want to allow the database user — yourself or other users — to edit the items in the drop-down menu from the Contact window, choose the Allow Editing option.

- ✔ **Show the descriptions:** If you want the descriptions to be displayed in the drop-down menu, choose the Show Descriptions option.

Exporting and Importing Drop-Down Menu Items

Putting in all the time and effort to create a drop-down menu is a tedious task that you don't necessarily want to do again and again. Fortunately, with ACT! you don't have to. Just save (or export) your menu as a delimited file, and you can apply (import) it to another ACT! field in the current database or in any other database.

Turning a Field into a Trigger Field

The Triggers tab turns ACT! into the center of your computing universe. Want to launch a program or run a macro when you enter or exit a selected field? Here are a few examples of ways to customize ACT! to suit your needs.

- Name an ACT! field "Excel," and every time you place the cursor in the field, ACT! opens a specific spreadsheet for you.

- Name a field "Word," and every time you get a new client or customer, you can create a form letter thanking them for doing business with you.

Creating Your Own Indexed Fields

Each time you enter contact information into ACT!, ACT! updates its index of all the contact's first names, last names, company names, city, state, zip, and so on. (The fields listed on the Lookup menu are all indexed.) When you perform a lookup, query, or sort, ACT! searches the index for the appropriate criteria. This is much faster than searching the entire database. These indexes are stored in separate ACT! files in the database directory.

The fields in an ACT! database are either indexed or non-indexed, and by choosing the Advanced tab in the Define Fields dialog box, you can add additional indexes to your ACT! database.

Creating a new index

This is how you create a new index:

1. **Select your record type, either Contact or Group, in the Record type field.**

   The list of available indexes is displayed.

2. **Click the New Index button and select the field to index from the drop-down list — which is a list of every field in the ACT! database — displayed in the Index On field.**

   This selection is added to the list of indexed fields.

3. **Select a second field in the Then On field to determine the new index field's sort order.**

   You can select None.

4. **Select a third field in the Then On field to determine this index field's sort order, if desired.**

5. **Click OK, and ACT! re-indexes your database.**

Performing a lookup on an indexed field

To perform a lookup on an indexed field, select Lookup⇨Other Fields from the menu bar, and the Lookup Other dialog box appears. Select the field you want to perform the lookup on from the drop-down menu, enter the lookup criteria, and click OK. (Lookups are discussed in Chapter 10.)

Deleting an index

To delete an indexed field (you're deleting the index, not the field), highlight the field in the Field List box and click the Delete button.

Part II
Using Your Database

The 5th Wave   By Rich Tennant

The Perls of Pauline

Help! I'm losing depth recursion!
My subroutines are confusing!!
My hash tables are degrading—
heeeeellp!!

In this part . . .

ACT! is nothing without a database full of information — information that you provide. Before ACT! can become a useful tool for you to use, you need to put some work into it. In other words, you need to fill up your ACT! database with the names, addresses, and phone numbers of everyone you know. In a way, ACT! is sort of like the Senate Un-American Activities Committee — except that it has nothing to do with witch hunts, communism, or Joseph McCarthy. Anyway, the chapters in this part show you how to use, abuse, and otherwise manipulate the information that you put into ACT!.

Chapter 7

Entering Information into Your Database

*T*o enter information into a contact record — yours or anybody else's — the only thing you have to do is type in the information. It's that easy. Just place the cursor in a particular field and start typing.

My Record Is Your Record

The first piece of information you enter into an ACT! database is information about yourself, which you record in the My Record contact record. To locate the My Record contact record, select Lookup⇨My Record from the menu bar.

When you create a new database, ACT! copies the My Record information from the open database to the new database.

When you create a new *empty* database by copying an existing database — select File⇨Save Copy As and then select Create Empty Copy option — ACT! copies the information from the currently open database and displays it in the Enter "My Record" Information dialog box. Here, you can change the My Record information before creating the database.

If you're sharing ACT! with other users (a multi-user database), you entered information about yourself in the My Record contact record when you first signed on as a network user.

It's your database, at least while you're using it

The My Record contact record contains information about the owner, manager, or user of the ACT! database, and that's probably you. (If you're sharing a database on a network, the My Record contact record belongs to the person who is currently using the database.)

Use your own contact record (My Record) to schedule activities that are not associated with other contacts. As you add more people to your ACT! database, you'll find that almost all of your activities will be associated with other contacts, and very few activities will be associated with your contact record. The My Record contact record can also be used to schedule activities for yourself.

ACT! has a new scheduling tool, SideACT!, enabling you to schedule activities — calls, meetings, and to-dos — without assigning them to a specific contact. You can even use SideACT! without using ACT!. I tell you all about SideACT! in Chapter 14.

My Record information

ACT! also uses some of the information in the My Record contact record, such as your name and address, when you create letters, memos, faxes, and custom reports. So make sure that each entry, especially your name, company name, and title, is entered the way you want it to appear in all these formats.

If you plan to use one of the e-mail systems that ACT! supports, add your e-mail address to your contact record (My Record). (To learn more about ACT! e-mail capabilities, see Chapter 20.)

Your contact record is ACT!'s home base

When you turn on ACT!, the contact record that appears on-screen is always your own contact record. If you want to look up your contact record when someone else's contact record is displayed, select Lookup⇨My Record, and your contact record appears. The My Record contact record for yours truly is shown in Figure 7-1.

When you're using ACT! on a network, the program knows who is using it based on the logon ID. When you log on, ACT! knows which My Record contact record to activate and which activities are associated with it.

Many people find ACT! works much faster when they use the keyboard instead of pointing and clicking with the mouse. For example, to look up the My Record contact record, all you have to do is press Alt+L+M (Lookup⇨ My Record). To look up a contact by the last name, press Alt+L+L (Lookup⇨ Last Name), and the Lookup Last Name dialog box appears. To look up a contact by the first name, press Alt+L+F (Lookup⇨First Name), and the Lookup First Name dialog box appears.

Whenever you delete a contact from your database, the date, time, and contact name are recorded in the History file of your contact record. This provides a record of each contact deleted from the database.

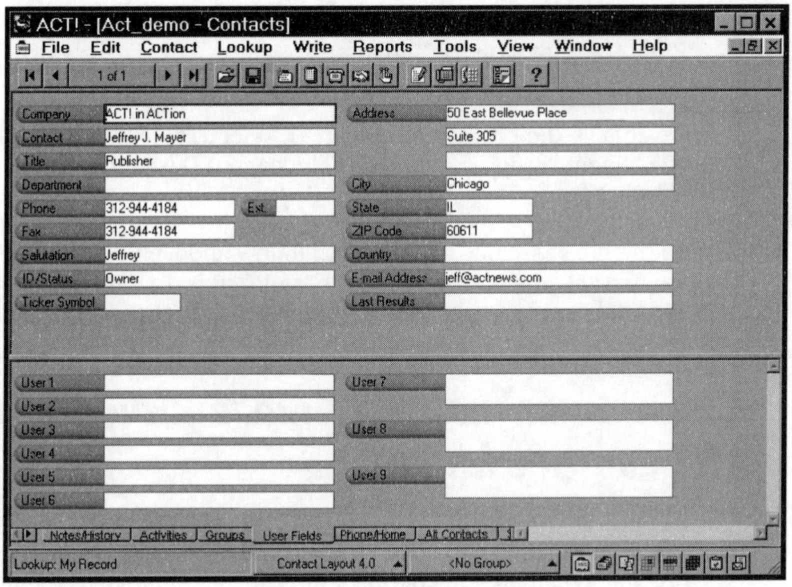

Figure 7-1:
Jeffrey
Mayer's
"My Record"
contact
record.

Entering Information into a Contact Record

To enter information into an ACT! contact record, you must be able to move around the contact layout, and ACT! offers you a number of different ways to do this. You can use the Tab key, the Enter key, or the mouse.

Using the Tab key to move from one field to another

ACT! has a predefined order for entering information into a contact record. When you're in the contact layout and the cursor is in the Company field, watch where the cursor goes when you press the Tab key. It moves to the Contact field. Press Tab again and it goes to the Title field. Each time you tab, the cursor moves down; when you get to the last field in the left-hand column, the cursor moves to the top of the right-hand column. Here are some ACT! tabbing tips:

- When you've tabbed your way through the fields in a User Field tab, Phone/Home tab, and so on, press the Tab key again, and the cursor moves to the next user field tab — that is, it moves from the User Field tab to the Phone/Home tab. This makes it easy for you to continue adding contact information.
- Pressing Shift+Tab moves your cursor backward.
- To change the predefined tab order, select Tools⇨Design Layouts from the Layout Designer menu bar. The Layout Designer is discussed in Chapter 23.

Having the tab sequence in an easy-to-follow and well-thought-out order makes entering contact information easy for you. To enter information in a specific field, just tab over to the field and type in the information.

Using your mouse to move around the contact layout

You can use your mouse to move anywhere on the contact layout. Just place the cursor in the field you want to enter information into, click once, and start typing. When you finish, press the Tab key to move to the next field or use the mouse to move to another field.

The secret of the semicolon

When you enter the name of a company in a contact record, consider how you want ACT! to sort it. For example, if you have a company named "The ABC Manufacturing Company" and you enter it into ACT! just like that, ACT! sorts it alphabetically under the letter "T." Though you would probably prefer that it be filed under the letter "A."

If you type the name as "ABC Manufacturing Company, The" (note the comma), ACT! sorts it under "A," but then, when you create any word-processing document, the company name appears in the letter or other document as "ABC Manufacturing Company, The."

However, using a semicolon (;) after the word "Company" followed by "The" gives you the best of both worlds. ACT! sorts the company alphabetically under the letter "A" but inserts the name in your documents as "The ABC Manufacturing Company."

If you want to insert a person's name in the Company field, type the last name followed by a semicolon, then the first name and the middle initial. For example, I type my name like this: Mayer; Jeffrey J. (Note the semicolon after Mayer.) This appears in ACT! as Jeffrey J. Mayer, but it is sorted alphabetically under "M." (I often place a person's name in the Company field because I want every person's name to appear when I'm doing a lookup by company, and if I leave the field blank, the names don't show up.)

Using the Enter key

With The ACT! Group Stop feature, you can select specific fields to edit when you press the Enter key. You set Group Stops from within the Layout Designer (select Tools⇨Design Layouts from the menu bar). The Layout Designer is discussed in Chapter 23.

Greetings and the Salutation field

When you add a new contact to your ACT! database (adding contacts is covered in Chapter 9), ACT! automatically inserts the person's first name in the Salutation field. This is a nice feature if you send out a lot of letters, memos, and other correspondence.

In the Names tab of The ACT! Preferences dialog box, shown in Figure 7-2, you can have ACT! insert the person's first name or last name. And if you don't want ACT! to insert the person's name at all, choose the Do Not Fill Salutation option. You open the Preferences dialog box by selecting the Edit⇨Preferences command.

Getting Names Right So That ACT! Can Find People

When you enter a person's name into your database, ACT! needs to know the person's first and last names so that ACT! can find that person when you perform a lookup. Now you'd think this would be easy, wouldn't you? But what happens when a person's name is Doctor Stephen Del Grosso, Sr.? (Steve Del Grosso is an ACT! Certified Consultant in Boston and a very good friend. If you have some ACT! questions, give Steve a call at 617-545-6500.) To my knowledge, Steve isn't a doctor, nor is he a senior, but this is just an example and you may know hordes of people who are both doctors and seniors. So, how does ACT! find such a person during a first name or last name lookup?

How does ACT! know to ignore the first name prefix (Doctor) or the last name suffix (Sr.)? And is his last name sorted under "D" for Del, or "G" for Grosso?

To solve this problem, open the Preferences dialog box, select Edit⇨ Preferences, and select the Names tab, which is shown in Figure 7-2.

ACT! name separators tell ACT! what first name prefixes (Doctor, Dr., Mr., Ms., and Mrs.) or last name suffixes (Esq., Jr., Sr., J.D., Ph.D., and M.D.) to ignore when performing either a first name or last name lookup.

The last name prefix options (Del, Von, Van, de, and da) tell ACT! to use this last name prefix as the beginning of person's last name when it sorts the database. (The answer to the Del Grosso question is that ACT! sorts Del Grosso under the letter "D" if the last name prefix was added to the list before his name was inserted in the database.)

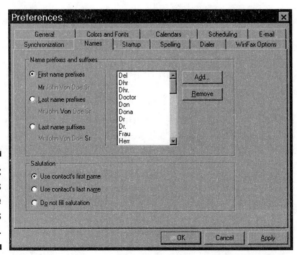

Figure 7-2:
The Names
tab of the
Preferences
dialog box.

You can also enter Steve's name as DelGrosso (without the space between the "L" and the "G"). This ensures that ACT! stores his last name under "D."

The name separator is an important feature because, if you don't enter the correct name separator entries in the Name Separator lists before you enter the name, ACT! won't be able to accurately locate contact records when you perform a lookup.

If you enter a contact with a name separator that is not included in the Name Separators list, the contact's name will not be found when you do a lookup. To find this contact, you must add the name separator to the Name Separators list. Then go back to the contact, delete the name from the contact field, press Ctrl+S to save the record, and re-enter the name. (You don't have to delete the contact record.)

ACT! comes with many pre-installed name prefixes and suffixes, but if you need to add additional name separators to the list, click the Add button.

The Many Data Fields of ACT!

ACT! has different data types available for each field. This diversity allows you to customize each individual field. You can designate a field as a Character field, an Uppercase Only field, a Lowercase Only field, an Initial Caps field, a Date field, a Phone Number field, a Numeric field (ACT! inserts commas), a Currency field (ACT! inserts commas and a $ sign), a Time field, and a URL Address field (where you can enter Web sites). To change a field's data type, you open the Define Fields dialog box by selecting Edit➪Define Fields from the menu bar. (Defining ACT! fields is discussed in Chapter 6.)

Working with drop-down menus and Edit List dialog boxes

The most time-consuming part of setting up and using a database comes when you have to enter information into individual fields. And because much of the information is repetitive, it is a big waste of time to retype the same basic information for one person after another, after another, after another. From my own experience, I can tell you that it gets mighty boring typing "Chicago, IL 60611" over and over and over and over again. ACT! has a simple way of dealing with this problem. It uses drop-down menus and Edit List dialog boxes. (For ACT! 2 users, Pop-up boxes are now called Edit List boxes.)

Let me take a moment to explain what a drop-down menu does. A drop-down menu is a list of items that can be inserted in a field.

The beauty of the drop-down menu is that it enables you to select contact information from a list that is automatically inserted into the field. ACT! offers enormous flexibility because any field in ACT! can be designated a drop-down menu field.

Let me give you an example. To enter information in the City field, you place your cursor in the City field, click the drop-down menu arrow that appears at the right edge of the field, and select a city from the list.

You can also select items from the drop-down menu by typing the first few letters of the item's name or by scrolling through the list by pressing the up- or down-arrow keys.

Customizing drop-down menus

Every field in ACT! can have a drop-down menu that you can customize to display the specific words or phrases you use to describe your daily business activities. If you have data that you enter frequently, you can use a drop-down menu to automate the process of entering that information.

To edit a drop-down menu item, select the Edit List command, which is the last item on the drop-down menu, or press the F2 key, and the Edit List dialog box appears.

From the Edit List dialog box, insert items into an ACT! field by highlighting the item and clicking OK. You can also add, delete, or modify existing drop-down menu items. Here are some Edit List dialog box tips:

✔ While in an Edit List dialog box, just press the first letter of the name you want to insert; for example, in a City field dialog box, press C for Chicago, N for New York, L for Los Angeles, and so on, and ACT! moves to that letter of the alphabet. (To select an item that is not the first entry under that letter, press the same letter again until you find the city you want.) Then press Enter, and ACT! automatically inserts the city's name. This ACT! feature is called *typing ahead*.

✔ To select multiple entries next to each other in an Edit List box, hold down the Shift key while using the mouse or arrow keys to move up or down the list. To select multiple entries that are not next to each other, hold down the Ctrl key while you select the individual items by clicking them with your mouse.

✔ When you use drop-down menus or Edit List dialog boxes to enter information, it ensures that all of the entries in your database will be consistent and spelled correctly, thus enabling accurate database searches.

Customizing descriptions

An ACT! drop-down menu can also insert items that are abbreviations of a word instead of the whole word. The State field is a good example of this feature. Put your cursor on the State field, press F2, and the State field's Edit List box appears. Click the Modify button, and the Modify dialog box appears where you can modify an item and its description.

If the description field isn't available or you're unable to edit the drop-down menu items, go into the Define Fields dialog box and enable the Allow Editing and Show Description options. If you're using ACT! in a multi-user environment, only the administrator can make these changes.

Making drop-down menu fields

If a field doesn't have a drop-down menu available, you can enable the drop-down menu feature by selecting the Edit⇨Define Fields command and clicking the Drop-down tab. Defining ACT! fields is covered in Chapter 6.

Whenever you tab over to a field designated as a drop-down menu, the list is automatically available. Let me give you an example. After I enter a person's company, I press the Tab key and enter the person's name in the Name field. when I get to the City field, I press "c" for Chicago, and Chicago appears in the City field. I press the Tab key once more, and the cursor then moves to the State field; I type **il** and Illinois is entered in the field. As you can see, this really makes the tedious process of entering information a breeze.

Customizing Individual Fields

The following is a list of fields that I suggest you customize with drop-down menus. These are just my suggestions — you should customize your ACT! database to fit your own individual needs, desires, and preferences — but they should give you some ideas as to how powerful and easy ACT! really is to use.

✔ **Title field:** If it's important to note someone's position, title, or occupation, you should populate the Title field's drop-down menu with the appropriate list of positions, titles, and occupations.

✔ **City field:** This drop-down menu should contain frequently entered cities. You use this information in your written correspondence and when you look people up.

✔ **Zip Code field:** If you enter the same zip codes over and over, put frequently entered zip codes in this drop-down menu.

✔ **Last Results field:** The Last Results field is uniquely designed for you to write a quick note to yourself indicating the results of your last contact with a person. You can either type this information into the field or use a drop-down menu item to insert the details of your most recent exchange.

If I may, I would like to ask you to open the Define Fields dialog box, by selecting the Edit➪Define Fields command, and select the Last Results field because I want to point something out to you.

Please note that a check is in the Generate History box. Whenever you write anything in this field, the information is automatically entered as a History item that can be viewed by clicking the Notes/History tab. (Generating ACT! histories is discussed in Chapter 5.)

If you have other fields whose information you would like ACT! to store as a history item, select the Generate History option for those fields.

✔ **ID/Status field:** This is the field that enables you to categorize your contacts. In theory, you can use any ACT! field to categorize your contacts, but the information in the ID/Status field is automatically indexed. This means that when you do a lookup in this field, ACT! gives you the results of your search in a fraction of a second. On the other hand, when you do a search in a field that is not indexed, ACT! must search the entire database. Depending upon the size of the database, this search can take some time. The indexed fields in ACT! are Company, First Name, Last Name, Phone, City, State, Zip Code, and ID/Status.

Any ACT! field can become an indexed field. Just select the Advanced tab in the Define Fields dialog box. (Creating indexed fields is covered in Chapter 6.)

To change the name of the ID/Status field from ID/Status to something like Category (that's what I did), open the Define Fields dialog box, and in the box that says Field Name, type **Category**.

Changing Information

Changing information in ACT! is easy. Just place the cursor in the field that you wish to edit and start typing. When you tab to a field that already contains information, ACT! highlights the entire field, and you replace the old information when you begin typing in the new information.

Editing Several Contact Records at Once

From time to time, you need to edit some of the information that appears in a contact's record. Perhaps a contact's address changes. But it can be a real time-consuming and time-wasting process to change the address for a group of people who work for the same company one at a time. Fortunately, ACT! has a feature that enables you to change contact information for a group of contacts all at once.

Changing field information

The first thing to do is group your contacts together by performing a lookup. (ACT! lookups are discussed in Chapter 10.) After grouping your contacts, open the Replace window. To open the Replace window, select Edit⇨Replace from the menu bar.

Type the new information you want to appear in the selected contact records in the appropriate fields. Using the preceding example, type in the new address of the company that moved. After you finish inserting the new information, select the Replace⇨Apply command from the menu bar, and a message box appears asking, This function modifies all records in the lookup. Are you sure you want to continue? Select Yes, and the new information is entered into each contact's records.

If you need to edit fields that do not appear in the currently selected layout, you must switch to the layout containing those fields. You can choose a different layout by clicking the Layout button at the bottom of the window and selecting a layout from the menu.

If you want to delete the contents of a field, place the cursor in the field and press Ctrl+F5, which inserts the BLANK command.

Keep in mind that all of the contacts in the current lookup are affected by this procedure. If the process is taking too long and you need to cancel it, press Esc. All changes already made will remain in effect.

Moving contact information between fields

You may from time to time want to move information between two fields (swap) or copy information from one field to another.

Swapping contact information between fields

Say that you enter contact information in one field and then decide that you want it in another field. For example, you start out entering a contact's spouse information in the User 1 field (which holds 50 characters), and golf scores in the User 6 field (which holds 75 characters). And now you realize that you want the spouse information in the longer field and want to swap it with the golf scores field. This is how you do it:

1. **Select Edit⇨Replace from the Contact window.**

   The Replace window opens.

2. **Select Replace⇨Swap Fields from the menu bar in the Replace window.**

   The Swap Field Contents dialog box appears.

3. **Select the first field whose contents you want to swap from the list of fields displayed on the drop-down menu in the Swap contents of field.**

4. **Select the second field whose contents you want to swap from the list of fields displayed on the drop-down menu in the With contents of field.**

5. **Click OK.**

Copying contact information from one field to another

Sometimes you may find it useful to copy information from one field to another. Instead of doing it manually, you can use the Replace⇨Copy A Field command from the menu bar in the Replace window. This is how you do it:

1. **Select Edit⇨Replace from the Contact window.**

   The Replace window opens.

2. **Select Replace⇨Copy A Field from the menu bar in the Replace window.**

   The Copy Field Contents dialog box appears.

3. **Select the field whose data you want to copy from the list of fields displayed on the drop-down menu in the Copy contents of field.**

4. **Select the field into which you want to copy the data from the list of fields displayed on the drop-down menu in the To field.**

5. **Click OK.**

Chapter 8

Viewing Your Contacts as a List

● ●

In This Chapter

▶ Viewing contact information

▶ Changing contact information

▶ Scheduling activities

▶ Doing all sorts of useful stuff from the Contact List

● ●

*A*CT! gives you two ways to view your contact data. From the Contact window, you can see your contact information in a field-by-field format; in the Contact List window, you can view and edit your contact information in spreadsheet form.

 To open the Contact List window, select View➪Contact List from the menu bar, click the Contact List button on the status bar, or press the F8 key. The Contact List window is shown in Figure 8-1.

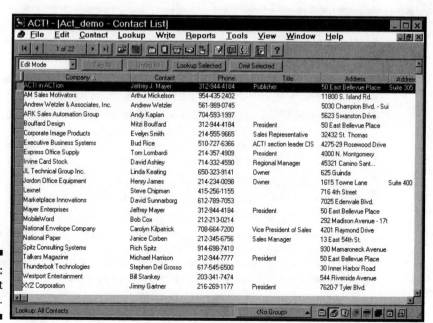

Figure 8-1:
The Contact
List window.

Viewing Contact Information

With the Contact List, you can change the way you view contact information. You can add or remove columns, change their position, change their sort order, and refine your lookups.

Changing from Edit Mode to Tag Mode

To edit contact information, you need to be in Edit Mode. To refine your lookups, you must be in Tag Mode. You can switch from one mode to the other by clicking the Edit/Tag Mode box with your mouse, selecting View⇨Edit/Tag Mode from the menu bar, or pressing Shift+F8.

Selecting the information you wish to view

In the Contact List window, you can change the way contact information is displayed. You have the following options:

TIP

- ✔ **Add a column:** To add a column, right-click a blank portion of the window and select the Add Columns command from the subsequent menu. The Add Columns dialog box appears. Select the column you want to add and click OK.

  Right-click a label on the column heading to get a shortcut menu you can use to add columns.

- ✔ **Change column positions:** To change the position of a column, click the column's heading and drag the cursor (which turns into a hand) to where you want the column; then release the mouse.

- ✔ **Remove a column:** To remove a column, click the column's heading and drag it upward and off the Contact List.

- ✔ **Change column width:** To change the width of a column, place the cursor on the line between two column headings or on the grid line if displayed. The cursor turns into a sizing tool, which you move left or right to make the column wider or smaller.

- ✔ **Show grid lines:** To display grid lines between your columns, select the Show Grid Lines option for the Contact List in the Colors and Fonts tab of the Preferences dialog box.

- ✔ **Lock columns:** To lock your columns in place, click the small bar located at the left-hand edge of the column heading and drag it to the right of the column(s) you want to lock. The columns to the left of the column lock remain in place when you scroll left or right.

Changing the appearance of the Contact List window

To change the font (type size, style, color), and/or the background color of the Contact List window, open the Preferences dialog box, select the Colors and Fonts tab, and then select the Contact List. You open the Preferences dialog box by selecting Edit⇨Preferences from the menu bar.

For all the details on how to change ACT! window and tab appearances, turn to Chapter 24.

Changing the order of contact information

Click a field label in the column heading (such as Contact, Company, City, and so on) and ACT! re-sorts the data in the column based on the information in that column. A little arrow appears in the selected field to indicate which field ACT! is sorting. Here are some sorting tips:

- ✔ Right-click a label on the column heading, and a shortcut menu appears from which you select your sort order — ascending or descending.
- ✔ You can change the sort order by holding down the Shift key while clicking a column heading with your mouse.
- ✔ You can also sort contacts by selecting Edit⇨Sort from the menu bar.

Sorting ACT! contacts is discussed in Chapter 10.

Changing Contact Record Information

To change contact information in the Contact List, select Edit Mode and put your cursor in the desired *cell* — a cell is where a row and a column meet in a spreadsheet — and enter the new information. If a drop-down menu is available, you can enter information from that menu.

Right-click the text in the cell and you find some basic Windows editing tools that are available. Highlight the text in the cell, and you can cut, copy, paste, or delete the text with just a click of your right mouse button. With the Select All command, you can highlight all the text in the cell. If you want to undo your changes, select the Undo command.

Scheduling Activities from the Contact List

Scheduling activities — calls, meetings, and to-dos — directly from the Contact List is a breeze. Select Contact⇨Schedule (Call, Meeting, or To-do) from the menu bar, or select one of the Schedule commands (Call, Meeting, or To-do) when you click the right mouse button, and the Schedule Activity dialog box appears. Scheduling activities is covered in detail in Chapter 13.

Phoning a Contact from the Contact List

You can phone a contact directly from the Contact List. Just select the Contact⇨Phone Contact command from menu bar, or click the right mouse button to access that same command. ACT!'s telephone and dialing features are covered in Chapter 17.

Writing Letters from the Contact List

To create a letter to a contact from the Contact List, just select the letter, memo, or fax you wish to send from the Write pull-down menu, or right-click to access the same command. Chapter 18 discusses correspondence.

Faxing from the Contact List

Send a fax to a contact from the Contact List by selecting the WinFax PRO icon from the toolbar. See Chapter 19 for more on sending faxes from ACT!.

Printing Your Contact List

You print your Contact List by selecting File⇨Print⇨Window from the menu bar. ACT! prints your Contact List just as it appears on your screen.

Managing Your Contacts from the Contact List

From the Contact List, you add new contacts to your ACT! database and remove unwanted contacts.

Adding a contact

Use the Contact⇨New Contact command from the menu bar, select the New Contact command after right-clicking, and press the Insert key to add a new contact using your default values. Information on default values is found in Chapter 6.

To copy information from an existing contact to a new contact, highlight the first contact by clicking the Contact button at the right side of the Contact List window, and then select the Contact⇨Duplicate Contact command from the menu bar. You can also use the Duplicate Contact command, which appears on the shortcut menu when you right-click within the Contact List window.

In the Duplicate Contact dialog box, you can duplicate contact data from the contact's primary fields or from all fields. Adding contacts to your ACT! database is covered in Chapter 9.

Deleting a contact

To delete a contact, highlight the contact by selecting the contact button at the right-hand side of the Contact List window; then select the Contact⇨ Delete Contact command from the menu bar. You can also select the Delete Contact command from the menu that appears after clicking the right mouse button, or you can press the Ctrl+Delete key combination. Deleting contacts is discussed in Chapter 9.

Deleting more than one contact

If you want to delete more than one contact, you must first highlight, or tag, the contacts before you select the Delete command. To highlight contacts that appear in sequence, hold down the Shift key while clicking the first and last contact in the sequence. To highlight contacts that do not appear in sequence, hold down the Ctrl key while you highlight each contact individually. When you've highlighted the desired contacts, select the Delete Contact command as described in the preceding section.

Refining Your Lookups Using the Tag Mode

In the Contact List Tag Mode, you refine your lookups by tagging or untagging your contacts. First create your lookup and then go through the list and tag the contacts by clicking them — a plus (+) sign appears in the left-hand column — one by one. (You can also "tag" a contact by pressing the space bar.)

Once you select the contacts, you can refine your lookup in one of two ways.

✔ You can click the Lookup Tagged button, which will create a lookup of only the tagged contacts.

✔ You can click the Omit Tagged button, which will create a lookup of the contacts who were *not* tagged.

The Tag All, Untag All, Lookup Tagged, and Omit Tagged commands are also available from the menu that appears when you right-click in the Contact List window.

Returning to the Contact Window

Once you've refined your lookup, double-click on one of the contacts in the Contact List, and ACT! opens the lookup in the Contact window and displays the chosen contact's record.

Chapter 9

Adding and Removing Contacts

● ●

In This Chapter

▶ Adding new contacts

▶ Deleting contacts

▶ Don't wipe out your ACT! database by mistake

▶ Undeleting deleted contacts

● ●

Adding New Contacts to Your ACT! Database

ACT! offers several ways to add new people to your ACT! database from either the Contact window or the Contact List window. The commands are the same in both windows. You can

✔ Insert a new contact without copying any information from the record of the currently displayed contact into the new contact record (also referred to as *default values*).

✔ Insert a new contact by copying some information from the record of the currently displayed contact into the new contact record (also referred to as *primary fields*).

✔ Insert a new contact by copying all the information from the record of the currently displayed contact into the new contact record (also referred to as *all fields*).

The ACT! software designers sometimes get rather technical and use a phrase such as "default value" without explaining what a value is. A *value* is anything that you enter in a specific field. When you enter someone's name in the Contact field, the person's name is the value. When you enter a phone number in the Phone field, that number is the value.

Using the New Contact command

When you add a new contact to your ACT! database by selecting Contact⇨New Contact from the menu bar, ACT! uses the default values that are selected in the Define Fields dialog box in creating the new contact record. Defining ACT! fields is discussed in Chapter 6. To open the Define Fields dialog box, select Edit⇨Define Fields.

You can also insert a new contact by pressing the Insert key or by selecting the New Contact command after clicking the right mouse button.

By entering default values in the Default Value field, you can enter contact information that you want ACT! to insert in every new contact record that you create using the New Contact command. To enter default information, just highlight the field (City, for example) in the List of Fields field and type the desired default value (Chicago) data in the Default Value field.

If you have repetitive information that you enter for almost every one of your new contacts, such as city, state, zip, or telephone area code, you can insert this specific information into the respective Default Value fields, and it will appear in every new contact record that you create. Don't worry, you can easily overwrite this information, as it isn't applicable to every contact you add to your ACT! database. Just highlight the text and enter the new information.

Using the Duplicate Contact command

When you add a new contact to your ACT! database by using the Contact⇨Duplicate Contact command, the Duplicate Contact dialog box appears, as shown in Figure 9-1. You can also access the Duplicate Contact command by clicking the right mouse button and selecting Duplicate Contact from the shortcut menu.

Figure 9-1:
The
Duplicate
Contact
dialog box.

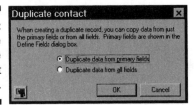

The Duplicate Contact dialog box gives you two choices:

✔ Duplicate data from primary fields
✔ Duplicate data from all fields

I describe these two choices in the following sections.

Duplicating data from primary fields

When you select the Duplicate Data from Primary Fields option to create a new contact record, ACT! copies the information from the primary fields of the current contact — Company, Phone, Address, and so on — into the new contact.

You can specify which fields are primary fields in the Define Fields dialog box.

When you select the Primary field attribute in the Define Fields dialog box, you specify that you want the information in a particular field to be copied into a new contact's record whenever you create a new contact by using the contact's primary fields.

Select the Duplicate Data from Primary Fields option when you want to create a contact record for a person who works for the same company or organization as one of your other contacts. This way, you have to type only the new person's name and phone number because the other information remains the same.

Duplicating data from all fields

When you add a new contact to your ACT! database by selecting the Duplicate Data from All Fields option, ACT! inserts all the information that's entered in the displayed contact record, except for the contact's name, into the new contact record.

Select the Duplicate Data from All Fields option when you want to copy all the information from an existing contact to a new contact.

Saving your new contact record

After you've selected one of the two options — Duplicate Data from Primary Fields or Duplicate Data from All Fields — a new ACT! contact screen appears. You then enter the information for the new contact into the individual fields, and ACT! automatically saves your new contact's contact record.

Adding new contacts from the Schedule Activity dialog box

When you're scheduling an activity for a person who isn't already in your ACT! database, you can now add the new person to your database. You do this by clicking the Schedule Activity's Contact button and selecting New Contact. The Add Contact dialog box appears, which is shown in Figure 9-2. Scheduling activities is covered in Chapter 13.

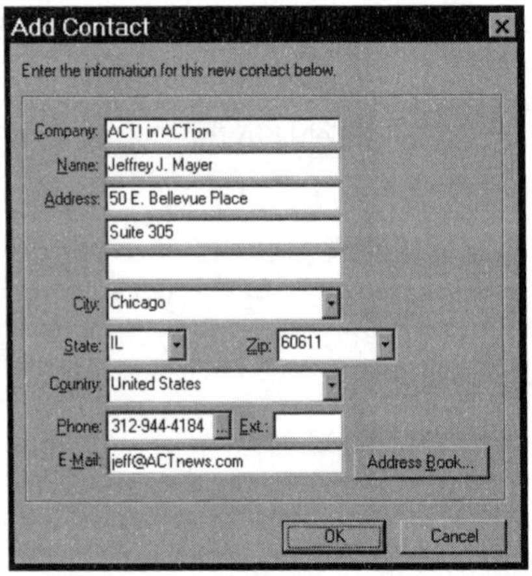

Figure 9-2:
Add
Contact
dialog box.

Adding new contacts to your database from the Internet Lookup Directory

ACT!'s Internet Directory Lookup enables you to find people over the Internet. To find someone, all you've got to do is select Lookup➪Internet Directory, type in a person's name, and select which directory service you want to use — Bigfoot, WhoWhere, or Yahoo!. ACT! then logs onto the Internet, accesses the directory, and displays a list of names.

To add a person to your ACT! database just highlight the name and click the Add Contact button. The Add Contact dialog box, shown in Figure 9-2, opens and enables you to enter the person's name, address, and other information. I just happen to cover the subject of how to find people in ACT! in Chapter 10.

Removing Contacts from ACT!

From time to time, you'll need to remove people from your ACT! database. People move away or change jobs. Or you may have a person in your ACT! database that you don't plan to call again, so you decide that this name needs to be removed from the database.

In ACT!, you can easily delete a contact record. All you have to do is bring up the contact's record in the Contact window and select Contact⇨Delete Contact from the menu bar. You can also select the Delete Contact command from the menu that appears after clicking the right mouse button, or you can press Ctrl+Delete. Any of these actions brings up the Delete Contact dialog box. Here, you are warned that deleting contacts cannot be undone, and a message box appears that states Deleting contacts cannot be undone. Would you like to delete the current contact or the entire contact lookup? To delete the current contact you click the Contact button.

When you select the Delete Contact button, a message box appears stating, Are you sure you want to permanently delete this contact? If you click Yes, the contact's contact record is permanently removed from your ACT! database and cannot be retrieved. (The default setting is No so that you can't accidentally delete a contact.)

In addition to being able to delete an individual contact record, you can also delete an ACT! lookup, which is a group of contact records. When you perform a lookup in ACT!, you can group a number of contacts together — for example, everybody who lives in Chicago or everybody who has the last name of Smith.

When you select the Contact⇨Delete Contact, a dialog box appears asking whether you want to delete the current contact or the entire lookup. Click the Delete Lookup button and ACT! asks you, Are you sure you want to permanently delete this lookup containing [number of records to be deleted] records? If you do, click Yes.

Don't Wipe Out Your ACT! Database by Mistake

During the past year I've received a number of telephone calls from ACT! users who were having a problem. Why were they calling? They had deleted their entire ACT! database by mistake.

This is what they had done: They deleted a lookup instead of deleting a single contact, and the lookup just happened to be every person in the database. Before they knew it, ACT! deleted every contact record. All that remained was the My Record contact record.

Most experienced ACT! users understand the difference between deleting a contact and a lookup. But many inexperienced users may not.

Today, many users across large networks may use the same ACT! database. That is why *every* ACT! user needs to know the difference between deleting a contact and deleting a lookup.

A *lookup* — lookups are discussed in the next chapter — is a collection of contact records within the database that are grouped together after a database search. And though only one contact record is displayed at a time, you can make a lookup of a single contact record, many contact records, or the entire database.

When you perform a lookup — first name, last name, company, city, and so on — you search your ACT! database for contact records with similar or identical information, such as everybody who has a last name of Smith or everybody who lives in Chicago. When ACT! finds these records, it groups them together.

The type of lookup you're performing is shown at the bottom-left corner of the Contact window.

Stopping the deletion of lookups

As the contacts in the lookup are being deleted, a status box appears that shows the progress of the deletion and the Record Counter begins counting backwards as ACT! removes contacts from the database.

To stop the deletion process, click the Cancel button on the status box.

Undeleting Deleted Contacts

ACT! has a utility — ACTDIAG.EXE — that enables you to undelete deleted contacts. This utility restores all deleted contacts since the database was last compressed and reindexed.

ACTDIAG.EXE does not have a help file or other documentation. I suggest calling ACT! technical support at 541-465-8645 and have them walk you through the undeletion process.

Part III
Working with ACT! Contacts

The 5th Wave   By Rich Tennant

FIRED
YOU

"NIFTY CHART, FRANK, BUT NOT ENTIRELY NECESSARY."

In this part . . .

1 explain how you find people in your ACT! database, and I also show you how to create groups of contacts, a great feature that will make your life much easier.

Chapter 10

Finding People in ACT!

· ·

· ·

*O*ne of the most important — and most powerful — features in ACT! is its lookup feature. With the lookup feature, you can find anyone in your ACT! database in just a fraction of a second. (You can also search your ACT! database for any piece of information, or key word, but searching can take a lot longer than a fraction of a second if you have a large database.) When you perform a lookup, you're searching your ACT! database for contact records that contain similar or identical pieces of information.

Lookup Basics

When you use the Lookup command, you're actually creating a *group* of contacts from within your ACT! database. For example, if you do a lookup of *Chicago* by selecting Lookup⇨City and typing **Chicago**, you create a group of contact records of people who live or work in Chicago. Or if you do a lookup of *Smith* by selecting Lookup⇨Last Name and typing **Smith**, you create a group of contact records of people who have the last name of Smith. Here are some lookup tips:

> ✔ A lookup remains active until you do another lookup.
>
> ✔ You can create specific groups of ACT! contact records while keeping your ACT! database intact. (I discuss how to do this task in Chapter 12.)
>
> ✔ To see your whole ACT! database after you've performed a lookup, select Lookup⇨All Contacts.

If you can't remember how a person's name is spelled, just type the first two or three letters of the name when you do a lookup, and ACT! creates a list of all your ACT! contacts whose names have those letter combinations. To see a list of the contact records that were grouped in a lookup, select View⇨ Contact List, click the Contact List icon, or press F8, and the Contact List window opens (see Figure 10-1). Then you can scroll through the list until you find the name that you're searching for.

The Lookup menu offers you a number of ways to look up information in ACT!. You can look up contact records by My Record, All Contacts, Company, First Name, Last Name, Phone, City, State, Zip Code, ID/Status, Other, Previous, Keyword, By Example, and Internet Directory.

Using Instant Lookups

Three selections in the Lookup menu are predefined — My Record, All Contacts, and Previous. All you need to do is make your selection.

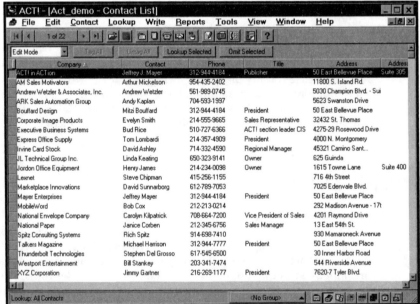

Figure 10-1:
The Contact
List
window.

Make ACT! your electronic Rolodex

Add to your ACT! database the names, addresses, and phone numbers of everybody you speak with or meet because you just don't know if — or when — you'll need to speak with that person again. And when you do need to find someone's phone number, just look up either the person's first or last name, and the contact record is displayed before you can blink your eye.

When performing lookups, I suggest that you use the keyboard because it's so much faster than using the mouse.

To look up a person by first name, just press Alt+L+F (Lookup⇨First Name), type in the first three or four letters of the first name, and press Enter. To look up a person by last name, press Alt+L+L (Lookup⇨Last Name), type the first three or four letters of the last name, and press Enter. Then, if you have a modem, use ACT! to dial the phone for you. As a result of the conversation, you'll probably have to schedule some type of activity with that person. Go ahead and schedule that activity now, before you move on to your next task.

Finding your My Record contact record

When you want to find *your* contact record, you can perform a lookup and search for either your first or last name, but in ACT!, you don't have to work that hard. Instead, you can just look up My Record by selecting Lookup⇨ My Record, which is the contact record that contains information about the owner or main user of the database, who is you when you're using it. (If you're sharing a database, the My Record contact record displays the contact information of the person who is currently using the database.)

When you're using ACT! on a network, you tell ACT! that you're the user when you enter your name and password. After you enter your name and password, ACT! knows which My Record contact record to activate.

Looking up everyone in your database

To find everyone in your ACT! database, or in the current group, select Lookup⇨All Contacts. ACT! lists all your contacts alphabetically, first by the company's name and then by the contact's name. So when you want to scroll through your entire database, just look up everyone and then press F8 to open the Contact List. Refining your lookups with the Contact List window is discussed later in this chapter. (I discuss the features of the Contact List in Chapter 8.)

Viewing your previous lookup

To view your previous lookup, select Lookup⇨Previous, and ACT! displays your previous lookup.

Use the Previous command when someone needs a phone number or address. Say, for example, you're talking to Jane on the phone, and she asks you for Tarzan's address. Do a lookup for Tarzan, and after you give Jane the information, use the Previous command to return to Jane's contact record.

Performing Standard Lookups

The majority of your lookups may be for information in the following ACT! fields: Company, First Name, Last Name, City, State, Zip Code, and ID/Status. ACT! considers these to be *standard lookups*.

When you do a lookup for Company, City, State, Zip Code, or ID/Status, you can access the same drop-down menus that are used in the respective fields in the Contact window — if the respective fields have been designated as drop-down menu fields in ACT!'s Define Fields dialog box. (To read more about defining ACT! fields, turn to Chapter 6.)

After you perform any of the lookups listed in this section, you can view the contact records individually by using the Page Up/Page Down keys or by clicking the Previous/Next Contact buttons on the toolbar. Or you can view the group as a list by pressing F8, which opens the Contact List window.

Looking up people who work for the same company

When you want to perform a search for the contact records of all the people who work for the same company, choose Lookup⇨Company from the menu. This lookup groups all the contact records of the people who work for a particular company together.

I discuss the Replace Lookup, Add to Lookup, and Narrow Lookup options (located in the Lookup for Company dialog box) later in this chapter.

Looking up people with the same first name

When you want to find someone by his or her first name, choose First Name from the Lookup menu, type in the person's first name, and ACT! creates a group of all the people in your database who have that same first name.

Many times, I look up people by their first names because I can't remember how their last names are spelled. I then open the Contact List so I can scroll through the list. After I locate the person, I double-click the Contact button to the left of the name, and ACT! brings up the contact record.

Looking up people with the same last name

When you want to find someone by his or her last name, choose Last Name from the Lookup menu, and ACT! creates a group of all the people in your database who have that same last name.

I use the ACT! Last Name lookup feature all day long. When I want to find a person's contact record, I just press Alt+L+L (Lookup⇨Last Name) to bring up the Last Name Lookup dialog box; I type in the first three or four letters of the person's last name, press Enter, and ACT! groups all the people together who have those letters in their last names. Then I use the Page Up/Page Down buttons to scroll through the list.

Looking up people who live or work in the same city

When you want to perform a search of all the people who live or work in the same city, choose City from the Lookup menu, type in the city's name or select it from the drop-down menu, and ACT! creates a group of all the people in your database who live or work in the selected city. If the City field has been designated as a drop-down menu field, you can access the City drop-down menu by clicking the drop-down menu button. (I cover designating fields as drop-down menu fields in Chapter 6.)

Every once in a while, I find that I want to call someone, but I can't remember the exact spelling of either his or her first or last name, so I perform a lookup of the person's city, and then I open the Contact List (by pressing F8) and scroll through the list.

The next time you plan an out-of-town business trip, search for all the people who work in the cities you'll be visiting to see whether you have any additional people that you need to meet with. You can then group-schedule a call, instead of scheduling a call one contact at a time. You can also send out a mass mailing to these people.

*Business*MAP PRO is a product that provides streets for every town in the United States. For more information, contact ESRI, 1202 Richardson Drive, Richardson, TX 75080; phone 800-257-0624 or 972-664-0456; Web site `www.esri.com/businessmap`.

Looking up people who have the same phone number prefix or area code

When you want to do a lookup based on a phone number prefix or area code, choose Phone from the Lookup menu, and ACT! creates a group of all the people in your database who have the same phone number prefix or area code. You must include the area code in the search criteria. For example, if you wanted to send a mailing piece to everybody in the northern suburbs of Chicago, you can do a lookup for the 708 area code, and ACT! groups everybody who has a 708 area code.

Looking up people who live or work in the same state

When you want to perform a search for all the people who live or work in the same state, choose State from the Lookup menu, and ACT! creates a group of all the people in your database who live or work in the same state.

Looking up people who live or work in the same zip code area

When you want to search for all the people who live or work in the same zip code, or Zip Code range, choose Zip Code from the Lookup menu, and ACT! creates a group of all the people in your database who live or work in the same zip code area.

Looking up people who have the same ID/Status

When you want to search for people who have the same ACT! ID/Status, choose ID/Status from the Lookup menu, and ACT! creates a group of all the people in your database who have the same ID/Status.

You can use the ID/Status field to assign your own categories to your contacts. For example, you may want to identify contacts as customers, prospects, clients, vendors, friends, family, relatives, and so on.

When you perform a lookup for contacts by their ID/Status, use the drop-down menu. This ensures that you're using the correct search criteria.

Looking up other indexed fields

By selecting Lookup⇨Other Fields, you can select from the list of available fields in the Lookup Other dialog box.

From the drop-down list in the Available Fields field, you can perform a lookup on any field that you have selected as an indexed field. (Any ACT! field can become an indexed field. I discuss defining ACT! fields in Chapter 6.)

Using ACT! and the Internet

ACT! has added some very powerful Internet features that enhance your lookup capabilities. I'm mentioning them in the section on ACT! lookups because I want you to know that you have more lookup power at your fingertips.

Internet Directory

With ACT!'s Internet Directory you can search for people by using several Internet directory services — Bigfoot, WhoWhere, and Yahoo!.

Internet Links

With ACT!'s Internet Links — which you can locate by selecting Tools⇨ Internet Links — you can log onto Symantec's Web site and get information about ACT!, reach ACT! technical support, and find out about a whole lot more cool stuff.

You can also log onto a number of Yahoo! sites where you can get driving directions to client's offices, find local maps, search for people, look up corporate information, and a whole lot more.

And best of all, you can add your own sites to the list.

To find out all about ACT!'s Internet links, check out Chapter 22. But before you do, finish reading the rest of this chapter.

Finding people on the Internet

ACT! 4 has a new feature that enables you to search for people by using several Internet directory services — Bigfoot, WhoWhere and Yahoo!.

To search the Internet, select Lookup⇨Internet Directory, and the Internet Directory dialog box appears. This is shown in Figure 10-2.

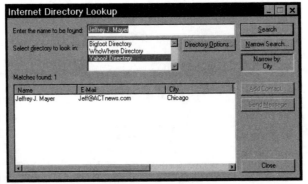

Figure 10-2: The Internet Directory dialog box.

You must have an Internet service provider (ISP) in order to use the powerful Internet Directory feature.

This is how you search the Internet:

1. **Enter a person's name in the Enter name to be found field.**

2. **Select the directory you want to look in.**

3. **Click the Search button.**

   ACT! logs onto the Internet, goes to the selected directory, and the search results are displayed.

Narrowing your Internet searches

If your search results are too large, you may want to narrow your search. You do this by clicking the Narrow Search button. From the Narrow Search dialog box you can narrow your search by selecting City, State, Country, Organization, or All.

Adding, removing, and editing Internet directories

Click the Directory Options button and the Directory Options dialog box appears. Here you can select the Add, Edit, or Remove options to search directories from your Internet Lookup directory.

Adding contacts to your database

After you find a contact, you can add it to your ACT! database by highlighting the person's name and clicking the Add Contact button. The Add Contact dialog box appears, and you enter the person's name, address, and so on. Adding contacts to your ACT! database is covered in Chapter 9.

Sending e-mail with the help of ACT!

If you want to send an e-mail message to someone you just located, highlight the person's name and click the Send Message button. Sending e-mail is covered in Chapter 20.

Refining Your Lookups

Sometimes you may want to expand or refine your lookups. Doing so saves you the time and trouble of performing sophisticated database searches.

Narrowing your lookups

When you narrow your lookup, you are refining the number of contacts that match certain search criteria. For example, say that you're going on a business trip and want a list of all your customers in Boston. This is what you do:

1. **Select Lookup⇨City, type** Boston, **and click OK.**

   ACT! creates a group of everybody who is in Boston.

2. **Select Lookup⇨ID/Status and type** Customer.

   This step assumes that you use the ID/Status field to categorize your contacts and that one of your categories is Customer.

3. Select the Narrow Lookup option.

Selecting this option tells ACT! to search the already existing lookup list for contacts matching the current lookup criteria. This option creates a smaller and more refined lookup.

4. Click OK.

ACT! creates a lookup of all your customers in Boston.

Expanding your lookups

When you expand your lookups, you're adding the results of two or more lookups together. For example, say that you're going to California and want a list of all your contacts in Los Angeles and San Francisco. This is how you can compile your list:

1. Select Lookup⇨City, type Los Angeles, **and click OK.**

ACT! creates a group of everybody who is in Los Angeles.

2. Select Lookup⇨City, and type San Francisco.

3. Select the Add to Lookup Option.

This option tells ACT! to add the contacts found using the lookup criteria to the current lookup.

4. Click OK.

ACT! creates a lookup of everybody you know in both Los Angeles and San Francisco.

Sorting Your Database

When you perform an ACT! lookup, the program sorts the contact information as shown in Table 10-1.

Table 10-1	The Sort Order of Contact Information
Sort By	*Sort Order*
Company	Company, Last Name, First Name
First Name	First Name, Last Name, Company
Last Name	Last Name, First Name, Company

Sort By	Sort Order
Phone	Phone Number, Last Name
City	City, Company, Last Name
State	State, City, Company
Zip Code	Zip Code, City, Company
ID/Status	ID/Status, Company, Last Name

Here's an example of how ACT! sorts the database when you do a lookup for a company. First, the lookup is sorted by the company's name; next, the contacts are sorted alphabetically by their last names; and finally, if two or more people have the same last name, they are then sorted alphabetically by first names.

Sorting alphabetically

To sort your ACT! database alphabetically, select the Lookup command that you want — such as Company, First Name, Last Name, and so on — leave the Lookup dialog box empty, click OK, and your lookup is sorted in alphabetical order.

Changing the sort order

To change the ACT! sort order, select Edit⇨Sort from the ACT! menu bar, and the Sort Contacts dialog box, shown in Figure 10-3, appears.

Figure 10-3:
The Sort
Contacts
dialog box.

You use the Sort Contacts dialog box to sort the database in ascending or descending order. You can use three fields to customize the sort:

✔ **Sort Contacts By:** In the Sort Contacts By section, you specify the first field (criteria) that you want to sort your lookup by. You can also choose whether to perform the sort in (A to Z) or descending (Z to A) order.

✔ **And Then By:** In the And Then By section, you specify the second-level criteria that you want to sort your lookup by. You can also choose whether to perform this sort in ascending or descending order.

✔ **And Finally By:** In the And Finally By section, you specify the third-level criteria that you want to sort your lookup by. You can also choose whether to perform this sort in ascending or descending order.

To sort by one set of criteria, choose None as the second and third sort criteria.

Searching Your Entire Database by a Key Word

To search your entire ACT! database — the contact database, notes database, history database, activities database, and your e-mail addresses — select Keyword from the Lookup menu, and the Lookup Keyword dialog box appears.

Enter the key word or string of words (a phrase), and ACT! creates a group of all the people in your database who have that key word or phrase somewhere within their contact record.

Keep in mind that a key word search can take a long time, and if you have a large database, it can take a *very* long time.

A word about key word searches

You can enter the data that you want ACT! to find in a key word search in any of the following ways:

✔ You can have ACT! search for a single word, such as "price."

✔ You can use wild cards (*) to search for an incomplete word. See the following section for more info on using wild cards.

✔ You can use Boolean operators to look for two or more words. For example, you can search for Chicago AND Detroit, Chicago OR Detroit, Chicago AND_NOT Detroit, Chicago OR_NOT Detroit. (Boolean operators are discussed later in this chapter.)

✔ You can search for complete phrases, such as "price list enclosed."

Key word lookups are not case sensitive. For example, if you do a search for the key word "National," ACT! includes the words "National" (first letter capitalized), "NATIONAL" (all caps), and "national" (all lowercase) in the search results.

Wild cards, you make my heart sing

When you want to look up words that have specific groups of letters in them, you use wild cards. You denote a wild card search by placing an asterisk (*) before or after a group of letters. The following is an explanation of how to use wild cards:

✔ **An asterisk at the end of the group of letters:** If you want to do a search for all the words that begin with the letters "con," type **con***. When your search is complete, you will find such words as contest, conversation, convoluted, and conversion.

✔ **An asterisk at the beginning of a group of letters:** If you want to do a search for all the words that end with the letters "con," type ***con**. After your search is completed, you will find such words as falcon, lexicon, and icon.

✔ **An asterisk at the beginning and ending of a group of letters:** If you want to do a search for all the words that have the letters "con" in the middle of the word, type ***con***. After your search is completed, you will find such words as intercontinental, economy, economical, and iconoclast.

Viewing the Status of Your Lookup

When ACT! completes your lookup, you see the first contact record of the lookup on-screen.

Determining the position of a contact record within a lookup

To determine the position, within the current lookup, of the contact record that's presently displayed on-screen, check the numbers that are displayed in the Status area on the toolbar (see Figure 10-4). For example, 7 of 15 means that this contact record is the 7th record out of a total of 15 records; 125 of 327 means that this contact record is the 125th record out of a total of 327 records.

Figure 10-4:
The Status
area on the
toolbar.

Moving through a lookup one record at a time

You have a couple of ways to move — one record at a time — through the contact records of your lookup. You can use the Previous/Next Contact buttons, or you can use the PageUp/PageDown keys.

- ✔ **The Previous/Next Contact buttons:** Click the Previous/Next Contact buttons, located on the toolbar (they're the buttons with the single arrows) to move to the prior or next contact in the lookup. The buttons are shown in Figure 10-4.

- ✔ **Ctrl+PageUp/Ctrl+PageDown keys:** The Ctrl+PageUp/Ctrl+PageDown keys move you to the prior or next contact in the lookup.

- ✔ **PageUp/PageDown keys:** The PageUp/PageDown keys move you to the prior or next contact in the lookup (if you selected the Move Between Records Using ACT! 2.0 Shortcut Keys command in the General tab of the Preferences dialog box).

Moving to the first or last record in a lookup

You have two or three ways in which you can move to the first or last contact record of your lookup. You can use the First/Last Record buttons on the toolbar or the Home and End keys.

✔ **The First/Last Record buttons:** Click the First/Last Record buttons (they're the buttons with the arrow facing a line) to move to the first or last record in the lookup. These buttons are shown in Figure 10-4.

✔ **Alt+Home/Alt+End:** You can move to the first record in your lookup by pressing Alt+Home, and you can move to the last record in your lookup by pressing Alt+End.

✔ **Ctrl+Home/Ctrl+End:** You can move to the first record in your lookup by pressing Ctrl+Home, and you can move to the last record in your lookup by pressing Ctrl+End (if you selected the Move Between Records Using ACT! 2.0 Shortcut Keys command in the General tab of the Preferences dialog box).

Scrolling through your contact list

To scroll through the Contact List from the keyboard, you can either use the up- and down-arrow keys or the Page Up and Page Down keys. To scroll through the Contact List with your mouse, click and hold the scroll buttons with your mouse pointer. Pressing Ctrl+Home takes you to the first item on the list; pressing Ctrl+End takes you to the last item on the list.

Typing ahead: Finding people by name

ACT! has a feature that's called *typing ahead*. To find people in your Contact List by name, click the Name column and begin typing the person's last name. ACT! highlights the first person whose name begins with those letters.

To find people in any Contact List column — Firm, Title, Address, and so on — just highlight the specific column and begin typing.

Using the Lookup indicator

The Lookup indicator, which is on the status bar at the bottom of the Contact window, tells you the type of lookup — Everyone, First Name, Last Name, City, State, and so on — that you have performed. This indicator helps you keep track of how you grouped your contacts.

For example, if the Lookup indicator says "All Contacts," all the contacts in the current group have been selected. (I cover grouping contacts in Chapter 12.)

Displaying a list of your contacts

With the Contact List window, you can see the results of your database search as a list. From the Contact List, you can select an individual contact's record from a list instead of having to scroll through each contact record in the Contact window.

 To open the Contact List window (shown in Figure 10-5), select View⇨ Contact List, press F8, or click the View Contact List button. I discuss ACT!'s Contact List in Chapter 8.

Using the Contact List to Further Refine Your Lookup

After you've performed a lookup to group a number of people together, the Contact List window enables you to remove selected people from the lookup.

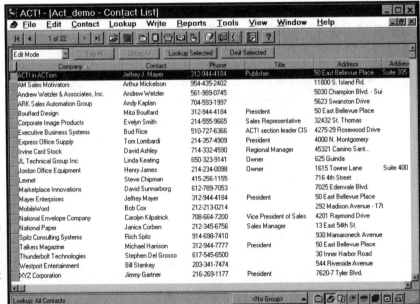

Figure 10-5:
The
Contact List
window.

Removing a single person from the lookup in the Edit Mode

In the Edit Mode you can change the way you view contact information. You can add or remove columns, change their position, change their sort order, and refine your lookups by selecting the Lookup Selected or Omit Selected commands.

To Tag contacts, before refining your lookup, you must be in Tag Mode.

You can switch from one mode to the other by clicking the Edit/Tag Mode box with your mouse, selecting View➪Edit/Tag Mode from the menu bar, or pressing the Shift+F8 keys.

This is how you remove a single person from a lookup:

1. **Highlight the person you want to remove from the lookup by clicking the person's Contact button.**

   Every person has a Contact button, which is located at the left edge of the Contact List.

2. **Click the Omit Selected button on the Contact List window.**

   You can also click the right mouse button and select the Omit Selected command from the menu that appears.

3. **Release the right mouse button.**

   The contact is removed from the lookup.

Removing more than one person from the lookup in ACT!'s Edit Mode

This is how you remove more than one person from a lookup:

1. **Highlight the people you want to remove from the lookup by holding down the Ctrl key and clicking each person's Contact button.**

2. **Click the Omit Selected button on the Contact List window.**

   You can also click the right mouse button and select the Omit Selected command from the menu that appears.

3. **Release the right mouse button.**

   The selected people are removed from the lookup.

   You can highlight a group of adjacent contact records by holding down the Shift key and clicking the Contact button of the first person and then clicking the Contact button of the last person in the sequence.

You can also refine your lookup by highlighting a group of contacts, clicking the right mouse button, and selecting the Lookup Selected command from the subsequent menu.

Tagging and untagging your contacts in the Tag Mode

To tag contacts, before refining your lookup, you must be in Tag Mode. If you're in the Edit Mode, you can switch to the Tag Mode by clicking the Edit/Tag Mode box with your mouse, selecting View➪Edit/Tag Mode from the menu bar, or pressing the Shift+F8 keys.

In Tag Mode, you can use the Contact List to refine your lookups. To do this, select a group of contacts by clicking them — a plus (+) sign appears in the left-hand column — or by pressing the Space Bar.

After you select the contacts, you have two ways to create a lookup. You can create a lookup by clicking the Lookup Tagged button, or you can remove them from the lookup by clicking the Omit Selected button.

Saving Your Lookups

After you've gone through the effort of creating a lookup, you may want to save it so that you don't have to go through the process a second time. With ACT!'s Group feature, you can save your lookups. I cover creating, using, and managing groups in Chapter 12.

Chapter 11

Performing Advanced Database Queries

*I*n ACT!, you're able to perform advanced database searches that go way beyond the commands that are available from the Lookup menu. (Performing ACT!'s instant and standard lookups was discussed in Chapter 11. If you haven't read that chapter already, you should do so now because this one is a bit more technical.)

Performing Advanced Lookups from the Query Window

To perform an ACT! advanced query, select Lookup⇨By Example from either the Contact or Group window, and the Query window appears, as shown in Figure 11-1.

From the Query window, you can instruct ACT! to search for contacts who match specific search criteria. When you perform a lookup for all the people who live or work in a particular city, such as Chicago, that's a *criterion*. When you perform a lookup for a person by his or her first name, last name, or anything else, that's also a criterion. If you were to combine these two criteria, for example, to lookup everyone who has the last name of Smith and lives in Chicago, you create an *advanced query*.

```
ACT! - [Act_demo - Contacts]                                    _ □ X
  File   Edit   Query   Tools   Window   Help                     _ 8 X
 □ 🖙 ■ 🖳 🕀 !  Close  ?

 Company    [              ]        Address    [              ]
 Contact    [              ]                   [              ]
 Title      [              ]                   [              ]
 Department [              ]        City       [              ]
 Phone      [        ] Ext. [  ]    State      [              ]
 Fax        [              ]        ZIP Code   [              ]
 Salutation [              ]        Country    [              ]
 ID/Status  [              ]        E-mail Address [          ]
 Ticker Symbol [        ]           Last Results [            ]


 User 1     [              ]        User 7     [              ]
 User 2     [              ]
 User 3     [              ]        User 8     [              ]
 User 4     [              ]
 User 5     [              ]        User 9     [              ]
 User 6     [              ]

 ◄│►│ User Fields │ Phone/Home │ Alt Contacts │ Status │
 Lookup: All Contacts                 Contact Layout 4.0 ▲ 🖾🖨🖾🖾🖾🖾🖾🖾
```

Figure 11-1:
The Query
window.

From the Query window, you can perform lookups for contacts who meet all sorts of criteria. You can, for example, perform a lookup of all your clients (as opposed to prospects) who live in Dallas, Detroit, or Los Angeles and who have placed an order with you within the last 90 days. (This assumes that you set up your ACT! fields in such a way that you store this type of information.)

All the drop-down menus and Edit List boxes that you use within your ACT! contact layouts are accessible from the Query window. Your ACT! layouts are also available. To change layouts in the Query window, click the Contact Layout button at the bottom of the window and select the layout from which you want to perform your query.

ACT! automatically erases search criteria after it performs a search. If you're creating a complex query, you may want to save it so you can use it over again. To save your query, select File➪Save or press Ctrl+S.

If you've started creating a query and want to erase it and start over, select Query➪Clear Query. You can also create a new query by selecting File➪New or pressing Ctrl+N.

Performing Advanced Contact Lookups

With ACT!, you can perform very powerful searches that enable you to find contacts who meet complex search criteria. In this section, I give you some examples of how you can search your ACT! database. The more you explore ACT!'s advanced query features, the better you'll get at performing database searches. In these examples, I introduce two new terms: Logical operators and Boolean operators, which I explain after these examples. My purpose in writing this part of the chapter in this manner is to give you the examples first and then explain how ACT! performs these custom lookups.

Example 1: Looking for clients in Dallas

Say that you want to perform a lookup for all your clients who live in a specific city; for illustrative purposes, I'll use Dallas. This is what you do:

1. **From the Query window, enter the criteria you want ACT! to use to perform an advanced query.**

   In this example, you enter the city's name — that is, Dallas — in the City field and the word Client in the ID/Status field of the Query window. (This assumes that you categorize your contacts in the ID/Status field and that one of the categories is "Client.") Remember to use your drop-down menus or Edit List boxes (press F2) to enter information.

2. **To run a query, select Query⇨Run Query.**

   Because I want to give you a more thorough explanation of what ACT! does to create this advanced query, I'm going to suggest that you not run the query just yet. After you enter the basic criteria, choose the Convert to Advanced Query command from the Query menu, and the Advanced Query window appears. ACT! has taken the entries that you made in the Query window and made the phrase ((City = "Dallas"*)) AND ((ID/Status = "Client"*)) out of it.

Proper spacing and the insertion of quotation marks are very important to an ACT! query. You must have a blank space between the left and right parenthesis marks and the first and last character in the statement. The word City identifies the ACT! field in the statement. The equal sign (=) is a Logical operator, and the word "Dallas" (note the quotation marks) is the *value*, which is the data you enter into a field. Because values are not case sensitive, you must always set them inside quotation marks ("__"). The word AND that connects the two statements in the phrase is a Boolean operator.

The asterisk (*) after the value — (City = "Dallas"*) — is the Logical operator for "begins with."

Example 2: Looking for clients who live in Texas but don't live in Dallas

To modify the previous example a bit, suppose that you want to look for all your clients who live in Texas but do not live in Dallas. Your search string looks like this: (((State = "TX"*) AND (City <> "Dallas"*))) AND (ID/Status = "Client"*).

Note the triple parentheses around the first part of this search string — (((State = "TX"*) AND (City <> "Dallas"))). The triple parentheses tells ACT! that you want it to look for everybody in Texas except for those who live in Dallas and who is a client.

Example 3: Searching for birthdays

Many people like to keep a record of the birthdays of their important customers, clients, family, and friends so that they can remember to send them a card, buy them a gift, or take them out to dinner. Here's an easy way to set up your ACT! Birthday fields.

1. **Designate a field as a Birthday field.**

   In this example, I designate the User 2 field as the Birthday field.

2. **Create a drop-down menu, with Descriptions, with the 12 months of the year — that is, January, February, March, and so on; and their abbreviations Jan., Feb., Mar. and so on — as the item.**

   You create drop-down menus from within the Define Fields dialog box. Open the Define Fields dialog box by selecting Edit⇨Define Fields. (I discuss defining ACT! fields and creating drop-down menus in Chapter 6.)

   Using a drop-down menu makes the entry of the month of birth easy and keeps all your entries consistent. January is abbreviated as Jan., for example.

3. **To find everyone who has a January birthday, choose Lookup⇨By Example to bring up the Query screen.**

4. **Type Jan.* in the User 2 field.**

5. **Select Query⇨Run Query, and ACT! searches for everybody who has a January birthday.**

That was easy, wasn't it?

If you were to convert your query to an advanced query before you clicked OK, your search string looks like (("User 2" = "Jan."*)).

When you type Jan.* in the User 2 field, it becomes (("User 2" = "Jan."*)). The asterisk (*), which is called a *wild card*, after the word "Jan." tells ACT! to look for a string of characters that *starts with* the word "Jan." Starts With is the Logical operator.

If you want to perform a lookup of your clients who have a January birthday, you type Jan.* in the User 2 field and Client in the ID/Status field. This is how your search string looks: (("User 2" = "Jan."*)) AND ((ID/Status = "Client"*)).

In the example above, note that in the phrase (("User 2" = "Jan."*)), the words "User 2" are enclosed in quotation marks. ACT! encloses fields that have two or more words in quotation marks.

Example 4: Searching for contacts based on dates

You can also search for contacts based on a date or range of dates. On the bottom of the Status tab, ACT! records the following:

- ✔ **Last Meeting:** The date of your last meeting with a person.
- ✔ **Last Reach:** The date that you last reached a person on the phone.
- ✔ **Last Attempt:** The date that you last attempted to reach a person on the phone.
- ✔ **Letter Date:** The date you last sent the person a letter, memo, or fax; and the date the contact record was created, merged, or edited. (This is why clearing your activities and logging your correspondence into the contact's History file is so important.)
- ✔ **Create Date:** The date a contact record was created.
- ✔ **Edit Date:** The date a contact record was last edited.
- ✔ **Merge Date:** The date a contact record was merged into this database.

To perform a search of all the people whom you haven't spoken with on the phone since, let's say, December 1, 1997, just enter < 11-30-97 in the Last Reach field. ACT! searches your database for every contact that has a Last Reach date that is *less than* December 1, 1997.

To find everybody you spoke with on the phone during the month of December 1997 (the period of time from December 1, 1997, through December 31, 1997), your search string in the Advanced Query window look likes this: `(( "Last Reach" >= "12/1/97"* )) AND (( "Last Reach" <= "12/31/97"* )).`

Another way to find everybody you spoke with on the phone during the month of December 1996 is to use the *range* (..) Boolean operator. With the range Boolean operator, you can search for a range of dates. Your search string looks like this: `(( "Last Reach" = "12/1/96"* )) .. (( "Last Reach" = "12/31/96"* )).`

When you're replacing an existing Logical or Boolean operator with a new operator in the Advanced Query window, highlight the operator that you want to replace in the search string and then double-click the operator that you want to replace it with, and the new operator overwrites the old operator. When you replace operators in this manner, you eliminate the possibility of typing the wrong characters in the search string.

To find everybody you had some type of contact with during the month of December 1997 (the period of time from December 1, 1997, through December 31, 1996), your search string looks like this: `(( "Edit Date" >= "12/1/97"* )) AND (( "Edit Date" <= "12/31/97"* )).`

Whenever you make any changes to a contact's information, ACT! automatically enters the date of that change into the Edit Date field. The next time your boss asks you for a list of everybody you spoke with on the phone, had a meeting with, sent a letter, memo, or fax to during the past week (or any period of time), perform your advanced database search on the Edit Date field. ACT! searches your database based upon the range of dates you selected in the Edit Date field, and you have your list in just a few moments.

Using the Query Helper Dialog Box

You use the Query Helper dialog box, which is shown in Figure 11-2, to create a new query or edit an existing query. The Query Helper dialog box spares you the trouble of entering the information from the keyboard, thus reducing the possibility or making a mistake. The Query Helper dialog box is also the easiest way to insert field names, Logical operators, and Boolean operators into a query.

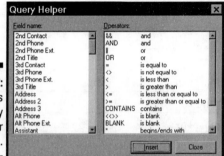

Figure 11-2:
ACT!'s
Query
Helper
dialog box.

ACT! places both Logical operators and Boolean operators together in the Query Helper dialog box. For explanation purposes, I refer to them separately.

To insert ACT!'s field names, Logical operators, or Boolean operators into a query, highlight the field name or operator you want to insert and click the Insert button.

Insert as much search criteria as you can into your query by entering information into the fields of the Query window. After you've entered this information, convert your query to an Advanced Query by selecting Query⇨Convert to Advanced Query. Then all you do is make changes to the Logical operators or Boolean operators. If you need to move, copy, or rearrange the statements or phrases within the query, use the Cut, Copy, and Paste commands. This method spares you the trouble of typing in the search statements and reduces the possibility of entering a statement incorrectly.

To hide the Query Helper dialog box, click the Close button, and the dialog box disappears. To show the Query Helper dialog box, choose Query⇨Show Query Helper, and it reappears.

Using Logical operators

Logical operators are words and symbols that show the relationship between a specific field and its value. In the example ((City = "Dallas"*)), City identifies the ACT! field, the equal sign (=) is the Logical operator, and "Dallas" is the value. (Note the quotation marks around the value Dallas.) Table 11-1 is a list of Logical operators.

Table 11-1	Logical Operators
Symbol	*Meaning*
=	Equal to
>	Greater than
<	Less than
<>	Not equal to
<=	Less than or equal to
>=	Greater than or equal to
!	Not
<<>>	Blank (The field is empty.)
Blank	Blank

The following list presents word-based operators:

- **Starts With:** The field that you are searching contains data that starts with a specific letter, number, word, or part of a word. Type ___* in a Query field, and it becomes ___* in the Advanced Query window. For example, if you wanted to search for all the zip codes in Atlanta, you type **303*** in the Zip Code field.

- **Ends With:** The field that you are searching contains data that ends with a specific letter, number, word, or part of a word. Type *___ in a Query field, and it becomes *___ in the Advanced Query window. For example, if you want to search for all your contacts who have contracts that are up for renewal in 1998, you type ***1998** in the Contract Expiration field.

- **Contains:** The field that you are searching contains a specified combination of letters and/or numbers. Type *___* in a Query field, and it becomes *___* in the Advanced Query window.

For example, say that you've designated a specific ACT! field as your "Products of Interest" field. In this field, you insert the names of the products — Widgets, Thingamajigs, and Whatchamacallits — that your customers have indicated they may be interested in purchasing.

The next time that you have a sale on Widgets, you search your database for everybody whose "Products of Interest" field contains Widgets. To perform this search, you type ***Widgets*** in the "Products of Interest" field, and in a few moments, ACT! creates a group of everybody in your database who has indicated that they may be interested in buying Widgets. Now all you have to do is call them.

To find a field that is empty — that is, one that contains no information — position the cursor in the field you want to check, press Ctrl+F5 to insert the *blank* characters ⟨⟨⟩⟩ in the field. Select Query⇨Run Query, and ACT! finds every contact in the active lookup or active group in which this field is empty. If, for example, you're looking up contacts that have an empty Zip Code field, your search string looks like this: (ZIP ⟨⟨⟩⟩).

To find a field that contains some information — that is, one that's not empty — position the cursor in the field you want to check and place an asterisk (*) in the field. Click OK, and ACT! finds every contact in the active lookup or active group in which this field is not empty. If, for example, you want to look up contacts that do not have an empty User 1 field, your search string looks like this: ("User 1" ! ⟨⟨⟩⟩). The statement reads "User 1 is not empty."

Using Boolean operators

You use *Boolean operators* to combine a series of simple queries into a sophisticated and extremely powerful advanced query. I suppose that's why ACT! calls these advanced queries.

Table 11-2 is a list of Boolean operators and what they mean.

Table 11-2	Boolean Operators
Symbol	*Truth Value*
AND	(Condition 1 is True) and (Condition 2 is True)
&&	(Condition 1 is True) and (Condition 2 is True)
OR	(Condition 1 is True) or (Condition 2 is True)
‖	(Condition 1 is True) or (Condition 2 is True)
AND_NOT	(Condition 1 is True) and (Condition 2 is False)
OR_NOT	(Condition 1 is True) or (Condition 2 is False)
(Range)	With the Range Boolean operator, you can search for a range of dates.

Using Advanced Query Commands

Here are some additional advanced query commands that can help you get more out of your advanced queries.

Sorting your query

After you've created your query and checked it for errors, you can select the field that you want ACT! to sort the database search on. You may want to do this when you're creating a report, for example. Or, when you perform a lookup for clients who live in Texas but don't live in Dallas, you can then tell ACT! how you want it to sort that database search — by last name, company, city, zip code, and so on.

To sort your query, select Query➪Specify Query Sort, and the Sort Contacts dialog box appears. I discuss sorting in Chapter 10.

Executing a query

When you're ready to execute a query from the Query window, choose Run Query from the Query menu, or press Ctrl+R, and ACT! executes your query.

Saving a query

After you've created an advanced query, you can save it by selecting the File➪Save command or by pressing Ctrl+S. If you want to save an existing query with a new name, select the File➪Save As command or press F12. Queries are saved in ACT!'s queries directory. Saving your queries has several useful benefits. Here are a couple:

- When you want to perform the same query in the future, you won't have to re-create the query.
- You can use a previous query as the foundation for another query.

Chapter 12

Grouping Your Contacts

· ·

In This Chapter

▶ Setting your group preferences

▶ Creating a new group

▶ Entering group information

▶ Defining group fields

▶ Viewing group information

▶ Changing group layouts

▶ Performing group lookups

· ·

*I*n addition to looking up or searching through your ACT! contact records, you can group a number of contact records together — creating a subset of your ACT! database. When you create a group of contacts from within your existing database, any individual contact record that has become a part of this group still remains a part of the main database and also remains a member of any other groups that it may already belong to.

When you have all your contacts in an ACT! database, you may find it useful to categorize them so that you can quickly bring up a collection of records based on a certain criterion. Groups also make managing sets of contacts easier. A group can have an unlimited number of members, and a person can be a member of an unlimited number of groups.

For example, you may want to categorize some of your contacts as personal and some as professional so that you can quickly print an address book for one of the two sets of contacts at a time. Or you may want to set up distinct categories for your contacts based on their business or profession so that you can send bulk mailings to certain categories of contacts. You can also create groups of contacts to help you manage your accounts, company contacts, or for that matter, any other collection of contacts who have something in common.

Using Group Records

Although setting up groups is slightly more complicated than setting an ID/Status for each contact, group records enable you to keep track of notes, history, and activities for the whole group instead of for each contact.

When you create a group, you can keep and view notes, histories, and activities for the whole group.

The following list shows a few examples of how you can use groups to manage information in your ACT! database:

- **Collections of contacts:** Groups are great when you need to view a bunch of diverse contacts at the same time. Your groups can contain the contact records of your customers, friends, vendors, and so on.

- **Project records:** When you're working on projects, use groups to keep track of all the people involved by recording notes, histories, activities, and the like.

- **Account records:** As with projects, you can create groups for all of the people related to your accounts. Again, doing so helps you to keep track of notes, history, and activities.

- **Sales opportunities:** Groups are a big help when you need to keep track of sales and business opportunities. By customizing the User fields, you can record revenue forecasts, the salesperson for the account, the closing date, and so on.

- **Company records:** It is often useful to create a group to record information about the companies with which you do business. You can keep track of all the notes, history, and activities that pertain to the company rather than for each individual contact who is associated with that company.

- **Saved lookups of contacts:** You can use groups to act as saved lookups of contacts that you need to access often. For example, if you're a team leader for a project at work, you probably need to schedule meetings with other team members, send e-mail messages, or schedule calls. By creating a group for the team, you can quickly access all their records.

✔ **Sharing a database with other users:** If you're sharing a large — 2,000, 3,000, 5,000, or 10,000 contacts — database with several other users, you may want to create a group of the people that you keep in touch with on a regular basis.

✔ **Lookups are faster:** Having different groups of contacts makes using your ACT! database more manageable. You can perform lookups much faster when you're searching through only 1,000 contact records rather than 5,000 to 10,000 contact records.

✔ **Group your committees and organizations:** If you're on a committee or involved in a charitable organization, you may want to create a specific group of the members of that committee or organization.

✔ **Manage your projects:** If you're working on a large project or program, you may want to create a group of the specific contacts who are part of the project or program. (A friend of mine who is a journalist has grouped his contacts by subject areas: the telecommunications industry, the auto industry, the computer industry, the media industry, and so on.)

✔ **Holiday mailing lists:** In my own case, I've created a number of different groups, including one for my holiday mailing list.

With ACT!'s grouping capabilities, you have lots of different ways to improve your productivity.

Opening the Groups Window

 To open the Groups window, where you can create, modify, and delete your groups, you select View⇨Groups from the menu bar or click the Groups button, and the Groups window appears, as shown in Figure 12-1.

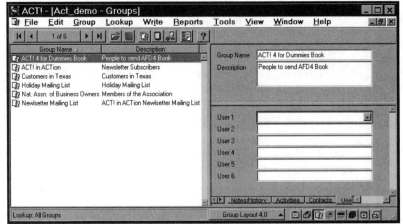

Figure 12-1:
The Groups
window.

Setting Your Group Preferences

Several preference settings apply specifically to ACT! groups. To open the Preferences dialog box, select Edit➪Preferences from the menu bar and select Preferences from the menu that appears; then select the Startup tab.

The Startup tab in the Preferences dialog box enables you to make several group startup selections:

✔ **Default group layout:** With the Default Group Layout option, you can choose a group layout to use as the default every time you start ACT!.

✔ **Make new groups private:** With the Make New Groups Private option, you can choose whether or not you want to make new groups public or private.

✔ **Second group column:** If you would like to display a second column in the list of groups window, choose which field you want displayed as the second column from the Second Group Column drop-down menu.

Creating a New Group

ACT! offers several ways to create a new group. You can

✔ Create a new group without copying any information from the currently displayed group (also referred to as *default values*).

✔ Create a new group by copying some information from the currently displayed group into the new group (also referred to as *primary fields*).

✔ Create a new group by copying all the information from the currently displayed group into the new group (also referred to as *all fields*).

Using the New Group command

When you create a new group by choosing Group⇨New Group from the menu bar, or by selecting New Group from the menu that appears after you click the right mouse button, or by pressing the Insert key when within the Group window, ACT! uses the default values that are selected in the Define Fields dialog box. (I discuss defining ACT! fields in Chapter 6.) To open the Define Fields dialog box, select Edit⇨Define Fields from the menu bar.

By entering default values in the Default Value field, you can enter group information that you want ACT! to insert in every new group that you create using the New Group command. To enter default information, just highlight the field (City, for example) in the List of Fields field and type the desired default value data (Chicago) in the Default Value field.

If you have repetitive information that you enter for almost every one of your new groups, such as city, state, zip, or telephone area code, you can insert this specific information into the respective Default Value fields, and it appears in every new group that you create. Don't worry, you can easily overwrite this information — by highlighting the text and entering the new information — when it isn't applicable to every group you create.

Using the Duplicate Group command

When you create a new group by choosing Group⇨Duplicate Group from the menu bar or by right-clicking and then choosing Duplicate Group from the menu that appears, the Duplicate Group dialog box appears.

The Duplicate Group dialog box gives you two choices:

✔ Duplicate data from primary fields.

✔ Duplicate data from all fields.

The Duplicate Data from Primary Fields option

When you select the Duplicate Data from Primary Fields option to create a new group, ACT! copies the information from the primary fields of the current group — Company, Phone, Address, and so on — into the new group.

You can specify which fields should be primary fields in the Define Fields dialog box. (I discuss defining ACT! fields in Chapter 6.) To open the Define Fields dialog box, select Edit⇨Define Fields from the menu bar.

When you select the Primary field attribute in the Define Fields dialog box, you specify that you want ACT! to copy the information in this field into a new group whenever you create a new group using the group's primary fields.

Use the Duplicate Data from Primary Fields option when you want to create a new group for the same company or organization. This way, you have to type only the new group's name because the other information remains the same.

The Duplicate Data from All Fields option

When you create a new group by selecting the Duplicate Data from All Fields option, ACT! inserts all the information that's entered in each group field into the new group.

Deleting Groups from ACT!

From time to time, you may find that you want to remove a group. (You're removing the group, not the contact records that make up the group.) In ACT!, deleting a group is very easy. All you have to do is highlight the group and select Group⇨Delete Group from the menu bar, or select Delete Group from the right mouse button menu, or press Ctrl+Delete, and the Delete Group dialog box appears. The Delete Group dialog box warns you that deleting groups cannot be undone and asks you whether you want to delete this specific group. Click Yes, and ACT! deletes the group.

Entering Group Information

You enter group information in the same way that you enter information into an ACT! contact record. (I discuss entering information into ACT! in Chapter 2.)

Defining Group Fields

You can customize each of the fields in a group. This flexibility enables you to customize each group to fit your individual work habits and work style and makes entering group information much easier.

The Define Fields dialog box is where you can set the individual characteristics, or properties, for each field in an ACT! group. To edit a field's attributes, select Edit⇨Define Fields.

The features for defining fields for ACT! contacts and groups is the same. You select which record type you want to modify — Contact or Group — from the Record Type drop-down menu.

After you customize your Group fields, you may want to change the layout of the group fields. To change the layout, you use ACT!'s Layout Designer by selecting Tools⇨Design Layouts from the menu bar. (I discuss customizing your contact and group layouts in Chapter 23.)

Editing the Membership of a Group

To edit the membership of an ACT! group, select Group⇨Group Membership from the menu bar or right-click and select Group Membership from the menu that appears. The Group Membership dialog box appears, as shown in Figure 12-2.

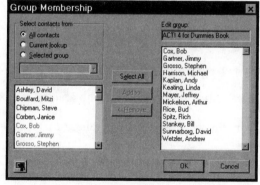

Figure 12-2:
The Group Membership dialog box.

You use the Group Membership dialog box to add members to a new group or to edit — add or remove — the membership of an existing group.

Selecting contacts for group membership

You can select contacts to become members of a group from three sources:

✔ **All contacts:** Choose the All contacts option to make all contacts in the database available for selection.

✔ **Current lookup:** Choose the Current lookup option to select contacts from the current lookup only.

✔ **Selected group:** Choose the Selected group option to select contacts from a specific group.

Adding people to a group

After you select the source of your contacts — all contacts, current lookup, or selected group — ACT! displays a list of all the contacts. To add new members to a group, highlight the names of the people you want to add from the available list. Next, highlight the name of the group that's displayed in the Edit Group field that you want to add these people to, and click the Add button. ACT! adds the names to the list of members of the selected group.

To add all the available contacts to a specific group, click the Select All button, and ACT! adds all the names to the list of members of the selected group.

You can add a contact to a group by clicking the contact record and dragging it into the group window.

Removing people from a group

To remove people from a group, you must first select the group from the list of groups in the Edit Group field. After you select a group, ACT! displays the names of all the members of that group in the Group Members box.

To remove members from the selected group, highlight their names and click the Remove button.

The Remove button is not available if no contacts in the list are highlighted.

Using the Contact window's Group Memberships command

From within the Contact window you can add or remove specific contacts to or from an ACT! group. You do so by selecting Contact⇨Group Membership from the menu bar, or from the menu that appears when you right-click within the Group tab, and the Group Membership dialog box opens.

From the Group Membership dialog box, you can see a list of all the available groups and the groups in which a person is presently a member.

Viewing Group Information

You can view information about each of your groups by clicking the tabs at the bottom of the Group window.

The Contacts tab

Click the Contacts tab, and ACT! displays a list of all the members of the selected group.

Highlight a contact by clicking the Contact button to the left of the contact's name; double-click the Contact button, and ACT! brings up the person's contact record in the Contact window and creates a lookup of everybody that is a member of the group.

Viewing information in the Contacts tab

In the Contacts tab, you can change the information that ACT! displays as well as the look and feel of your columns. You can do the following things:

- ✔ **Add columns:** Click the right mouse button and select Add Columns from the menu. The Add Columns dialog box appears. Select the column you want to add and click OK.

- ✔ **Change the position of columns:** To change the position of a column, click the column's heading and drag it to its new position. (The cursor turns into a hand.)

- ✔ **Remove a column:** To remove a column, click the column's heading and drag it upwards and off the Contacts tab.

- ✔ **Change the width of a column heading:** To change the width of a column heading, place the cursor on the line between two column headings — it turns into a sizing tool — and move it left or right to make the column wider or smaller.

- ✔ **Show Grid lines:** To display grid lines between your column headings, select the Show Grid Lines option in the Colors and Fonts tab of the Preferences dialog box.

Changing the appearance of the Contacts tab

To change the appearance — font, font size, font style, font color, and background color of the Contacts tab — open the Preferences dialog box by selecting Edit⇔Preferences from the menu bar and click the Colors and Fonts tab. To read more about how to change ACT! window and tab appearances, turn to Chapter 24.

The Activities tab

Click the Activities tab, and you can see a list of all the activities that are scheduled for members of this group.

With the Filtering command, you can choose which activities to display in the Activities tab by user, activity, priority, and date. ACT! displays your filtering options by clicking the Filter button at the top of the Activities tab.

You can also change your filtering options by opening the Filter Activities dialog box. You do this by selecting View⇨Filter Current Tab View from the menu bar or by selecting Filter from the menu that appears when you right-click in the Activities tab.

You can also customize the appearance of the Activities tab by changing the sort order, column headings, the position and width of the column headings, as well as the font, font size and font color, and background color.

The Notes/History tab

Click the Notes/History tab, and you can see a list of all the notes, history items, and attachments that are part of a group.

Other Group window tabs

You find additional tabs in the Group window:

- ✔ **The User Fields tab:** In the User Fields tab, you can record information in User Fields 1 through 6.
- ✔ **The Address tab:** In the Address tab, you record basic group information, such as the group's mailing address.
- ✔ **The Status tab:** In the Status tab, you have group status information, such as Create Date, Edit Date, Record Manager, and so on.

Writing Group Notes

To enter notes of meetings or conversations that pertain to a group, select Group⇨Insert Note from the menu bar, press the F9 key, click the Insert Note button on the Notes/History tab, or select the Insert Note command from the menu that appears after you click the right mouse button. Here are a couple of group note tips:

✔ **Entering a note:** After you select the Insert Note command, ACT! automatically inserts the date in the Date column and inserts "Note" in the type column. All you have to do is type the note.

✔ **Modifying a note:** To modify the date a note was entered, click the Date column with your mouse; then click the drop-down menu and pick a new date from the calendar. To modify the note itself, just place your cursor in the Regarding field and make your changes.

Attaching Files to a Group

You can attach files to both ACT! contact records and to ACT! groups. Attaching a file to a group is very easy. This is what you do:

1. **Select the group you want to attach the file to.**

2. **Select Group⇨Attach File from the menu bar. The Attach File dialog box appears.**

   You can also press Ctrl+I or choose the Attach File command from the menu that appears after you right-click.

3. **Select the file you want to attach and click OK.**

   The file is attached to the contact record.

You can attach any file to a contact record by dragging it from the desktop or from Windows Explorer and dropping it onto the Notes/History tab in the Group window. For example, you may have created a spreadsheet to track orders from a specific contact. Drag the spreadsheet file to the group's Notes/History tab, and that file will always be part of the group's record.

Once you've attached a file to a group record, you can open it and/or view its details.

- ✔ **Opening an attached file:** To open an attached file, double-click the attached file icon with your mouse. ACT! launches the program that created the file and opens the file.

- ✔ **Viewing the details of a note, history entry, or attachment:** To view the details of a note, history entry, or attachment, highlight the specific item by clicking its icon. Click the Details button, and the Details dialog box appears.

Changing Group Layouts

To change Group layouts, select a layout from the Group Layout button at the bottom of the Group window. With the Layout Designer, you can create your own custom group layouts. I cover the features of the Layout Designer in Chapter 23.

Performing Group Lookups

You perform lookups on ACT! groups in the same way that you perform lookups on ACT! contact records. To perform an ACT! group lookup, select Lookup from the menu bar. You can then choose from the following lookup options:

- ✔ All Groups
- ✔ Other Fields
- ✔ Previous
- ✔ Key Word
- ✔ By Example
- ✔ Internet Directory
- ✔ Contact

I cover lookups in Chapter 10.

Part IV

Scheduling: A Play in Four Acts

The 5th Wave   By Rich Tennant

"IT'S ANOTHER DEEP SPACE PROBE FROM EARTH,
SEEKING CONTACT FROM EXTRATERRESTRIALS.
I WISH THEY'D JUST INCLUDE AN E-MAIL ADDRESS."

In this part . . .

This part is really the centerpiece of the book because scheduling is probably the most important and most used feature of ACT!. In the next four chapters, I cover all of the ways that you can schedule activities. I walk you through the Schedule Activity dialog box, I show you how to use SideACT!; and I explain how to get the most out of ACT!'s calendars and Task List.

Chapter 13

Scheduling Your Activities

- -

In This Chapter

▶ Setting your default scheduling preferences

▶ The art of scheduling activities

▶ Scheduling activities with one or more people

▶ Setting alarms

▶ Additional scheduling features

▶ Clearing and erasing activities

- -

*A*CT! offers you many ways to schedule an activity — a call, meeting, or to-do. You can schedule activities from the Contact window, the Contact List window, the Task List window, in addition to the Day, Week, and Month calendars. Because we all have different work styles and work habits, ACT! gives each of us many ways to schedule and view our activities. I'm leaving it to you to find the ones that work best for you. Here are some ACT! scheduling tips:

✔ Add everybody you know to your ACT! database. In ACT!, an activity is always associated with a specific contact. And before you can schedule an activity for a specific contact, he or she must be in the database. That's why it's important for you to get as many people into your database as quickly as you can.

✔ Don't list your calls, meetings, and to-dos under your own "My Record" contact record. Instead, you should list your activities under the contact record of the person with whom you're doing the activity.

✔ Use SideACT! to schedule activities that aren't associated with a particular contact. SideACT! is a new ACT! scheduling tool that enables you to schedule activities and keep them as a list. I explain SideACT! in the next chapter.

Scheduling Preferences

Before I go into the specifics of how to schedule activities, I want to spend a moment explaining ACT!'s scheduling preferences. The scheduling options in ACT!'s preferences are some of the most important components of setting up your ACT! database. These settings allow you to customize how ACT!'s scheduling features will act when you schedule a new call, meeting, or to-do.

To open the Preferences dialog box, select Edit⇨Preferences either from the menu bar or from the right mouse button menu, and then select the Scheduling tab. ACT!'s scheduling preferences are shown in Figure 13-1.

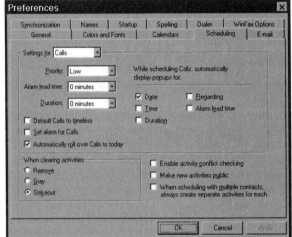

Figure 13-1:
ACT!
scheduling
preferences.

Setting your activity defaults

With the Activity defaults settings, you can have a separate set of settings for your calls, meetings, and to-dos. In the Settings For box, choose the type of activity you want to set preferences for: Calls, Meetings, or To-dos. You have the following scheduling options:

- **Priority:** The Priority option enables you to choose a High, Medium, or Low default priority for the selected activity.

- **Alarm Lead Time:** The Alarm lead time is the amount of time before the activity that you want the alarm to sound. You can choose a default alarm lead time from 5 minutes to 30 days.

The Set Alarm option must be selected for the Alarm Lead Time option to work.

✔ **Duration:** You can choose a duration default from 5 minutes to 30 days.

✔ **Default To Timeless:** Use this option if an activity type can be completed at any time during the day and doesn't need to be scheduled for a specific time.

✔ **Set Alarm For** *[Activity Type]*: When the alarm is turned on, ACT! reminds you of the activity you set the alarm for as long as ACT! is running, even if you're using another Windows application.

It's my suggestion that you set alarms only for activities that are *really* important; otherwise *every* activity becomes really important.

Automatically rolling over unfinished activities

If you would like ACT! to automatically reschedule your unfinished calls, meetings, and/or to-dos, select the Automatically Roll Over To Today option.

Basically, if you didn't get something done yesterday, ACT! moves the unfinished task(s) forward to today.

With this feature, you'll never forget about or lose track of any of your calls or to-dos. When you start ACT!, a pop-up message box displays a message like the one shown in Figure 13-2.

Select this option only for your unfinished calls and to-dos. It makes no sense to — at least to me it doesn't — to roll over your previously scheduled meetings.

Figure 13-2:
The
Automatic
Rollover
Message
box.

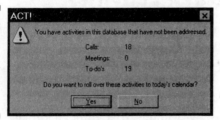

You then click either the Yes or No button. If you click Yes, all of your unfinished activities are rolled over to today's date. If you click No, the date of the activities remains unchanged.

 If you decide not to have ACT! roll over your unfinished tasks, they will remain on the date they were originally scheduled. One way to find them is to use the Task List, which I cover in Chapter 16. (To access the Task List, select View⇨Task List or click the Task List icon. You can also press F7.)

When the Task List window opens, click the Filter button at the upper-left edge of the Task List to change the Task List's view. (You can also select Edit⇨Filter from the menu bar or right-click the Task List to access the Filter command.)

From the Filter Activities dialog box, select the Past option, and all your past activities — activities that have not been completed or activities that have been completed but you haven't cleared — are displayed.

Adding Auto Pop-ups

When scheduling activities, ACT! makes it easy for you to enter information. It does this by giving you the option to have calendars and lists pop up automatically when you move to the next field in the Schedule Activity dialog box.

If you want any of the calendars or lists that are available in the Date, Time, Duration, Regarding, and/or Alarm Lead Time fields to pop up automatically when you schedule a call, meeting or to-do, just make a selection in the While Scheduling *[Activity Type]*, Automatically Display Pop-ups For check boxes.

Dealing with cleared activities

You choose how you want cleared activities to appear on a contact's Activities tab, the Task List, and the calendars. You have these choices:

- ✔ **Remove:** Deletes the activity.
- ✔ **Gray:** Colors the activity gray.
- ✔ **Strikeout:** Displays the activity in the strike-through format.

Making your scheduled activities public or private

When you schedule activities, ACT! gives you the option of making these activities public (everybody on the network or shared database can view the activity) or private (you are the only person who has access to your scheduled activities). If you would like your default selection to be public, check the Default Activities to Public check box.

Configuring conflict checking

This feature instructs ACT! to notify you when you are scheduling an activity that conflicts with a previously scheduled activity. When you do this, the Conflict Alert dialog box appears.

If you accept the conflict, ACT! goes ahead and schedules the activity. If you don't want this new activity to conflict with the previously scheduled activity, click Reschedule to access the Schedule Activity dialog box, where you can change either the date or the time of the new activity.

To disable conflict checking, choose the Disable Activity Conflict Checking option in the Conflict Alert dialog box. (I've found the conflict checking feature to be a nuisance because I often assign times to my calls or to-do items, and I don't need to be reminded that I have two items for 9 a.m. on the same day.)

Scheduling multiple activities

When you schedule an activity with more than one person, you can have ACT! schedule a single activity so that it applies for each of the people. If you modify or clear the activity for one person, the changes will be made for each person.

If, on the other hand, you want ACT! to schedule separate activities for each of the people, select the When Scheduling With Multiple Contacts, Always Create Separate Activities For Each option.

The Art of Scheduling Activities

In ACT!, you schedule activities from the Schedule Activity dialog box, shown in all its glory in Figure 13-3.

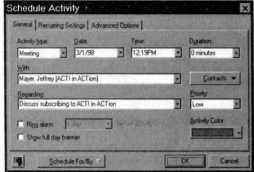

Figure 13-3:
The
Schedule
Activity
dialog box.

To access the Schedule Activity dialog box, do one of the following:

- ✔ Click the appropriate button (see Figure 13-4).
- ✔ Select Contact⇨Schedule (Call, Meeting, or To-do) from the menu bar or select a schedule command after right-clicking with your mouse.
- ✔ Press Ctrl+L for a call, Ctrl+M for a meeting, or Ctrl+T for a to-do, for those of you who prefer to use the keyboard.
- ✔ Drag and drop a contact from the Contact window to the Day, Week, or Month calendar; or to the Task List.
- ✔ Drag and drop a contact record from the Contact window to the Mini calendar.

Figure 13-4:
The Call,
Meeting,
and To-Do
buttons.

Scheduling activities from the Day, Week, and Month calendars is discussed in Chapter 15. Scheduling activities from the Task List is discussed in Chapter 16.

You modify a previously scheduled activity by highlighting the activity and selecting the Reschedule Activity command. Rescheduling activities is discussed later in this chapter.

What type of activity would you like to schedule?

When you schedule an activity using the Schedule (Call, Meeting, or To-do) commands, ACT! automatically selects the call, meeting, or to-do as the activity in the Activity type field. If you want to change an activity, all you have to do is make a selection from the drop-down menu.

With Practical Sales Tools's *FindersKeepers! Pro,* you have a practical way to manage multiple databases! With *FindersKeepers!* you can effectively use more than one database to manage your contacts better. You no longer have to open and close databases to look for your scheduled activities, task lists, and contact information. It's like having two or more databases open at once! *FindersKeepers! Pro* is available from Practical Sales Tools, Inc.; phone 888-433-2891; Web site: www.pstools.com.

Write notes to yourself

Whenever you schedule a new activity, it probably came about because of a meeting or a telephone conversation. And when you receive correspondence in the mail, an e-mail message, or a voice mail message, you'll probably have some additional items to add to your to-do list.

When adding these additional activities to ACT!, write yourself a brief note so that you'll be able to remember what was said during the meeting or phone conversation. This way, you won't forget who said what, what you're going to do, and when you're going to do it.

You should also write a brief description of the letter you received, the voice mail message

that was left for you, or your e-mail (you can attach the e-mail message to the contact's record) so that you'll remember what you received and when you received it.

You can write these notes to yourself in one of two ways: You can press the F9 key, or click the Insert Notes icon to insert a note in the contact's Notes/History tab. You can also use the Record History box to enter a brief note. (You open the Record History box by selecting Contact⇨Record History.) Or you can write a brief note in the Last Results field, which is automatically recorded in the Notes/History tab. The features of ACT!'s Notes/History tab are discussed in Chapter 5.

What is the activity's date?

The Date field identifies the date selected for an activity. You select a date from the drop-down calendar.

Right-click on the displayed month's name — January, February, March, for example — and a menu appears that enables you to move to today's date or a past or future month.

You can change the date that is displayed in the Date field, forward or backward one day at a time, by pressing the equals (=) or the hyphen (-) keys. To move forward or backward a month, use the Shift+Plus (+) or Shift+Hyphen keys. When the calendar is already displayed, you can change the year by pressing the Shift+PageUp or Shift+PageDown keys.

To insert a date manually, all you have to do is type in the numbers, and ACT! automatically inserts the slash marks (/) between the day, month, and year. ACT! is very intuitive, so you don't even have to type in the entire date. For example, to insert 5/3/98, just type 53, and ACT! displays the date as 5/3/98, assuming that you're in the calendar year 1998. (To enter a January date, always enter it as 01.)

ACT! makes it super easy for you to select dates using the calendar. Whenever the calendar appears, the current date is always highlighted. Or, if you're rescheduling an activity, the date of the scheduled activity is highlighted.

What is the activity's time?

You should always select a starting time for your meetings, though you may or may not want to select a time for either a call or a to-do. ACT! makes it easy to schedule times for all of these activities.

In scheduling a new activity, the Mini calendar, shown in Figure 13-5, aids you in selecting a time and duration for the activity. To help prevent conflicts, currently scheduled activities are displayed.

To make an activity timeless (that is, not associated with a particular time), select the Timeless bar at the bottom of the Mini calendar or type **NONE** in the Time field.

Figure 13-5:
The Mini
calendar.

Here are some tips for using the Mini calendar:

✔ The length, or duration, of an activity is automatically displayed in the Duration field.

✔ ACT! makes it easy for you to insert times into the Time field directly from the keyboard. To insert 9:15 a.m., just type **915a**. Press the Tab key to move to the next field, and ACT! displays 9:15AM in the Time field. Type **115a** and ACT! displays 11:50AM in the time field; **150p** appears as 1:50PM.

To set the increments of the time slots, go to the Calendars preferences by selecting Edit⇨Preferences from the menu bar and then selecting the Calendars tab. In the Daily Calendar Increments box, you can select time increments, which range from 5 minutes to an hour. You can also select the starting time that you want to appear on your calendar.

What's the activity's duration?

The Duration field displays the length of time, or duration, an activity is scheduled to take. When you use the Mini calendar to schedule an activity, the duration of that activity is automatically displayed in the Duration field. You can also select the duration of an activity from the Duration drop-down menu.

Duration times can also be entered from the keyboard. For example, when you type **4h**, ACT! displays it as 4 hrs; **35m** becomes 35 min.

What are your priorities?

You can assign each of your tasks a priority of High, Medium, or Low, depending upon the level of importance. On the Activities tab, the Task List, and the Day, Week, and Month calendars, all high-priority activities appear in red, medium-priority activities appear in blue, and low-priority activities remain black.

What is the activity regarding?

As long as you're scheduling an activity, you should make a notation to yourself as to the purpose, or nature, of the activity. You make this notation in the Regarding field by typing it in from the keyboard, or you can select a notation from the drop-down menu. (The Regarding field can also be left empty.)

To add, modify, or remove an item from the drop-down menu, press F2, or select the Edit List option at the bottom of the drop-down menu, and the Edit List dialog box, shown in Figure 13-6, appears. Modifying drop-down menu items is discussed in Chapter 7.

 Figure 13-6: The Edit List dialog box.

Type the first letter of the entry you're looking for, and ACT! automatically highlights the first item in the list that starts with that letter. Use the arrow keys to highlight the specific item you're searching for and then press OK, and that item is inserted into the Regarding field.

To enter more than one item from the Edit List dialog box into the Regarding field, open the Edit List dialog box and hold down the Ctrl key while you highlight the individual items with your mouse. Then click OK.

With whom are you scheduling the activity?

ACT! gives you two ways to select, or change, the person with whom you're scheduling an activity. You can select from the list in the With field, or you can click the Contact button and select from the Select Contacts dialog box.

In the With field, just click the down-arrow with your mouse, or place your cursor in the With field and press Alt+Down Arrow, and the list of contacts in the database opens. This list is shown in Figure 13-7.

Scroll through the list until you find the name of the person with whom you wish to schedule the activity. You can also locate people by pressing the first letter of the person's last name.

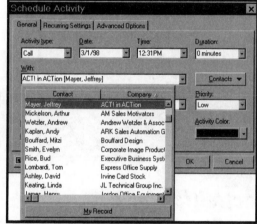

Figure 13-7:
The list of contacts with whom you can schedule an activity.

You can sort your list by last name or by company name by clicking the Contact or Company button located at the top of the window. To quickly locate your "My Record" contact record, click the My Record button.

Scheduling an Activity with One or More People

The Select Contacts feature is a very powerful scheduling tool because it saves you time, which helps you to become even more productive. The Select Contacts feature enables you to do the following:

> ✔ Schedule a new activity for someone other than the person whose contact record is currently displayed on the contact screen.
>
> ✔ Transfer an activity from one contact to another contact.
>
> ✔ Schedule an activity for several contacts at once.
>
> ✔ Add a new contact to your ACT! database.

To open the Select Contacts dialog box, shown in Figure 13-8, click the Contacts button and choose Select Contacts. The next sections explain how to use this dialog box.

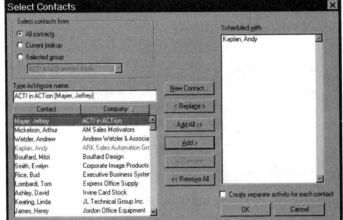

Figure 13-8:
The Select
Contacts
dialog box.

Scheduling activities for a different contact

Let's say that you're on the phone talking with Jane, who asks you to call Tarzan and give him a message. From the contact window, click the Call icon (you can also use this technique to schedule a meeting or a to-do), which brings up the Schedule Activity dialog box.

Click the Contacts button and choose Select Contacts from the drop-down list, and you bring up the Select Contacts dialog box. From the Select Contacts dialog box, you can select any person in your ACT! database and schedule an activity with that person. In the Select contacts from area, you can choose from All contacts, the Current lookup, or a Selected group, and the list of contacts is displayed in the Select contacts from box.

To schedule an activity with a different person, highlight the person's name and click the Replace button. This action replaces the contact whose name had been highlighted in the Scheduled with box.

Transferring activities from one contact to another contact

You can also use the Select Contacts dialog box to transfer an activity from one contact to another contact. To change the previous example just a bit, let's say that you have a meeting scheduled with Tarzan, who calls to tell you that he's going to be in the jungle and asks you to meet with Jane instead.

To transfer this activity from Tarzan to Jane, bring up your scheduled meeting with Tarzan by using the Reschedule Activity command. Click the Select Contact button, highlight Jane's name in the Select contacts from box, click the Replace button, and ACT! inserts Jane's name in the With field in the Schedule Activity dialog box. Click OK, and ACT! automatically transfers the scheduled meeting from Tarzan to Jane.

Scheduling activities for a group of people

In the first example, I scheduled a new activity for one person. Now I'm going to tell you how you can use the Select Contacts dialog box to schedule a meeting (it can also be a call or to-do) with two or more people. (You may want to use this scheduling feature when you need to schedule a sales or staff meeting with two, three, or more people.) Here's how you do it:

1. **From the Schedule an Activity dialog box, bring up the Select Contacts dialog box.**

2. **Choose the list of contacts from which you want to select your contacts. You can select from All contacts, the Current lookup, or a Selected group, and the list of contacts is displayed in the Select contacts from box.**

3. **Highlight the contacts you want to schedule the activity with.**

4. **Click the Add button, and their names are added to the list of names in the Scheduled with box.**

You can use your mouse to highlight a group of contacts. To select a group of contacts whose names are next to each other, highlight the name of the first contact and drag your mouse pointer upward or downward to highlight the names of the additional contacts. If the names are not next to each other, hold down the Ctrl key and highlight the individual names with your mouse. Then click the Add button.

Another way to schedule an activity for a group of contacts is to perform a Lookup so that you can group the contacts together before you schedule the activity. Then when you open the Select Contacts dialog box, choose the Select contacts from current lookup option, click the Select All button, and then click the Add button. (If you're not familiar with ACT!'s lookup features, see Chapter 10.)

Removing a person from an activity

From time to time, you may find that you need to remove a person from a scheduled activity. To do so, highlight the person's name in the Scheduled with box of the Select Contacts dialog box and click the Remove button.

Creating a separate activity for each contact

When you schedule an activity with more than one person, you can have ACT! schedule a single activity that will be applicable for each of the people. When the activity is modified or cleared for one person, the changes will be made for each person.

If on the other hand, you would like ACT! to schedule separate activities for each of the people, select the Separate Activity For Each Contact option.

Adding a new contact

From time to time you'll find yourself attempting to schedule an activity with a person only to discover that he, or she, isn't in your ACT! database. To solve that problem, ACT! now enables you to add contacts directly from the Schedule Activity dialog box. To add a new contact, just select Contact⇨ New Contact and the Add Contact box appears, as shown in Figure 13-9.

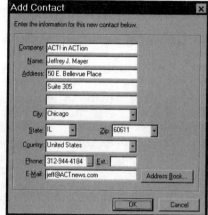

Figure 13-9:
The Add
Contact
dialog box.

Enter the contact information, click OK, and continue scheduling your activity.

You can also add a new contact to your ACT! database by clicking the New Contact button from inside the Select Contacts dialog box.

Setting the Alarm

One of the neat things you can do in ACT! is use its alarm to remind you to do something. When the alarm goes off at the appointed time, ACT!'s Alarms dialog box appears. To turn on the alarm, click the Ring alarm check box in the Schedule Activity dialog box.

Here are some ACT! alarm tips:

- ✔ As long as ACT! is open, you will receive your activity alarms — a beep sounds every 15 seconds — even when you're using another application.

- ✔ Use the alarm to remind yourself to make telephone calls. When you really want to reach someone, go to the Time field, select the time you want the alarm to go off, and turn on the alarm by clicking it with your mouse.

- ✔ When someone says, "Call me in 20 minutes," turn on the alarm.

- ✔ Don't set an alarm for every activity you schedule. Do it only for the important ones.

Setting the alarm's lead time

When you turn on ACT!'s alarm, you need to select the lead time so that ACT! will know how far in advance you want to be reminded of the upcoming activity. In the Ring alarm *[insert number of minutes or days]* before activity field of the Schedule Activity dialog box, you select how far in advance of an activity you want ACT! to remind you of the activity. To insert a lead time, select it from the drop-down menu or enter it from the keyboard.

Using ACT!'s alarm and the Alarm lead time field, you can be reminded of an upcoming activity long before the 59th minute of the 11th hour.

When an ACT! alarm goes off, the activity still appears on your to-do list for the day it's scheduled, not the day you were reminded of the activity.

With Practical Sales Tools's *HeadsUp! Pro,* you can see alarms from all your ACT! databases without running ACT!. You'll never miss another call, meeting, or to-do! You can get alarms from one database while working in another. And with the dialer, you can call the contact right from the alarm window. With *HeadsUp! Pro* you no longer have to open and close databases just to see your scheduled alarms. *HeadsUp! Pro* available from Practical Sales Tools, Inc.; phone 888-433-2891; Web site www.pstools.com.

Using the Alarms dialog box

When an ACT! alarm goes off, the Alarms dialog box appears, as shown in Figure 13-10. ACT! provides you with this information:

- ✔ A list of the alarms that have gone off
- ✔ The type of activity that the alarm or alarms represents
- ✔ The name of the contact, the phone number, and the alarm's date and time

Figure 13-10:
The Alarms
dialog box.

Alarms	☒
Ringing alarms: 3	
3/4/98 - 10:00 AM Rich Spitz	Select All
914-698-7410	
Discuss legal points	Snooze...
3/4/98 - 10:23 AM Stephen Del Grosso	Clear Alarm
781-545-6500	
Left message for me to call	Clear Activity
3/4/98 - 10:00 AM Andrew Wetzler	Reschedule...
561-989-0745	
Write another article	Go to

How much lead time would you like?

The Alarm lead-time setting is very important when you want to be reminded of a call, meeting, or to-do in advance. (Remember, the alarm must be on.) Here are some examples:

✔ You may want a 15-minute lead time to remind yourself of your next appointment.

✔ You have an important project that's due on, let's say, the 10th of the month, and you want to get started on it early, so you set the lead time for ten days. The alarm goes off when you turn on your computer ten

days prior to the activity's scheduled date and time.

✔ You want to be reminded to make a telephone call in an hour.

✔ If you want to be reminded of someone's birthday or anniversary, schedule that important day into ACT! as either a call or a to-do and give it a lead time of 7 to 14 days (and set the alarm) so that you can be reminded to purchase a gift or card.

When an ACT! alarm appears, you can select individual activities by highlighting them individually. Or you can select all the activities by clicking the Select All button.

You have the following alarm options:

✔ **Snooze:** When you click Snooze, the Snooze Alarm dialog box appears. Just like your favorite feature on your bedside alarm clock, ACT!'s snooze enables you to silence the alarm associated with the current contact record for a specific period of time, such as five minutes, ten minutes, and so on. When your time's up, the alarm goes off again.

To move within the Snooze Alarm dialog box, you can use the mouse, arrow keys, or just press the underlined numbers or letters. For example, press 5 for 5 minutes, 1 for 10 minutes, H for hour, D for day, and so on.

✔ **Clear Alarm:** When you select Clear Alarm, the alarm is turned off, but the activity remains on your schedule.

✔ **Clear Activity:** When you select Clear Activity, the Clear Call, Clear Meeting, or Clear To-do dialog box appears, and you can clear the activity from your schedule. (Clearing activities is covered later in this chapter.)

For calls, ACT! asks whether you completed the call, attempted the call, received the call, left a message, or erased the task. ACT! also asks you whether the meeting you want to clear was held and whether the to-do that you want to clear was completed. The information is then recorded in that contact's history. ACT! doesn't let you get away with anything. It sure is a vigilant task master.

If you have more than one contact who has a critical alarm, you can go through the list of alarms, one contact at a time. After you make a decision as to what you want to do with this contact's alarm — by selecting Snooze, Clear Alarm, Clear Activity, or Reschedule — you can then decide what you want to do with the next person's alarming activity.

✔ **Reschedule:** When you choose to reschedule the activity, the Schedule Activity dialog box pops up, enabling you to change the activity's date, time, or anything else about the activity.

✔ **Go To:** When you select Go To, you go to that contact's record. If there is more than one critical alarm, select the contacts whose records you want to go to or click the Select All button before you click the Go To button.

Additional Scheduling Features

I needed to cover the following ACT! scheduling features somewhere, so I put them all together in this section.

Displaying a banner

If you've scheduled an activity whose duration is longer than eight hours, click the Show full day banner option, and ACT! will display a full banner in the Month Calendar window.

Adding color to your activity

You can select colors for your activities. By default, a high-priority item is red, a medium-priority item is blue, and a low-priority item is black. The activity's color is displayed in the contact's Activities tab and the Task List. When you view activities in the Day, Week, or Month calendars, a colored bar appears that shows the duration of the activity. If the activity is scheduled for more than one day, the bar will span the scheduled days when viewed on the Week or Month calendars.

Scheduling activities for another ACT! user

If you're using ACT! on a network or sharing your ACT! database with other ACT! users, you can schedule activities for your colleagues. Just take these steps:

1. **Click the Scheduled For/By button at the bottom of the Schedule Activity dialog box.**

    The Scheduled For and the Scheduled By boxes appear.

2. **Select the user for whom you want to schedule the activity from the list of available users in the Schedule For field.**

    The Scheduled By field shows the user scheduling the activity.

Advanced scheduling options

On the Advanced Options tab of the Schedule Activity dialog box, you can make an activity public or private, send an e-mail message as a reminder, and associate an activity with a group.

Making activities public or private

If you're using ACT! within a multi-user database, you have the option of designating your activities as either public or private. Selecting Public in the Schedule Activity dialog box enables other ACT! database users to view your scheduled activities. By leaving the Public activities box empty, you ensure that all of your activities remain private.

Sending e-mail

When you select Send E-Mail Message To Activity Participants Reminder from the Schedule Activity dialog box and click OK, the Create E-Mail window appears. Specific information about the scheduled activity — the type of activity and what it's regarding — is automatically taken from the Schedule Activity dialog box and inserted in the e-mail message's subject line and message body. Using ACT!'s e-mail features is covered in Chapter 20.

Associating an activity with a group

To associate an activity with a group so that the activity can be viewed in the group's Activities tab, select the group from the drop-down menu in the Associate With Group field.

Scheduling a Recurring Activity

The Recurring Activity dialog box appears when you select the Recurring Settings tab on the Schedule Activity dialog box. The Recurring Activity dialog box enables you to schedule activities that occur on a repeated basis. The frequency of these activities can be specified for as often as daily or as rarely as once per year. The duration can be set for as little as one day or for as far into the future as you wish.

You have the following options:

- ✔ **Daily:** With the Daily option, you specify the number of days between each occurrence of the activity and the date on which the activity is to end.

- ✔ **Weekly:** With the Weekly option, you specify the number of weeks between each occurrence of the activity, the day of the week that the activity is to be repeated, and the date on which the activity is to end.

- ✔ **Monthly:** With the Monthly option, you specify the number of months between each occurrence of the activity, the day of the week that the activity is to be repeated, the weeks in the month when the activity is to be repeated, and the date on which the activity is to end.

- ✔ **Custom:** With the Custom option, you specify the time between each occurrence of the activity, select the specific day(s) of the month that the activity is to be repeated, and the date on which the activity is to end.

When you're viewing your activities on the Day, Week, or Month calendars, you can schedule recurring activities by using the Copy and Paste commands. Just highlight the activity you want to copy and press Ctrl+C to copy the activity to the Windows Clipboard. Then place the cursor on the new date and time and press Ctrl+V to paste the activity into your calendar.

Here are some ways to use ACT!'s recurring activity feature:

- ✔ If you have a weekly or monthly staff or sales meeting, schedule it as a recurring meeting.

- ✔ If you have a regularly scheduled conference call, schedule it as a recurring call.

- ✔ If you're a member of an organization that holds regularly scheduled meetings, schedule these as recurring meetings.

- ✔ If you want to take your important customers and clients out to lunch on their birthdays, schedule their birthdays as recurring activities.

- ✔ If you want to take your best customers out for a special day once a year — to play golf, go to a sporting event, the opera, the symphony, or whatever — schedule a recurring activity.

Saving an activity

When you've indicated the date, time, and all the other specifics of your activity, click OK to save your activity and return to the Contact window. If you change your mind and decide that you don't want to schedule a new activity or don't want to modify an existing activity, click Cancel or press Esc to return to the contact screen, and none of the changes you made to the Schedule Activity dialog box go into effect.

Rescheduling an activity

It's easy to modify or change the particulars — the date, time, or what it's regarding, for example — of a scheduled activity.

Highlight the activity on the Activity tab in the Contact window, the Task List, or one of ACT!'s calendars, and you can do any of the following to bring up the Schedule Activity box:

- ✔ Double-click the activity.
- ✔ Right-click with your mouse and select the Reschedule Activity command from the menu that appears.
- ✔ Select Contact⇨Reschedule Activity from the menu bar.
- ✔ Press the Ctrl+Shift+D keys.

When you finish making your changes, click OK.

Clearing and Erasing Activities

In ACT! you can clear an activity, clear multiple activities, and erase activities.

Clearing a single activity

To clear an activity, you must first highlight the activity on the Activity tab in the Contact window, the Task List, or one of ACT!'s calendars; then select Clear Activity from the Contact menu or the right mouse button menu, and the Clear Activity dialog box appears. You can also press Ctrl+D. The Clear Activity dialog box for a call is shown in Figure 13-11.

Figure 13-11:
The Clear
Activity
dialog box
for a call.

The Clear Activity dialog box enables you to select any of the appropriate results for clearing a call, meeting, or to-do. When the activity is cleared, it is added as a history item in the contact's Notes/History tab. The following sections discuss the result selections for clearing a call, meeting, or to-do.

Clearing a call

You have the following Result choices for clearing a call:

- ✔ **Completed:** This choice clears a call you've successfully made (you spoke with the contact) and updates the contact's history to indicate that this call was completed. The date of the call is also recorded in the Last Reach field.

- ✔ **Attempted:** This choice clears a call that you made, even though you did not get through to the contact. ACT! updates the contact's history to indicate that the call was attempted and also records the date in the Last Attempt field.

- ✔ **Received Call:** This choice clears a call when the contact called you. ACT! updates the contact's history to indicate that the call was received.

- ✔ **Left Message:** This choice clears a call for which you have left a message. ACT! records a notation in the contact's history indicating that you left a message.

- ✔ **Erased:** This choice completely erases a scheduled call. ACT! clears the previously scheduled call and does not record it in the contact's history.

Clearing a meeting

You have the following Result choices for clearing a meeting:

- ✔ **Held:** If the meeting was held, ACT! clears the meeting and makes a notation in the contact's history stating that the meeting was held.

- ✔ **Not Held:** If the meeting was not held, ACT! clears the meeting and makes a notation in the contact's history stating that the meeting did not take place.

- ✔ **Erased:** This choice completely erases a scheduled meeting. ACT! clears the previously scheduled meeting and does not record it.

Clearing a to-do

You have the following Result choices for clearing a to-do:

- ✔ **Done:** ACT! clears the to-do and makes a notation in the contact's history stating that the to-do was completed.

- ✔ **Not Done:** ACT! clears the to-do and makes a notation in the contact's history stating that the to-do was not completed.

- ✔ **Erased:** This choice completely erases a scheduled to-do. ACT! clears the previously scheduled to-do and does not record it.

Always clear your completed activities. When you clear an activity, it's recorded as a history item in the contact's Notes/History tab. This information becomes extremely valuable when you want to gauge or analyze your relationship with a person — especially when you're preparing for an upcoming meeting.

The items in the History file provide you with lots of useful information about the quality of your relationship. It shows you, for example, how many times you attempted to call a person or how many times you left messages for a person that weren't returned. It also shows you how many meetings you scheduled that were not held, and much more.

Scheduling a follow-up activity

Many times, the clearing of one activity will necessitate the generation of another activity. For example, when someone asks you to send them something, you schedule a to-do item as a reminder that something needs to be sent. After that something has been sent, the to-do item needs to be cleared and a follow-up call needs to be scheduled (because you want to know the response to the item you sent).

By clicking the Follow Up button on the Clear Activity dialog box, you bring up the Schedule Activity dialog box and can schedule a follow-up activity.

Clearing multiple activities

To clear multiple activities, highlight the activities in the contact's Activity tab or in the Task List, and select Clear Multiple from the menu that appears when you click the right mouse button. ACT! gives you three clearing choices: Completed, Not Completed, Erase.

Erasing activities

To erase an activity, highlight the activity in the contact's Activity tab, in the Task List, or in the Daily, Weekly, or Monthly calendar, and select the Erase command from the menu that appears when you click the right mouse button. ACT! erases the activity.

Chapter 14

Scheduling Activities with SideACT!

• •

In This Chapter
▶ Installing SideACT!
▶ Using SideACT!
▶ Moving or copying SideACT! activities into ACT!
▶ Using SideACT!'s right mouse button menu

• •

*U*p until now, many ACT! users have been frustrated because they had no place to store miscellaneous lists of things to do or people to call. They felt this way for two reasons:

✔ They didn't want to add these people to their ACT! database because they had no intention of contacting again.

✔ They had no place within ACT! to record the name and phone number of a person that wasn't work or business related.

If you use a previous version of ACT!, you probably experience the frustration of having no place to store miscellaneous lists of things to do or people to call.

One-time-only contacts aren't worth putting into the ACT! database, and there's no place to record the name and phone number of a person who isn't work or business related.

What to do? Write notes to yourself on little pieces of paper, or sticky notes, and let them accumulate on your desk. (I often think the reason we got computer monitors was to give us another place to stick notes.)

Another alternative is entering the person under My Record. This way, you do have a place to store the task inside ACT!, and don't have lists of things to do or people to call spread out on the top of your desk. But if you're like most ACT! users, this is a cumbersome process.

Enter SideACT!. SideACT! is a new ACT! program that runs independently of ACT!. Its sole purpose is to give you a place to record miscellaneous calls, meetings, and to-dos.

I suggest that you *always* schedule meetings inside ACT!. This guarantees that you won't forget about any of them.

Installing SideACT!

When you first install ACT! 4, you're asked if you want SideACT!'s icon installed on your desktop. If you answered yes, SideACT! should be there now.

If SideACT!'s icon isn't on your desktop, you put it there by opening the ACT! 4.0 for Windows folder and using the Windows copy and paste features. If you want to launch SideACT! each time you start Windows 95, you can also put the SideACT! icon in your Startup folder (if it's not there already).

Opening SideACT!

You have several ways to open SideACT!:

- ✔ Click the SideACT! icon on your Windows 95 desktop.
- ✔ Click the SideACT! icon on your Windows 95 menu bar (if SideACT! is in your Startup folder).
- ✔ Click the SideACT! icon on your ACT! toolbar.
- ✔ Select Tools➪SideACT! from the ACT! menu bar.
- ✔ Press Ctrl+Q.

SideACT! is shown in Figure 14-1.

Setting SideACT! preferences

SideACT! gives you several default preference settings. You open the preferences by selecting Edit➪Preferences. You have the following choices:

- ✔ **Which activity do you want as your default?** With this selection you make your default setting for new items.

My Tasks.SPD - SideACT!

File   Edit   View   Item   Send to ACT!   Help

Type text here and press Enter

	✔	Item #	Regarding	Date	Type
		1	Andy Kaplan - Write an article for May issue	3/1/98	☎
		2	Bill Stankey - Call aboutTM Speech	3/1/98	☎
		3	Mitzi Bouffard - Send follow-up letter for C...	3/1/98	📖
		4	Confirm shipment of AFD 4 books	3/1/98	☎
		5	Carolyn Fitzpatrick - Follow up on delivery	3/1/98	📖

Ready   NUM

Figure 14-1:
SideACT!

✓ **What happens to completed items?** With this setting, you choose whether SideACT! moves a completed item to the bottom of the list or leaves it in the current position.

✓ **Where are new activities placed?** This setting determines whether SideACT! places new activities at the top or the bottom of the list.

✓ **Where do these activities go when they're sent to ACT!?** SideACT! either automatically sends each activity to your My Record contact record or prompts you to select a contact.

✓ **Would you like SideACT! to display a confirmation box?** Select the Display Confirmation Dialog Before Transferring Activities to ACT! option if you want to be reminded before you transfer the activity.

Using SideACT!

Now that you've set your preferences, this is how you use SideACT!.

Entering and modifying activities

To enter an activity, just begin typing the activity's specifics and press the Enter key.

To modify an activity, click any of the activity's fields — Item #, Regarding, Date — and begin typing. To change a call, meeting, or to-do to a different type of activity, click the Type field and select a new activity type.

To change the activity type for more than one activity, highlight the activities (by holding down the Shift or Ctrl key and clicking the activities with your mouse) and then select Item⇨Set Item Type from the menu bar.

Clearing, unclearing and deleting activities

To clear a SideACT! activity, click the Cleared Activity column. The Cleared Activity column is the one with the Check Mark in it. You can also mark an item as completed by highlighting the item and selecting Item⇨Mark as Completed, or pressing Ctrl+M.

To unclear a cleared item, just click on the Cleared Activity column. You can also unclear a cleared item by highlighting the item and selecting the Item⇨Unmark Item command, or by pressing Ctrl+Shift+M keys.

To delete an activity, or several activities, highlight the activity and select Edit⇨Delete Selected, or press the Delete key.

Changing an activity's position

To move an activity higher or lower on the list, just highlight the item and select Item⇨Move Item Up or Item⇨Move Item Down. You can also press the Ctrl+Up Arrow or Ctrl+Down Arrow keys.

Printing your list of SideACT! activities

To print your list, select File⇨Print, or press Ctrl+P.

Moving or Copying SideACT! Activities into ACT!

SideACT!'s real power comes from its ability to move and copy items from SideACT! into ACT!. This is how you move a SideACT! activity to ACT!:

1. **Highlight the activity (or activities).**

2. **Select Send to ACT!⇨Move to Database. The SideACT! dialog box appears, as shown in Figure 14-2. The database that the item(s) are moving to is shown in the Details section of the SideACT! dialog box.**

3. **Click the Change Database button if you want to change databases.**

   The Select ACT! database dialog box appears and you select your database.

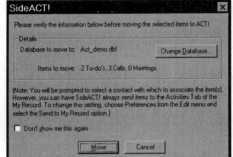

Figure 14-2:
The
SideACT!
dialog box.

4. **Click the Move button.**

   The Associate with Contact dialog box appears, as shown in
   Figure 14-3.

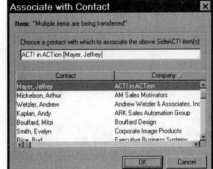

Figure 14-3:
The
Associate
with
Contact
dialog box.

5. **Select the contact to assign the activity to.**

   Type in the first letter of the contact's last name, or of the company's
   name, and ACT! locates the contact. To change the lookup from Contact
   to Company, click on the Contact or Company bar.

6. **Click OK.**

   ACT! moves the activity from SideACT! to the selected contact's activity
   tab within ACT!.

Once the activity moves into ACT!, you may want to modify the activity's
particulars, such as duration, priority, and so on.

Cleared activities move to the selected contact's Notes/History tab.

To copy an activity from SideACT! to ACT!, select the Send to ACT!➪Copy to
Database command. The rest of the process is identical to moving an activity.

You can also copy an activity from to SideACT! to ACT! using the Windows 95 drag-and-drop capabilities. Just highlight the SideACT! activity, drag it over to ACT!, and ACT! adds the activity to the contact's activity tab or places a cleared activity in the contact's Notes/History tab.

SideACT! activities can be dragged and dropped onto any of the following ACT! windows:

- ✔ **The Contact window.** Select the ACT! contact you want to associate the activity with, and drop the activity on the Contact window or any of the tabs.

- ✔ **The Contact List window.** Drop the SideACT! activity on the ACT! contact to whom you want to assign the activity from the list displayed in the Contact List window.

- ✔ **The Task List window.** Drop the SideACT! activity on ACT!'s Task List window and the Associate with Contact dialog box appears. From this box, you select which contact to assign the activity to.

- ✔ **The Calendar window.** Drop the SideACT! activity on ACT!'s Daily, Weekly, or Monthly calendars and the Associate with Contact dialog box appears. From this box, you select which contact to assign the activity to.

All activities are assigned as timeless activities.

Using SideACT!'s Right Mouse Button Menu

Many SideACT! commands can be selected by highlighting an activity and selecting the menu that appears when the right mouse button menu is clicked. From this menu you can do any of the following:

- ✔ Cut, copy, or paste an activity within SideACT!.

- ✔ Delete the selected activity.

- ✔ Mark an item as completed. A completed item can also be unmarked.

- ✔ Send the activity to ACT!.

- ✔ Change the activity type.

Chapter 15

Using ACT!'s Calendars

*I*n ACT!, you can view your activities in a Daily, Weekly, or Monthly calendar by just clicking an icon. In this chapter, I'm going to explain how to use each of these views.

Your activities are displayed in color when you view them in any of ACT!'s calendars, in the Activities Tab, or in the Task List. High-priority activities are displayed in red, medium-priority activities in blue, and low-priority activities in black.

Setting Your Calendar Preferences

ACT!'s specific preference settings enable you to customize the look and feel of your ACT! calendars. To open the ACT! Calendar preference settings, select Edit⇨Preferences from the menu bar and select the Calendar tab or select Preferences from the right mouse button menu. The Calendar preferences are shown in Figure 15-1.

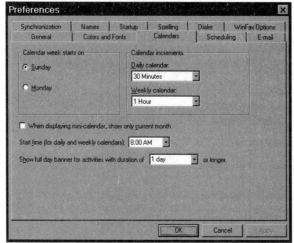

The Calendar tab offers these options:

- ✔ You can choose to have your Mini, Weekly, and Monthly calendars start on either Sunday or Monday.

- ✔ You can choose separate time increments for your Daily and Weekly calendars of 5, 10, 15, 30, 45, or 60 minutes.

- ✔ If you would like ACT! to show a full-day banner for activities that are displayed on the Monthly calendar, select the Show full day banner for activities with duration of option.

- ✔ The Mini calendar, which is discussed later in this chapter, normally displays the current month, the past month, and the next month. If you would like it to display only the current month, choose the When displaying mini-calendar, show only current month option.

Viewing Your Activities a Day at a Time

 To activate the Daily calendar, click the Day Calendar icon with your mouse, select View⇨Calendar⇨Daily Calendar from the menu bar, or press Shift+F5, and the Daily calendar appears. The Daily Calendar is shown in Figure 15-2.

The commands for using the Daily, Weekly, and Monthly calendars are the same, so I'm going to explain them all here.

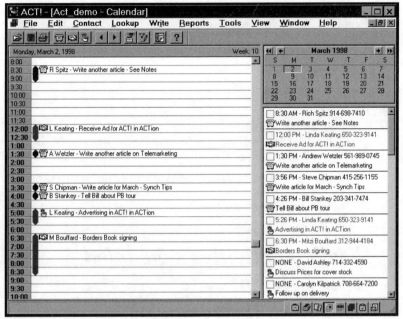

Figure 15-2:
The Daily
calendar.

When you activate the Daily calendar, the activities you've scheduled for today are displayed. The same icons you use to schedule an activity from the Toolbar are used to display the type of activity you've scheduled. The contact's name, the regarding information, and the activity icon are displayed. A colored bar, or band, shows how long each activity is scheduled for.

Any activity you schedule with yourself does not show your name; instead, it shows what the activity is regarding.

Scrolling through the calendar

Depending upon the size of your monitor and the time increment you've chosen, the Daily calendar may display only a portion of the work day. If you need to view times of the day that are not displayed, you can use the up-arrow key or the Scroll Upward button to view early morning hours and the down-arrow key or the Scroll Downward button to view late afternoon or evening hours.

In the Daily calendar, the activities you assigned to a specific time of day are displayed. All of your activities — those to which you have assigned a specific time of day, and the ones that have no specific time associated with them (your timeless activities) — appear in the activity box at the right of the Daily calendar window.

Here are some Daily calendar tips:

✔ If you have activities scheduled prior to the earliest time shown on the calendar, the calendar displays an up arrow in the upper-right corner of the calendar, just to the left of the Scroll Upward button.

✔ If you have activities scheduled after the latest time shown on the calendar, the calendar displays a down arrow in the lower-right corner of the calendar, just to the left of the Scroll Downward button.

Viewing activities scheduled for a different date

To see what your scheduled activities look like on any specific date, just select that date on the Navigator calendar (the calendar displayed in the upper-right corner of the Daily calendar).

Right-click a date and ACT! opens a window that displays a list of all of your scheduled activities for the selected date. This Activity List is shown in Figure 15-3.

Figure 15-3:
The Activity
List
window.

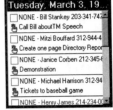

Tuesday, March 3, 19...
☐ NONE - Bill Stankey 203-341-747
🔊 Call Bill aboutTM Speech
☐ NONE - Mitzi Bouffard 312-944-4
🔊 Create one page Directory Repor
☐ NONE - Janice Corben 212-345-6
🔊 Demonstration
☐ NONE - Michael Harrison 312-94
🔊 Tickets to baseball game
☐ NONE - Henry James 214-234-00

You can move within the Daily calendar using the keyboard by doing the following: To move one day at a time, use the left- and right-arrow keys. To move one week at a time, use the up- and down-arrow keys. To move one month at a time, use the Page Up and Page Down keys.

Changing your views

If you want to change your view from the Daily calendar to either the Weekly or Monthly calendars, you can do it with the click of your mouse:

 To change to the Weekly calendar, click the Weekly Calendar icon.

 To change to the Monthly calendar, click the Monthly Calendar icon.

Printing your calendar and taking it with you

To print your calendar, select the File⇨Print command from the menu bar or press Ctrl+P, and the Print dialog box appears. From this dialog box, you can print your calendar and address book in any one of several popular daily-planning book formats, including full page, half page, large pocket, or small pocket calendar/address book. (All the details of printing your calendars are discussed later in this chapter.)

View activities

You can choose which activities you would like to view by using the Filter Calendar dialog box. Select View⇨Filter Calendar from the menu bar or right-click in the Daily calendar and select the Filter Calendar command from the menu that appears.

The Filter Calendar dialog box offers the following options:

- ✔ In the Users box, you can view the activities of selected users or all users.
- ✔ In the Activity Type box, you can choose to filter out calls, meetings, or to-dos.
- ✔ In the Activity Priority box, you can choose to filter out all activities with a high, medium, or low priority.
- ✔ If you would like your cleared activities to appear on your calendar, select the Show Cleared Activities option.

Scheduling a new activity

There are several ways to schedule a new activity from the Daily calendar. Any of the following actions opens the Schedule Activity dialog box.

- ✔ Click the time on the left edge of the Daily calendar.
- ✔ Highlight a time on the Daily calendar and select Contact⇨Schedule (Call, Meeting, or To-do) from the menu bar. You can also access the Schedule commands from the right mouse button menu, or press Ctrl+L, Ctrl+M, or Ctrl+T, to schedule a call, meeting, or to-do, respectively.
- ✔ Click an activity's starting time and drag the mouse pointer down to the ending time.
- ✔ Double-click the activity's starting time.
- ✔ Click a blank portion of the Contact window and drag the contact from the Contact window onto the calendar.

Scheduling activities with the Schedule Activity dialog box is covered in Chapter 13.

Modifying a previously scheduled activity

To modify a previously scheduled activity, highlight the activity with your mouse and double-click on the activity. You can also select the Reschedule Activity command from the right mouse button menu. Either way, the Schedule Activity dialog box appears, enabling you to modify your previously scheduled activity.

To change the date of a timeless activity, highlight the activity, drag it onto the Navigator calendar, and drop it on the desired day.

Changing the date or time of your activities by dragging and dropping

If you're really into your mouse, you can even change the date and time of an activity by using the drag-and-drop technique. To do so, highlight the activity, drag it to a new time, and then release the mouse button. Be sure to hold down the left mouse button as you drag the text. Here are some more ACT! mousie tips:

✔ To change a timeless activity to a timed activity, highlight the activity, drag it to the desired time and release the mouse button.

✔ To change the date of a specific activity, highlight the activity and, while holding the left mouse button, move the pointer to the right of the border of the calendar. This action moves the calendar forward one day at a time. Move the mouse pointer to the left of the calendar's border to go backward one day at a time. To move forward or backward more than one day at a time, keep the mouse pointer outside the border of the calendar; the date changes every second.

✔ When you view your activities on the Daily, Weekly, or Monthly calendars, you can schedule recurring activities by using the Copy and Paste commands. Highlight the activity you want to copy and press Ctrl+C to copy the activity to the Windows Clipboard. Then you place the cursor on the new date and time and press Ctrl+V to paste the activity into your calendar.

✔ Use the Cut and Paste commands to move an activity from one date to another. Highlight the activity you want to move and press Ctrl+X to remove it from your calendar and copy the activity to the Windows Clipboard. Place the cursor on the new date and time and press Ctrl+V to paste the activity into your calendar. Presto! Your activity has been rescheduled.

The duration of an activity can be changed by highlighting the activity and dragging the colored activity bar to an ending time.

Clearing, unclearing, and erasing activities

Once you've completed an activity, you clear, unclear and erase it from the Daily calendar.

Clearing an activity

After you complete an activity, you can clear it directly from the Daily calendar. To do so, highlight the activity you wish to clear and select Contact⇨Clear from the menu bar, or choose the Clear Activity command from the right mouse button menu. The Clear Activity dialog box appears.

You can also clear an activity by clicking the box just to the left of the activity's time in the Activity List field. The cleared activity will then have a check in the box.

Unclearing a cleared activity

To unclear a cleared activity, click on the cleared activity check box that was just described. A message box appears asking, `The activity is currently cleared. Do you want to unclear it?` To unclear the activity, click Yes.

Erasing an activity

To erase an activity, highlight the activity and select the Erase Activity command from the right mouse button menu.

You can also erase an activity by using the Edit⇨Cut command, or by pressing Ctrl+X.

When you erase an activity, ACT! does *not* make a record of this activity in the contact's History file.

Creating lookups and going to contacts

To create a lookup of your scheduled activities, highlight any portion of the calendar, right-click, and select Create Lookup from the menu that appears. ACT! brings up the Contact window with all of the contacts that have an activity scheduled for that day.

From the Weekly calendar, you can create a group of everybody with whom you have an activity scheduled for that week, and from the Monthly calendar, you can create a group of everybody with whom you have an activity scheduled for that month.

To view a complete list of the contacts that are included in this group, select View⇨Contact List from the menu bar or press F8.

If you would like to go to a specific contact's record, highlight the contact, click with the right mouse button, and select Go To Contact from the menu that appears. ACT! brings up the Contact window, and the highlighted contact's record is displayed.

Using ACT!'s Mini Calendar

ACT!'s Mini calendar is a small calendar you can use to schedule new activities or modify previously scheduled activities. To bring up the Mini calendar, which is shown in Figure 15-4, select View⇨Mini-Calendar from the menu bar or press the F4 key.

Mini-Calendar

Figure 15-4:
The Mini
calendar.

In ACT!'s Calendar preferences, you can select whether you want to view a one- or three-month Mini calendar.

Opening the Daily calendar

To view your scheduled activities for a specific date, double-click the date, and the Daily calendar appears.

Viewing your scheduled activities

To view a list of your scheduled activities for a specific date, single-click the date with the right mouse button, and the Activities List dialog box appears. From the Activities List dialog box, you can modify or clear an activity.

Scheduling a new activity

To schedule a new activity from the Contact window with the Mini calendar, follow these steps:

1. **Locate the contact with whom you wish to schedule the activity.**

2. **Click the contact screen with your mouse. (Don't click a field.)**

3. **Drag the mouse pointer onto the Mini calendar and drop it onto the desired date.**

   The Schedule Activity dialog box appears so that you can schedule your activity.

Scheduling activities for more than one contact

With the Mini calendar, you can schedule activities for one or more contacts. This is how you do it:

1. **Open the Contact List window.**

2. **Highlight a contact(s).**

3. **Drag the mouse pointer onto the desired date on the Mini calendar.**

 The Schedule Activity dialog box appears where you enter the activity's particulars.

Modifying an activity for more than one contact

With the Mini calendar, you can also change the date of several activities at once. This is how you do it:

1. **Open the Task List window.**

2. **Highlight a contact.**

3. **Drag the mouse pointer onto the new date on the Mini calendar.**

 ACT! changes the activity's date.

Viewing Your Activities a Week at a Time

When you select the Weekly calendar, the calendar for the current week appears. The Weekly calendar lists the date, time, and regarding information. The calendar also displays the contact's first and last name for each activity that you schedule during the week.

 To activate the Weekly calendar, click the Weekly Calendar icon.

All of the commands and features of the Weekly calendar are identical to those of the Daily calendar and were explained earlier in this chapter.

You can change your view from the Weekly calendar to either the Daily calendar or Monthly calendar with the click of your mouse.

 To change to the Daily calendar, you can click the Daily Calendar icon, select View⇨Daily Calendar, or press Shift+F5.

You can also move from the Weekly calendar to the Daily calendar by double-clicking on the gray bar that displays the specific day of the week.

 To change to the Monthly calendar, you can click the Monthly Calendar icon, select View⇨Monthly Calendar, or press the F5 key.

Viewing Your Activities for a Whole Month

The Monthly calendar lists the contact's name for each activity you've scheduled. The particulars for the selected day's activities are displayed in the Activities List.

 To activate the Monthly calendar, click the Monthly Calendar icon with your mouse, select View⇨Monthly Calendar, or press the F5 key.

All of the commands and features available in the Monthly calendar (including scheduling) are also available in the Daily calendar and are explained earlier in this chapter.

 When you have an activity that spans more than one day, its banner extends over those days in the Monthly calendar.

Customizing the Look and Feel of Your Calendars

To change the appearance — font, font size, font style, font color, and background color — of the Daily, Weekly, or Monthly calendars, open the Preferences dialog box (Edit⇨Preferences) and select the Colors and Fonts tab. Changing colors and fonts works the same way for every ACT! window and tab. All the information you need is in Chapter 24.

Printing Your Calendar

If you absolutely love the leather-bound daily planning book you've been using for years, ACT!'s calendar-printing options give you the ability to print your schedule on pages that will fit almost any daily planner. Now you can take your schedule along with you whenever you leave the office.

You can access the Print dialog box from a number of different places within ACT!:

- ✔ Click the Print button in the Daily, Weekly, or Monthly calendars or the Task List.
- ✔ Choose the File⇨Print command.
- ✔ Press the Ctrl+P key combination.

From the Print dialog box, you can also print your phone number and address book on pages that fit in your favorite daily planner. I discuss this feature in the chapter on ACT! phone features, Chapter 17. And you can print your ACT! reports, envelopes, and your mailing labels from the Print dialog box, too. I discuss ACT! reports in Chapter 21.

Selecting the printout type

Before you can print your calendar, you need to choose the type of calendar you wish to print: Day, Week, or Month. To choose the type of calendar, select Printout Type with your mouse pointer, or use the up- and down-arrow keys to highlight the desired calendar format from within the Printout type field. (You can also use the Printout type drop-down menu. Just place your cursor in the Printout type field and press the Alt+down-arrow key combination.)

If you would like to see a preview of your selected printout, select the Show Preview option.

Selecting the size and type of your paper

After you select the type of calendar you want, you must decide what size paper you want to print your calendar on. Just scroll through the list in the Printout Type box to select a form. After you highlight the paper size you want, you can preview the layout in the Preview window just to the right of the Printout Type field by selecting the Show Preview option.

If you ever try to access the Print dialog box and get an error message that reads something like There are no Layouts in this Directory (or you don't get an error message but the layouts don't appear), you didn't lose your layouts. You've simply lost the availability of your Windows resources. To get your Windows resources back, all you have to do is close ACT! and all of your other active software programs, exit Windows, and restart your computer. After you've restarted your computer, all your Windows resources will once again be available to you. If you don't close everything down and restart your computer, there is a very high probability that it will lock up on you.

Choosing your calendar options

After you've selected your calendar format and paper size, you can select the information you want to have printed on your calendar. To select the information, click the Options button, and the Calendar Options dialog box appears.

From the Calendar Options dialog box you can select whether or not you want to print the Company Name, Saturday and Sunday, a column for priorities, and a five-week view on your calendar.

You can also select the starting hour when you print the Day calendar.

Filtering your calendar

Click the Filter button and the Filter Calendar Printout box appears. From this box, you can decide which user(s) you want to include activities from, and which activities to include in your printed calendar.

You can also include the priority of the activity by clicking the Priorities check box and indicating the range of dates that you want to include.

Getting ink on paper

After you make your selections in the Calendar Options dialog box, click OK to return to the Print dialog box. When you're ready to print your calendar, click the OK button, and the Windows Print dialog box appears.

Click OK to start the printing process. (This may sound confusing because the dialog box in which you make all of your calendar printing selections and the dialog box where you make your printing selections are both called Print.)

The first few times you print out your calendar, print it on regular paper (not your expensive calendar paper) so that you can determine the right format and layout for your calendar.

Chapter 16

Using the Task List

● ●

In This Chapter

▶ Filtering your activities

▶ Managing your activities from the Task List

▶ Sorting the Task List

▶ Creating lookups from the Task List

▶ Printing your Task List

● ●

I find the ACT! Task List to be one of the most important productivity-improving features in the entire program. I refer to it throughout the day because it provides me with a visual list of all my unfinished activities. In my best-selling time management book, *Time Management For Dummies* (published by the fine folks at IDG Books Worldwide, Inc.), I went into great detail about how you can use a Master List to take control of your day.

With ACT!, you can manage all the items that were formerly on your Master List — your calls, meetings, and to-dos — using your computer, thus eliminating the need to write and rewrite information on a pad of paper. And then, by pressing a button or clicking an icon, you can bring up your electronic Master List, the ACT! Task List.

 To view the Task List, which is shown in Figure 16-1, do any of the following: Select View⇨Task List or click the Task List icon (shown to the left of this paragraph) with your mouse or press F7.

 Items on the Task List are displayed in color. High-priority activities are displayed in red, medium-priority activities in blue, and low-priority items in black.

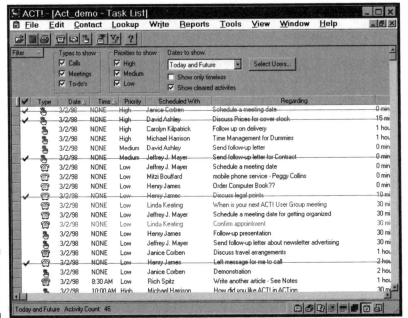

Figure 16-1:
The ACT!
Task List.

The one difference between the Task List and the Activities tab

The features of the Task List and Activities tab — which are discussed in Chapter 5 — are identical. However, you find one difference between these two ACT! features:

✔ In the Activities tab, you view the calls, meetings, and to-dos that you've scheduled with a single person.

✔ In the Task List, you're looking at *all* the calls, meetings, and to-dos that you've

scheduled with everybody in your database for the selected date.

In this chapter, I'm explaining how to use the Task List, but keep in mind that the functions of the Task List and the Activities tab are identical.

Filtering Your Activities

With the Filter command, you can select which activities you want to view, the dates of the activities you want to view, which type of activity you would like to view, and which level of priority you would like to view.

A Filter button has now been placed at the top of the Activities tab. Click the button, and you can make the same selections that are described in the Filter Activities dialog box.

To open the Filter Activities dialog box, select View⇨Filter Task List from the menu bar, or right-click in the Task List to select the Filter Activities command from the menu that appears.

The Filter Activities dialog box offers these options:

✔ In the Users area, you can choose to view the activities of selected users or all users.

✔ From within the Task List, you can view your scheduled activities for many different periods of time:

  • To display a list of today's activities, select Today.

  • To display a list of all your activities — past, present, and future — select All.

  • To display a list of your past activities — you know, the things you should have done but didn't get around to — select Past.

  • To display a list of today's activities and your future activities, select the Today and Future option.

  • If you want to view a list of your activities for a specific date or range of dates, select Date Range, and a drop-down calendar appears. From the calendar, you can view a range of dates by highlighting the dates with your mouse.

✔ In the Activity Type area, you can choose which activities you want to view or not view by checking the boxes for calls, meetings, or to-dos.

✔ If you want to see your activities based upon a specific level of priority — high, medium, or low — select the desired priority level in the Activity Priority area. To list all activities, regardless of priority, select all three boxes.

✔ If you would like to view *only* your *timeless activities* — the activities to which you haven't assigned a time to — select the Show Only Timeless option.

✔ If you would like to view your cleared activities, choose the Show Cleared Activities option.

Managing Your Activities from the Task List

From the Task List, you can schedule new activities, clear completed activities, and modify previously scheduled activities.

Scheduling a new activity from the Task List

To bring up the Schedule Activity dialog box, do any of the following from the Task List:

- ✔ Select Contact⇨Schedule [Call, Meeting, or To-do] from the menu bar.
- ✔ Select Schedule [Call, Meeting, or To-do] from the right mouse button menu.
- ✔ Press Ctrl+L, Ctrl+M, or Ctrl+T to schedule a call, meeting, or to-do, respectively.

Scheduling activities is covered in Chapter 13.

Clearing, unclearing, and erasing an activity from the Task List

From the Task List, you can clear an activity, unclear an activity, and erase an activity.

Clearing an activity

To clear a completed activity, you can do any of the following:

- ✔ Click the box underneath the check mark that is located to the left of the activity. (If you aren't displaying grid lines, you just see white space. Showing and hiding grid lines is discussed later in this chapter.)
- ✔ Highlight the activity you want to clear and select Contact⇨Clear Activity from the menu bar.
- ✔ Highlight the activity you want to clear and select Clear Activity from the right mouse button menu.
- ✔ Highlight the activity you want to clear and press Ctrl+D.

Each of these actions brings up the Clear Activity dialog box.

Clearing multiple activities

To clear several activities at the same time, highlight the activities, by clicking the box to the left of the activity, and select the Clear Multiple option from the right mouse button menu. ACT! then asks you whether these activities were Completed, Not Completed, or whether you want to erase them.

Unclearing an activity

If you've cleared an activity and want to unclear it, this is what you do:

1. **Select the Show Cleared Activities option on the Task List Filter, if it isn't already selected.**

   Cleared activities appear as stricken or grayed out, depending upon the selection you made in the Scheduling tab of the Preferences dialog box; a check mark appears in the Completed column of the Task List.

2. **Highlight the activity by clicking the box to the left of the activity.**

3. **Click the check mark in the Completed column. A message box appears asking whether you want to unclear the cleared activity.**

4. **Click Yes.**

   ACT! unclears the cleared activity.

Erasing activities

To erase an activity, highlight the activity by clicking the box to the left of the activity, and select the Erase Activity command from the right mouse button menu. Release the right mouse button, and ACT! erases the activity.

Modifying activities with the Schedule Activity dialog box

To modify a previously scheduled activity, highlight the activity by clicking the box to the left of the activity. Then click the right mouse button and select the Reschedule Activity command from the menu. The Schedule Activity dialog box appears, where you can make changes to the activity.

You can also bring up the Schedule Activity dialog box to modify a scheduled activity by double-clicking the box to the left of the activity.

Modifying activities directly from the Task List

In addition to being able to modify the particulars of an activity from the Schedule Activity dialog box, you can modify an activity's particulars directly from the Task List itself.

Because the Task List is laid out like a spreadsheet, I'm going to use spreadsheet terms. A *column* is the information at the top of the list: Scheduled With, Date, Time, Regarding, and so on. A *row* is the list of activities that is displayed going down the side of the table. A *cell* is where a column and a row come together.

- ✔ Click an activity in the Type column, and you can change the activity from whatever it is to a call, meeting, or to-do.

- ✔ To change the person with whom an activity is scheduled, double-click the contact's name in the Scheduled With column, and the Select Contacts dialog box appears.

- ✔ To change the priority of an activity, highlight the activity's priority in the Priority column and select High, Medium, or Low from the drop-down menu.

- ✔ To change the particulars of what an activity is regarding, highlight the information in the Regarding column and select an option from the drop-down menu if one appears. You can also enter the regarding information directly from the keyboard.

  To bring up the Regarding Edit List dialog box, press the F2 key.

- ✔ To change an activity's duration, highlight the duration in the Duration column and select a duration from the drop-down menu.

- ✔ To change an activity's date, highlight the date in the Date column, and select a new date from the drop-down calendar.

- ✔ To change an activity's time, highlight the time in the Time column, and select a new time from the drop-down calendar.

- ✔ To make an activity a timeless activity, select the Timeless bar at the bottom of the Mini calendar.

- ✔ To clear an activity, highlight the activity by clicking the Activity Selection button at the left edge of the Task List window, right-click with your mouse, and select the Clear Activity command from the menu. The Clear an Activity dialog box appears, where you can clear an activity.

If you've selected the Show Cleared Activities option in the Filter Activities dialog box, ACT! displays your cleared activities. (They appear as stricken or grayed out, depending upon the selection you made in the Scheduling tab of the Preferences dialog box; a check mark appears in the Completed column of the Task List.)

To unclear a cleared activity, click the check mark and a message box appears saying, `This activity is currently cleared. Do you want to unclear it?` To unclear it, click Yes.

✔ To change the group that an activity's associated with, click the group in the Group column and select a new group from the drop-down menu.

Messing Around with Columns

In the preceding section, I discussed the different ways that you can modify an activity directly from the Task List. What I didn't mention was how you can add and remove columns, change their position, and change their size. That's what I'm going to do now.

Using two new columns: Company and Phone

ACT! 4 can now display two new columns on the Task List. These are the Company field and the Phone field.

If you've been using an earlier version of ACT!, you were asked whether you wanted to convert your old ACT! database to the ACT! 4 format when you first opened the database in ACT! 4. If you said yes, the Company and Phone fields were added to the list of available fields in the Task List.

If you will be sharing your ACT! database with someone who is still using ACT! 3, you DO NOT want to convert to the ACT! 4 database format because the two formats are not compatible. However, if you use two versions of ACT!, all is not lost. If you want to export your ACT! database in the ACT! 3 format, just select File⇨Save Copy As and select the Save Copy in ACT! 3.0 Format option.

Adding columns to the Task List

To display a new column in the Task List, right-click the Task List and select the Add Columns command from the menu. The Add Columns dialog box appears. Select the column you want to add and click OK.

Changing the position of your columns

To change the position of a column, click the column's heading (the cursor turns into a hand), drag it to its new position, and drop it there by letting go of the mouse button.

Removing a column from the Task List

To remove a column, click the column's heading, drag it upwards (the cursor turns into a garbage can), and release the mouse button.

Changing the width of a column heading

To change the width of a column heading, place the cursor on the line between two column headings — it turns into a sizing tool — and move it left or right to make the column wider or smaller.

Locking your columns

To lock your columns so that only columns to the right move when you scroll, click the Column Lock bar that is located at the left-hand edge of the column headings with your cursor — your cursor turns into a sizing tool — and drag it to the right of the column(s) you want to lock in place. When you scroll left or right, the columns to the left of the column lock remain in place.

Showing and hiding grid lines

To display grid lines between your column headings, you must first open the Preferences dialog box (Edit⇨Preferences). Next, select the Colors and Fonts tab and then select the Task List in the Customize box. To show grid lines, select the Show Grid Lines option.

Sorting Your Task List

To change the Task List's sort, just click any of the column headings (Date, Time, Priority, and so on), and ACT! re-sorts the Task List.

You can also place your cursor on these column headings and click the right mouse button. A menu appears where you can select Sort Ascending or Sort Descending. Make your selection, and ACT! re-sorts the items. An upward or downward arrow shows the sorting selection.

Grouping Your Contacts from the Task List

Now that you're familiar with how you can display your different activities in the Task List, you can use the lookup feature to create a grouping of selected contacts.

For example, if you want to group all the activities you've scheduled for today, select the Today option from the Task List Filter, and ACT! displays all the contacts that have activities scheduled for today.

Or if you want to create a list of all your high-priority calls, just select Calls as the Activity type and High as the Activity priority in the Filter Activities dialog box, and ACT! displays all the calls that have a high priority.

Or if you want to create a list of all your to-dos for the next week, just select To-do as the Activity type and select your date range from the drop-down calendar in the Date Range field in the Filter Activities dialog box, and ACT! displays all of next week's to-dos.

After you've grouped these selected activities together, you create your lookup by right-clicking the Task List to bring up the right mouse button menu. Then select the Create Lookup from this menu, and ACT! creates your lookup.

Creating a lookup for a single contact

To select a specific person's contact record, just highlight the contact's activity in the Task List by clicking the Activity button at the left edge of the Task List window. Then select the Create Lookup command from the right mouse button menu, and that person's contact record appears in the Contact window.

Creating a lookup of selected contacts

To create a lookup of all the contacts whose activities are displayed on the Task List, just select the Create Lookup command from the right mouse button menu, and the contact records appear on the Contact window.

To create a lookup of selected contacts, highlight the contact's activity in the Task List. (Simply hold down the Ctrl key while you click the activity button at the left edge of the Task List window.) When you've highlighted the selected activities, select the Go To Contact command from the right mouse button menu, and the contact records of the people with the selected activities appear on the Contact window.

To highlight activities that are next to each other, hold down the Shift key while you click the Activity button.

Printing the Task List

ACT! gives you several ways to print your Task List.

- ✔ If you want to print the activities of your Task List just as you see them on your computer screen, select File⇨Print Task List from the menu bar.

- ✔ If you want to print the activities of your Task List on the pages of your favorite daily planner, select File⇨Print from the menu bar, select a form, click the Print button with your mouse, or press Ctrl+P, and the Print dialog box appears. Choose the appropriate options and click OK.

- ✔ You can also print your Task List by selecting Report⇨Task List. (For a detailed discussion on printing ACT! reports, see Chapter 21.)

Part V
Communicating with the Outside World

"Now, when someone rings my doorbell, the current goes to a scanner that digitizes the audio impulses and sends the image to the PC where it's converted to a Pict file. The image is then animated, compressed, and sent via high-speed modem to an automated phone service that sends an e-mail message back to tell me someone was at my door 40 minutes ago."

In this part . . .

In addition to being a scheduling tool and contact manager, ACT! is filled with features that can help you stay in touch with your contacts.

In Chapter 17, I present ACT! phone features. In Chapter 18, I show you how to create letters and other documents within ACT!. In Chapter 19, I detail ACT's fax-related features. Chapter 20's focus is ACT! e-mail features. Chapter 21 is all about creating and working with reports.

I know that it seems like I'm trying to cover an awful lot in this part; that's because I am. Just take it one chapter at a time, let the material sink in, maybe play with your newly-learned ACT! features, and then move on to the next chapter. There's no rush. You didn't rent this book; you bought it, didn't you?

Chapter 17

Using ACT!'s Telephone Features

● ●

In This Chapter

▶ Keeping track of your calls

▶ Recording the history of your calls

▶ Setting your dialing preferences

▶ Adding phone fields

▶ Printing your address and phone book

● ●

*A*CT! makes it easy to store all the different phone numbers that you may have for your contacts, including their numbers at work, at home, and in the car, as well as their fax numbers and the phone numbers of their assistants. If you have a modem attached to your computer, and if your computer shares a phone line with your telephone, you can even have ACT! dial the phone for you.

The Easy Way to Make an ACT! Call

The easiest way to make a call in ACT! is by using the Phone Contact command, which brings up the Dialer dialog box (shown in Figure 17-1). (If you haven't set up the Dialer, ACT! asks whether you want to do so.)

 You execute the Phone Contact command by selecting Contact⇨Phone Contact from the menu bar, selecting the Phone Contact command from the right mouse button menu, or clicking the Phone Contact icon. (I'm assuming that you're viewing the contact record of the person you want to call. If you aren't, just use ACT!'s powerful Lookup feature to find the person you want to call. If you aren't familiar with lookups, check out Chapter 10.) The Dialer also has a Browse button that enables you to select a different contact to phone. The Dialer dialog box is discussed next.

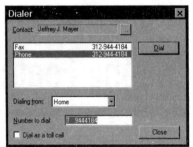

Figure 17-1:
The Dialer
dialog box.

Dialing your calls

After you open ACT!'s Dialer dialog box, you can use it to dial any contact in your database. (In the Dialer Preferences dialog box, which is discussed later in this chapter, you have the option of hiding or showing the Dialer after you've dialed a call.) The name and phone numbers of the contact whose contact record that ACT! is presently displaying in the Contact window appears in the Dialer dialog box.

Always enter a person's extension in the Extension field so that you don't have to go through a phone system's menu when you dial the main number.

To speed up your calling, always record the number(s) of the phone system's menu items. This way, you don't have to waste your time listening to a description of each menu item. (I usually store this information in a blank user field.)

Choosing whom to call

If you would like to phone a different contact, select the Browse button to the right of the contact's name in the Dialer dialog box, and the Select Contact dialog box appears where you can select a different contact to phone.

Using the Dialing From field

In the Dialing From field of the Dialer dialog box, you tell ACT! where you're dialing a call from. You can, for example, be making a call from your office, your home, a regional office, or an out-of-town hotel. The location settings are important because ACT! needs to know the area code you're dialing from (so that ACT! knows whether you're making a local or long-distance call). ACT! also needs to know what numbers it must dial in order to access a local or long-distance line. (These settings are created in ACT!'s Dialer Preferences dialog box, which is discussed later in this chapter.)

Managing your calls from inside ACT!

If you are using a telephone equipped with TAPI (Telephone Application Programming Interface) hardware and software, or if you are using a modem that supports call-management features, you can use ACT! to manage your telephone calls.

TAPI functions as a link between your computer and your modem or telephone, enabling you to place and manage calls using your computer. (ACT!'s dialer uses the TAPI technology that comes with the Windows 95 or Windows NT 4.0 operating systems.) ACT! supports the following call-management features: hold, call forwarding, call transfer, and three-way conference calling.

Unless you have TAPI hardware and the appropriate telephone driver software installed on your computer, you do *not* have access to these features.

If you have questions about which features your modem supports, refer to the documentation that came with your modem or contact your modem vendor.

If you have questions about using your telephone with your ACT! dialer, contact your company's telephone administrator or your telephone system vendor.

Dialing as a toll call

If your call is a toll call, select the Dial as a Toll Call option.

Having ACT! dial the phone for you

One of the neat things you can have ACT! do for you is dial the phone. If you have a modem and you can share a voice line with your computer, then ACT! can dial the phone for you. To dial the phone, select the phone number you wish to dial (phone, fax, home phone, second phone, and so on), and the number is displayed in the Number to Dial field. Click the Dial button, ACT! dials the phone, and the Call Status message box appears and instructs you to "Lift the receiver and click Talk."

When ACT! has dialed the phone number, pick up the telephone receiver, click Talk to disconnect the modem from the telephone call, and then you can talk to the person at the other end of the phone line. I do this all day long; it saves me a great deal of wear and tear on my fingers, and I don't dial too many wrong numbers.

If you don't have a modem, or if you do but it doesn't share a line with your telephone, you can still use ACT! to find the telephone numbers you want to dial, but you'll have to dial them manually.

When you add a contact's phone number to your ACT! database, always include the area code.

Keeping Track of Your Calls with the Record History Dialog Box

ACT!'s Record History dialog box, which is shown in Figure 17-2, opens automatically for your outgoing calls after you select the Talk or Hang Up button in the Call Status dialog box. From the Record History dialog box, you can record a note to yourself about the results of a call. You can view these notes in the contact's Notes/History tab.

You can also open the Record History dialog box by selecting Contact⇨Record History from the menu bar, by selecting the Record History command from the right mouse button menu, or by pressing Ctrl+H.

Using ACT!'s timer

If you select the Start Timer Automatically on Outgoing Calls option in the Dialer Preferences dialog box (discussed later in this chapter), ACT!'s timer starts automatically when you dial the phone. When the call ends and you click the Timer's Stop button, the Record History dialog box opens.

Figure 17-2:
The Record
History
dialog box.

To start the timer manually — when you're receiving a call, for example — select Tools⇨Timer, or press Shift+F4, and the timer appears. Click the Start button to start the timer. Click the Stop button, and the Record History dialog box appears.

Improve your productivity by using a telephone headset

Does your neck ever get stiff from cradling the telephone handset between your ear, chin, and shoulder? Do you find it difficult to take notes while you're on the phone because you just can't find an easy way to hold the phone to your left ear, use your left elbow to keep the pad of paper from moving while writing with your right hand, and remain comfortable, all at the same time?

If you answered "yes" to any of these questions, you should be using a telephone headset instead of the traditional handset. In fact, if

you spend any time at all on the phone, you should be using a telephone headset. I've been using one for years and have found that it's not only comfortable, but has greatly improved my productivity and efficiency as well.

Today's headsets are so light and comfortable that after you put one on, you'll quickly forget that you're even wearing it. And when you're on the phone, you'll have the use of both your hands, so you can concentrate on the conversation instead of the pain in your neck or the tenderness in your ear.

ACT! enters the duration of the timed call in the note's Regarding field along with your notation.

You can also bring up the Record History dialog box by selecting the Record History command when you right-click in the Notes/History tab.

Recording the history of your telephone calls

When you want to write a note to yourself about the status or purpose of a call — a completed call, an attempted call, a received call, or a message left — select Record History from the Contact menu, or right mouse button menu, or press Ctrl+H, and the Record History dialog box appears (refer to Figure 17-2).

In the Activity Result field, you can select from the following call results: Completed, Attempted, Left Message, or Received. (You can also select items for meetings and to-dos.) You can either type the note yourself in the Regarding field or select from the drop-down list of frequently used Call Regarding phrases.

Click OK when you're finished, and ACT! places a notation that you can view in the contact's Notes/History tab. ACT! also inserts the date of this call in the Last Reach field on the Status tab. The features of ACT!'s Record History dialog box are discussed in Chapter 5.

If you would like to enter more than one item from the Call Regarding list, press the F2 key to bring up the Edit List dialog box, highlight your items by holding down either the Shift or Ctrl key, and click OK.

As an alternative to recording the status of your calls as history items, you may want to record notes of your phone conversations. These notes are also stored in the contact's Notes/History tab. To write a note, select Contact⇨Insert Note from the menu bar or press F9. (From the Notes/History tab, you can click the Notes button.) Inserting notes is covered in more detail in Chapter 5.

Using ACT! with Caller ID

Caller ID tells you who is calling before you answer a telephone call. (Contact your local phone company to see whether Caller ID is available in your area.) If Caller ID is available, you can set the Lookup Contact Using Caller ID option in the Dialer Preferences dialog box, which is discussed later in this chapter, to display the contact record on a caller.

Don't forget to schedule an activity

One of ACT!'s greatest strengths is that it associates tasks to contact records. And almost every time you speak with someone on the phone, it's going to generate some kind of follow-up activity.

Tip: You can schedule a new activity from within the Record History dialog box by clicking the Follow Up Activity button.

Let me give you some examples:

✔ You have an appointment scheduled with someone, and that person's assistant calls to tell you that he or she won't be able to keep it. At the conclusion of the call, add a call item to the person's contact record so that you won't forget to reschedule the

appointment. At the same time, remove the appointment from your calendar.

✔ When the person you're talking to says, "I want to think it over," schedule a call for seven to ten days in the future so that you won't forget to call again.

✔ When you're asked to do or send something, schedule a to-do as soon as you get off the phone.

I know that I could go on and on with these examples, but I'll stop here. The key to being successful in business is to have a good and efficient follow-up system, and nothing works better than ACT!.

Don't forget to schedule and clear your calls

Whenever you need to speak with someone, you should add a Call activity to that person's contact record. This way, you won't forget to make the call because ACT! will continue to roll it over from one day to the next. And after you've made the call, don't forget to clear it from your list of activities.

When you clear a call, the Clear Activity dialog box, shown in the following figure appears. The Clear Activity dialog box has five Results selections to choose from, each of which

makes a different history notation that can be viewed in the contact's Notes/History tab, to indicate the final outcome of this particular call. The choices are Completed Call, Attempted, Received Call, Left Message, and Erase. You can also edit the information in the Regarding field, change the activity's date or time, and schedule a follow-up activity. Scheduling and clearing activities is covered in Chapter 13.

As you probably know, in order for you to use ACT!'s Caller ID features, your local telephone company must provide the Caller ID service, Caller ID must be enabled on your telephone line, and your telephone equipment must be new enough to support Caller ID.

When the telephone rings, ACT! looks at the number of the incoming caller and searches its database for a contact record with a matching number. If ACT! finds a matching number, ACT! displays the first contact record of a lookup based on that telephone number. If ACT! finds more than one contact record containing that telephone number, it displays all the contact records containing that number in the lookup.

Setting Your Dialer Preferences

To set your dialing preferences, you first open ACT!'s Preference dialog box and then select the Dialer tab. To open ACT!'s Preferences dialog box, select Edit⇨Preferences from the menu bar or select the Preferences command from the right mouse button menu.

Using the dialer

If you would like to use the dialer (the feature that dials the phone for you if your hardware is properly set up), select the Use Dialer option.

Setting up your modem

In the Modem or Line field, select your modem from the long list of available modems. After you select your modem, click the Setup button, and in the subsequent dialog box, you tell ACT! where to find your modem, as well as a few other things.

Indicating your location

In the Location field, you tell ACT! where you are dialing from. Click the Properties button, and the Dialing Properties dialog box, shown in Figure 17-3, appears. In the Dialing Properties dialog box, you enter the particulars of each location from which you'll be dialing.

In the Where I am section of the My Locations tab, you enter the following information:

- **I am dialing from:** In the I Am Dialing From field, select a location (for example, office, home, regional office, summer home, and so on). To add a new location, click the New button and enter the name of the new location in the Create New Location dialog box. To remove an unused location, select the location from the drop-down menu and click the Remove button.

- **The area code is:** In the Area Code Is field, you enter the area code of the location you're dialing. The information in this field lets ACT! know whether you're making a local or long-distance call.

- **I am in:** In the I Am In field, you enter the country you are dialing from. The number in parentheses is the country's country code.

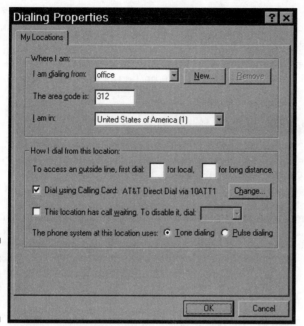

Figure 17-3:
The Dialing
Properties
dialog box.

In the How I dial from this location section of the My Locations tab, you
enter the following information:

- **To access an outside local line:** In this field, enter a number in the local
  box. (This number is often 9.)

- **To access an outside long-distance line:** In this field, enter a number in
  the long distance box. (This number is often 9,1.)

  To insert pauses — because your computer may be dialing a set of
  numbers faster than the phone company's computer can recognize
  them — insert one or more commas (,) between sets of numbers.

- **To use a calling card:** If you are using a calling card from the current
  location, select the Dial using Calling Card option, and the Change
  Calling Card dialog box appears. In the Change Calling Card dialog box,
  select the calling card you are using and its access number. (AT&T, for
  example, is 10ATT0.) In the Calling Card Number field, you enter (what
  else?) your calling card number.

  When you've selected the Calling Card option, ACT! displays the access
  number in the Dialer's Number to dial field.

✔ **To disable call waiting:** If the location you're calling from has call waiting, and you want to disable it, select the This location has call waiting option.

✔ **Tone or pulse dialing:** Select tone or pulse dialing by clicking the appropriate button at the bottom of the Dialing Properties dialog box.

Specifying your "address"

In the Address field, you choose the telephone extension or modem address you want to use from the drop-down list. (This feature is applicable only if you're dialing from a corporate telephone system.) Confused? A telephone or modem "address" is actually a telephone number. Some telephone lines can support multiple addresses. For example, the telephone line in your office may have two extensions, and each of those extensions is considered a separate address.

Setting other dialing options

In the Dialer tab of the Preferences dialog box, you have some additional options:

✔ **Hide dialer after dialing:** Pretty self-explanatory.

✔ **Lookup contact using caller ID:** If you have Caller ID, you can have ACT! look up the caller when you receive a call.

✔ **Start timer automatically on outgoing calls:** ACT! can start the timer on your calls if you so desire.

✔ **Modem has speaker phone capabilities:** If your modem has speaker phone capabilities, select this option.

What about the country code?

You can find the command for displaying or not displaying the country code in phone fields in the General tab of the Preferences dialog box. (Why it's there, don't ask me!) If you want ACT! to display the country code in the phone fields, select the Always display country code in phone fields option.

Creating Phone Formats for Foreign Telephone Numbers

If you would like to change a phone field's format from the standard 123-456-7890 to some other format, this is what you do:

1. **Open the Contact window if it's not open already.**

2. **Place your cursor in the phone field whose format you wish to change.**

3. **Click the phone field's Browse button or press F2. The Country Codes dialog box appears, as shown in Figure 17-4.**

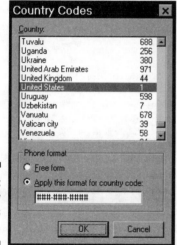

Figure 17-4:
The Country
Codes
dialog box.

4. **Select a country's country code and phone format.**

If you select the Free Form option, you can create a phone format that applies only to that specific contact's phone field. If you select the Apply this format for country code option, you can create your own format that applies to every contact in the database.

Adding New Phone Fields

ACT! comes with a number of fields that are already designated as Phone fields, but if you want to include more telephone numbers, ACT! offers you a lot of flexibility. In ACT!, you can designate any field as a Phone field. To make a field a Phone field, open the Define Fields dialog box by selecting Edit⇨Define Fields from the menu bar. From the subsequent dialog box, take these steps:

1. **Select the field that you want to make a Phone field from the list of fields box.**

2. **Select Phone as the Attribute type in the Type field.**

3. **Change the field name to a name that's appropriate.**

4. **Click OK to save your changes.**

With the flexibility to make any field a Phone field, you can include a person's car phone, cell phone, home phone, vacation home phone, fax machine, home fax machine, beeper, and every other phone number that person may have. Defining ACT! fields is discussed in detail in Chapter 6.

The name that you select as the field's field name appears in the Dialer when you select the Phone Contact command.

If you're wasting a lot of time chasing down wrong phone numbers due to area code splits, Tele-Support Software's Split Wizard for ACT! solves the problem. Split Wizard tracks the area code changes of more than 11,000 prefixes. For more information, call 800-386-1623 or visit Tele-Support Software's Web site at www.tssw.com.

Printing Your Address and Phone Book

In ACT!, you can print the names, addresses, and phone numbers of your ACT! database on various page sizes — full page, half page, large pocket, or small pocket — that are designed to fit in the most popular daily planning books.

To print your name-and-address book, choose File⇨Print or press Ctrl+P, and the Print dialog box appears. From this dialog box, you can print your calendars, as well as your address book, on pages that fit in your favorite organizer format. You can also print your ACT! reports and your mailing labels from the Print dialog box. I discuss printing calendars in Chapter 13 and printing reports in Chapter 21.

If you ever try to access ACT!'s printing features and get an error message that reads something like "There are no Layouts in this Directory," don't worry. You didn't lose your layouts. What you've lost is the availability of your Windows resources. To get your resources back, all you have to do is close ACT! and all your other software programs, exit Windows, restart your computer, and all your Windows resources will once again be available to you.

Selecting printout and paper options

Use the Printout Type drop-down menu to select the type of printout you want. You can choose from Address Book, Day calendar, Week calendar, Month calendar, and Reports, Labels, and Envelopes.

Before you can print your name-and-address book, you must decide which size form you want ACT! to print it on. Just scroll through the Paper Forms list to select a form. If you want to see a preview of your form after you select the paper size you want, select the Show Preview option, and ACT! previews the layout in the Preview window just to the right of the Paper Forms list.

Selecting your Address Book options

When you click the Options button, the Address Book Options dialog box appears. (You must of course select Address Book as your printout type.)

Print options

In the Print section of the Address Book Options dialog box, you select the information you want printed on your name-and-address book. You have the following print options: Primary Address, Secondary Address, Phone Numbers, Alternate Contacts, and E-mail Addresses.

With the three additional fields options (Fields 1, 2, and 3), you can include additional ACT! information in your name-and-address book, which can include information from any field in your ACT! database.

Print settings options

From the Print Settings section of the Address Book Options dialog box, you select how you want your name-and-address book printed. You have these options: Double Sided Printing, Break Page On New Letter, Letter At Top Of Page, Lines Between Contacts, or European Postal Format.

Contact options

From the Create Printout For section of the Address Book Options dialog box, you can select the group of contacts whose names and addresses will appear in your name-and-address book. You can select the Current contact, the Current lookup, or All contacts.

Font options

By clicking the Font button in the Address Book Options dialog box, you can select the specific font, font style, and font size that you want ACT! to use when it prints your name-and-address book.

When printing your name-and-address book, you may want to experiment with different layouts, different formats, and different fonts before you decide which one you like best. So use regular printing paper, not your expensive custom paper, while you're experimenting. When you're fully satisfied with the appearance of your address book, then put your good paper in the printer.

Producing hard copy

After you've set up your printer and selected all of your Address Book options, it's time to print. From the Print dialog box, click the OK button. It doesn't get much easier than that.

Chapter 18

Writing Letters

● ●

In This Chapter

▶ Selecting your word processor

▶ Writing a letter, memo, or fax

▶ Printing, faxing, and e-mailing

▶ Creating form letters

▶ Some useful third-party products

▶ Using ACT!'s word processor

● ●

*A*CT!'s creators realized that ACT! users can be more productive if they have the capability to merge the names and addresses in their database with form letter templates. To fill this need, they give you three choices. You can use the word processor included as part of ACT!. Or you can use either WordPerfect or Word as your word processor.

Selecting Your Word Processor

In the General tab in the Preferences dialog box, you tell ACT! which word processor you'd like to use. To open the Preferences dialog box, select Edit⇨Preferences from the menu bar or select the Preferences command from the right mouse button menu.

In the Default Applications section of the General tab, select your word processor from the Word Processor drop-down list. You can choose from WordPerfect, Word, or ACT!'s word processor. You select your faxing software from the Fax software drop-down list.

If you want to use ACT! with Word or WordPerfect, you should have at least 16MB of RAM, though 32MB would be even better. Today, the price of RAM is so inexpensive, you'll thank yourself for increasing it to 64MB.

I run my publicity campaigns from ACT!

I do all my own promotion and publicity — for my books and my time-management consulting practice — and ACT! has helped me improve my efficiency four- or five-fold.

Over the years, I've spoken with several hundred newspaper reporters, magazine writers, and radio and television broadcasters. Before I got ACT!, I stored all their names in a WordPerfect merge file. When I needed to send someone a press release, a copy of a new book, or some other material, I used WordPerfect to merge the recipient's name and address into a letter, and then I had to run the merge a second time to print the envelope or mailing label.

I've since imported all of these people into ACT!, and my media database has grown to more than 3,000 people.

I get the same results — quicker, faster, and better — using ACT!, and I've greatly improved my productivity. When someone tells me that he or she is interested in reviewing one of my books, I just select the publicity letter from the Write menu, and ACT! automatically merges the contact's name and address into my form letter. All I have to do is click the Print button.

I now do in seconds what used to take me several minutes, and I do it over and over and over again, day after day. This ACT! feature alone saves me two hours of work each week.

Writing a Letter, Memo, or Fax

One of the neat things about the letter-writing capabilities of ACT! is that contact information (the Contact Name, Company Name, and Address, for example) automatically merges into a form letter when you select Letter, Memorandum, Fax Cover Page, or Other Document from the Write menu to create a new document. This feature — which works the same way in Word, WordPerfect, or ACT!'s word processor — makes you much more productive and efficient because you don't have to waste your valuable time retyping your contact's name and address into your correspondence.

Writing a letter

 When you select Write⇨Letter or click the Letter icon, ACT! automatically inserts specific contact information — the contact's name, address, and salutation, as well as the date — into the letter. (In case you're interested, the name of the ACT! letter template is LETTER.TPL; if you're using Word, the template is called LETTER.ADT; and in WordPerfect it's LETTER.AWT. All of these templates are in ACT!'s template directory.)

ACT! also automatically inserts your name and title on the letter's signature line. ACT! takes this from the My Record information of the current database user, presumably you. This feature is another way that ACT! is so intuitive. Because each ACT! user on a multi-user database has his or her own My Record contact record, ACT! always knows who is using the program and is then able to insert that person's name on the signature line in a letter.

Figure 18-1 shows a letter I'm sending to Linda Keating. (Linda is an ACT! Certified Consultant in Palo Alto, California, who specializes in database marketing. She's a very good friend and also happens to help run the San Francisco Bay Area ACT! Users Group.)

Linda also makes some real neat ACT! utilities. For more information about the ACT! Users Group, or Linda's utilities, call 415-323-9141, or send her e-mail at `lkeating@jltechnical.com`. You can also visit her Web site at `www.jltechnical.com`.

As you can see, ACT! inserted Linda's name and address into the letter. (What you can't see is the closing and my signature line because the word processor viewing area isn't large enough.) So all I have to do now is type in the text of the letter and print it. Doesn't that sound easy? (If you're wondering why my letterhead is in the template, it's because I created my own letterhead inside my ACT! Letter template. This way, I don't have to have letterhead printed anymore.)

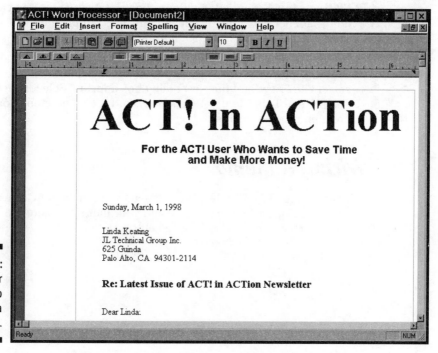

Figure 18-1:
A letter
from me to
Linda
Keating.

When you add a new contact to your ACT! database, you can have ACT! automatically insert the person's first or last name in the Salutation field. (The default is first name.) This is a nice feature if you send out a lot of letters, memos, and other correspondence. To make your selection, Open ACT!'s Preferences dialog box by selecting Edit⇨Preferences, and select the Names tab. In the Salutation section of the Names tab, you can have ACT! insert the person's first name or the person's last name. Make your choice and click OK.

Printing envelopes and labels

ACT! comes with a rather elaborate label and envelope printing program, but for myself, I think a program called DAZ-zle is much easier to use. (I talk about DAZ-zle in the last section of this chapter.) These are the things you can do with labels and envelopes:

- ✔ **Printing a label or envelope:** To print an envelope or label, select File⇨Print or press Ctrl+P, and the Print dialog box appears. This is the same dialog box you use to print your address book, and Day, Week, and Month calendars.

  Select Labels or Envelopes as your Printout type. Then select the label or envelope you wish to print from the list of available labels or envelopes and click OK.

- ✔ **Editing a label or envelope:** From the Print dialog box, you can also edit a label or envelope by clicking the Edit Template button, which opens ACT!'s Report Designer. For information on the features of the Report Designer, read Chapter 21.

- ✔ **Creating a new label or envelope:** To create a new label or envelope, select File⇨New, and the New dialog box appears. Select Envelope Template or Label Template, click OK, and the label or envelope creation process begins.

Writing a memo

To write a memo in ACT!, select Write⇨Memorandum, and ACT! inserts the contact's name opposite the word To and your name opposite the word From. The current date is also inserted automatically.

Creating a fax cover page

Select Write⇨Fax Cover Page, and ACT! inserts the contact's name opposite the word To, the contact's phone number opposite the word Phone, and the contact's fax number opposite Fax Phone. It also inserts your name, company name, and fax and phone numbers, as well as the current date.

Printing, Faxing, and E-Mailing

After you've created your document, you can print it, fax it, e-mail it, or just save it to a file. These are the options that I discuss next.

Printing your letter, memo, or fax

When you print your letter, ACT! does some very interesting things. To print an ACT! letter, select File⇨Print from the menu bar (the Print command is the same for WordPerfect, Word, and the ACT! word processor). The Print dialog box appears, where you can change your printing options if you wish. Then click OK and ACT! prints the document and opens the Create History dialog box, shown in Figure 18-2, even when you're in Word or WordPerfect.

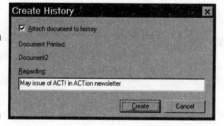

Figure 18-2:
The Create
History
dialog box.

The Create History dialog box appears when you print, fax, or e-mail a document. From the Create History dialog box, you have the following options:

✓ **Attach Document to History:** This option enables you to attach the document to the contact. Click the Attachment icon in the contact's Notes/History tab, and ACT! opens the document.

   If you have selected the Attach document to history option but haven't saved the document, the Save As dialog box appears when you click the Create button. Give the document a name, click the Save button, and you're done.

✔ **Document Printed:** The Document Printed section of the Create History dialog box displays the name of the document that was printed, faxed, or e-mailed.

✔ **Regarding:** In the Regarding field, you can enter a description of the document that will appear in the Attachment's Regarding field in the Notes/History tab.

After you've made your selections, click the Create button, and the information appears in the contact's Notes/History tab, and the letter's date is automatically inserted in the Letter Date field located on the contact's Status tab.

Always spell-check your letters, memos, and faxes before you print them. ACT!'s word processor comes with an 80,000-word dictionary. To activate the spell checker, select Spelling⇨Check Document from the word processor's menu bar.

All ACT! documents created in the ACT! word processor have the *.AWP extension and are saved to the ACT!'s Document directory.

Sending your document as a fax from WinFax PRO

This is how you send your document as a fax:

1. **Select File⇨Send⇨Fax.**

   Your document is faxed, using the fax number entered in the contact record, and the Send Fax dialog box appears (shown in Figure 18-3).

   In WordPerfect and Word, you select the File⇨Send Fax Using ACT! command.

2. **Make your Create History choices and click the Continue button.**

   The WinFax PRO Send dialog box opens and gives the following options:

   • **Subject:** Enter the subject of the fax in the Subject dialog box.

   • **Record History for This Fax:** To make a record of the fax in the contact's Notes/History Tab, select this check box.

   • **History Options:** ACT! gives you two history options. You can attach the fax to the contact as a document and/or you can attach the fax to the contact as a WinFax file. If you want to save the file, this is where you give it a name.

Figure 18-3:
The Send
Fax dialog
box.

3. **From the WinFax PRO Send dialog box, choose from the additional faxing options available.**

4. **Click the Send Button.** ACT! launches WinFax PRO, if it's not already running, and the WinFax PRO Preview window opens so you can view your fax.

5. **Click the Send Fax button. WinFax PRO sends your fax.**

ACT! and WinFax PRO now have complete integration. I discuss using WinFax PRO and ACT! in Chapter 19.

If you send a lot of faxes, it's best to launch your faxing software prior to faxing a document. This will save you time since ACT! doesn't have to launch WinFax PRO.

Sending your document as e-mail

This is how you send your document as an e-mail message:

1. **Select File➪Send➪E-Mail from the menu bar in your word processor.**

   The Send E-mail dialog box appears (see Figure 18-4).

Figure 18-4:
The Send
E-mail
dialog box.

In WordPerfect and Word, you select the File⇨Send E-mail Using ACT! command.

2. **Make your sending selection.**

Your choices are as follows:

- **Entire document as file attachment:** Choosing this option attaches your entire document to an e-mail message.

- **Entire document in message body:** Selecting this option sends your entire document in the body of an e-mail message.

- **Selected text in message body:** This option lets you send selected text — highlighted text — in the body of an e-mail message.

3. **Click OK.**

ACT! sends your e-mail message, and the Create History dialog box appears.

4. **Make your Create History choices, and click Create.**

The Save As dialog box appears. (The Create History choices are discussed earlier in this chapter.)

5. **Give the file a name in the Save As dialog box (if you want to save it) and click Save.**

You're done.

Using ACT! to send e-mail is covered in more detail in Chapter 20.

Saving your document

After you write a letter, memo, fax, or other document, you'll probably want to save it.

To save a document, just select the Save (or Save As) command from the File Menu. The Save As dialog box appears, where you give the document a name. In Word or WordPerfect, you save an ACT! document in the Word (.DOC), or WordPerfect (.WPD) format. Using ACT!'s word processor, you can save the document as an ACT! word processing document, which has the .WPA extension. You can also save as a Rich Text Format (*.RTF) document, which is a file that retains basic formatting codes and can be read by other word processors. An ACT! word processing document can also be saved as an ACT! form letter template or as an ACT! report template.

Deleting, renaming, or doing other things to your document

From within the Save As dialog box, you can delete, rename, or do other things to your document by highlighting the file and selecting the desired option from the menu that appears when you click the right mouse button. This is a basic Windows 95 file management feature.

Creating Form Letters

The strength of ACT!'s word processing functionality comes from its ability to merge contact information into form letter templates. Earlier in this chapter, I describe how you can use ACT! to merge a contact's name and address into a Letter, Memo, or Fax template. Now it's time to think this through a bit further. Instead of writing all your letters from scratch, why not create some boilerplate form letters that you can use to send to your customers, clients, prospects, or anyone else?

That's the beauty of ACT!'s mail merge functions: You create a form letter template and then merge that letter with one contact, a dozen contacts, or several hundred contacts, all at once. Now you're working smarter and saving lots of time by automating the entire process of creating letters.

You can create a form letter template from scratch (by selecting File⇨New and then choosing your word processing template from the New dialog box), but you'll find that it's much easier to modify an existing form letter template than it is to create a new template from scratch.

Before you start editing an existing template, save the template file with a new name (using the File⇨Save As command) because you don't want to make changes to the original template. This way, if you make a mistake or if you don't like the way the modified template turned out, you can delete the modified template and start over. If you do mess up your original ACT! templates, you can perform a custom installation from your original ACT! CD-ROM and reinstall your letter and report templates. (The people at ACT! Technical Support (phone 541-465-8645) can help you reinstall these files.)

Using form letter templates

ACT! stores all form letter templates in the Template directory. ACT! templates carry the .TPL extension. All Word form letter templates have the .ADT extension, and the WordPerfect template extension is .WPT. LETTER.TPL is the ACT! template for the standard letter. The following is a list of ACT! templates:

✓ **LETTER.TPL:** The Letter template is a business letter with the date line at the top, followed by Contact Name, Address, Salutation, and Closing lines. (This is the template ACT! uses when you select Letter from the Write menu.)

✓ **FAXCOVER.TPL:** The Fax template is a fax cover sheet with Title, Date, Pages, To, Phone, Fax Phone, From, and Subject lines included in the fax.

✓ **MEMO.TPL:** The Memo template carries the Memorandum title at the top, followed by Date, To, From, and Subject lines. (If you select Memo from the Write menu, this is the template ACT! uses.)

Sending a form letter to a group of ACT! contacts

Here's how you send a form letter to a group of ACT! contacts:

1. **Select Write⇨Mail Merge.**

   The Mail Merge dialog box opens, as shown in Figure 18-5. From the Mail Merge dialog box you make the following selections:

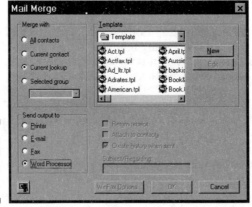

Figure 18-5:
The Mail
Merge
dialog box.

• **Merge with:** Select the contacts to whom you're sending this letter — Current contact, Current lookup, All contacts, or a Selected group.

• **Send output to:** Select where you want to send the finished documents. You can choose either Printer, Fax, E-mail, or the Word Processor.

- **Template:** Choose your form letter template from the displayed list. You can also create a new template or edit an existing one.

- **Regarding:** If you selected either the Printer, Fax, or E-mail options, you can enter information about the document in the Regarding field.

2. **Make your selections.**

3. **Click the OK button.**

   ACT! merges the selected ACT! contacts with the selected form letter template.

To record a History Notation for your document, select the Create History When Sent option. You can also enter information in the Regarding field.

When sending a form letter to a group of people, make sure that the text of the form letter is appropriate for everyone you're sending the letter to. You don't want to have to customize each and every letter.

Converting ACT! 2 templates to ACT! 4

If you're an ACT! 2 for Windows user and you're converting to ACT! 4, you probably have some ACT! form letter templates you would like to continue using.

Since ACT! 2 and ACT! 4 templates use the same format — this assumes you're still using the ACT! word processor — all you do to convert your templates is copy them from your actwin2\template directory to ACT! 4's Template directory.

The easiest way to do this is to open Windows Explorer and use the Copy and Paste commands.

Inserting ACT! merge codes into a form letter template

On the following few pages, I'm going to explain how the LETTER.TPL Letter template was created. (For this example, I've modified the LETTER.TPL template to include my letterhead, as shown in Figure 18-6.) Once you understand this process, it's easy to create any ACT! form letter template.

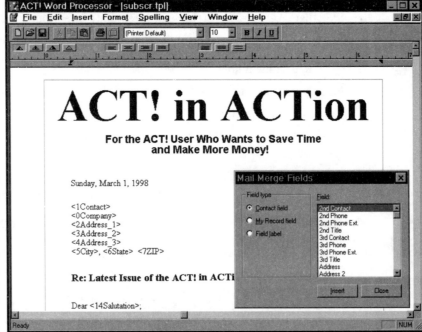

Figure 18-6:
The
LETTER.TPL
Letter
template
with ACT!'s
Mail Merge
Fields
dialog box.

The process of creating a word processing template is the same if you're using Word or WordPerfect, but you must remember to save your template with either the .ADT or .WPT extensions, respectively.

To open LETTER.TPL, select Write⇨Edit Document Template, and the Open dialog box appears. Scroll through the list of files until you find the LETTER.TPL file. Highlight the file and click Open and the LETTER.TPL file opens, in the ACT! word processor, as shown in Figure 18-6.

To create a new document or form letter template from scratch, select File⇨New, and the New dialog box appears. Highlight the word processing document or template for your word processor (ACT!, WordPerfect, or Word), and click OK.

The strange-looking codes you see in Figure 18-6 are ACT!'s merge codes. (The < > marks are called delimiters.) These codes tell the word processor which fields of information to extract from the contact record and where to place them on the form letter template. In this letter template, ACT! extracts the Contact, Company, Address 1, Address 2, Address 3, City, State, and ZIP fields from the contact's record and inserts them in the new letter.

You have two ways of inserting merge codes into an ACT! template. You can type them in, which is a big waste of time, or you can open ACT!'s Mail Merge Fields dialog box, and let ACT! enter them for you.

To access the Mail Merge Fields dialog box, select Insert⇨Mail Merge Fields from the menu bar in the word processor.

Here are some tips for using the mail merge fields and the Letter template:

- The Mail Merge Fields dialog box is active only while you're working in a Letter template.

- The basic LETTER.TPL template uses the contact address displayed on the Contact window. To create a Letter template that sends correspondence to the contact's home address, insert the following codes in place of the present codes in the LETTER.TPL template:

```
<Contact:26>
<Home Address 1>
<Home Address 2>
<Home City>, <Home State> <Home Zip>
```

Then give this file a new name, such as HOMEADDR.TPL.

Testing your letter template

After create your new Letter template, you probably want to test it to see how it really looks. (If you like the way it looks, save it. If you don't, go back to work.)

To preview your template, select the File⇨Mail Merge command, and the Mail Merge dialog box, which was shown back in Figure 18-5, appears. The Mail Merge dialog box gives you the opportunity to select which contacts you want to include in this letter merge and where you want to send the output: Printer, E-mail, Fax, or Word processor.

When you're experimenting with a new template design, it's best to select the active contact (the contact record presently displayed on the ACT! contact screen), and to send the output to the document screen where you can view your creation.

ACT! template tips

Here are some miscellaneous ACT! template tips:

✔ If you have standard, boilerplate phrases you frequently use in your letters or documents, create separate document files for each one of these phrases and then choose File➪Insert from the menu bar to insert the phrases into your document.

✔ Use form letter templates to create order forms, create quotation or bid forms, and create invoice forms.

Saving your form letter template

When you are satisfied with your new template, you'll probably want to save it. Do this by selecting File➪Save or pressing Ctrl+S. If the file already has a name — you should always be working with a copy of a form letter template, not the original — ACT! saves the updated version of the file, replacing the previous version.

If the file doesn't have a name, the Save As dialog box appears. Give the file a name and click Save. (The .TPL extension is automatically attached to the template, and the file is saved in the ACT! Template directory.)

Be very careful when editing an original ACT! template. If you accidentally save the modified version, you replace the original version with the template you just made. For this reason, use the File➪Save As command or press F12, and the Save As dialog box appears.

If you're modifying an ACT! template in WordPerfect or Word, you must remember to add the .WPT or .ADT extension to the template and save these templates in ACT!'s Template directory.

Other word processing programs may not be able to read documents created on ACT!'s word processor. To get around this problem, you can save your document in the Rich Text Format (with the .RTF extension), which retains the formatting codes and can be read by other word processors.

Merging an ACT! form letter with a group of contacts

Now that you've created and saved a form letter, it's easy to send it to a group of people. First you use the Lookup feature to group your contacts together (you can use the Contact List to refine your lookup). Then you select Write➪Mail Merge, and the Mail Merge dialog box appears, which was shown back in Figure 18-5.

The secret of the ampersand

If you're a touch typist and like to use the keyboard instead of the mouse, you can assign underlined letters to your ACT! custom menu items so that you can initiate ACT! commands by pressing the the Alt key plus an underlined letter. When you're adding a new item to an ACT! menu, such as your Write Modify Menu, place an ampersand (&) before the letter you want to have ACT! underline. If you number your documents, use &1 as 1 and &2 as 2. To open document number 1, you press Alt+W+1.

Select which contacts you want to send this letter to and how you want these letters produced (in the word processor, sent directly to your printer, routed to your faxing software, or sent as e-mail). Click OK, and ACT! creates your form letter. What could be easier?

Adding form letter templates to the Write menu

ACT! makes it easy for you to use any form letter template you've created by enabling you to add it as an additional option on the Write menu. To add your form letter template to the Write menu, select Write⇨Modify Menu, and the Modify Menu dialog box appears. From the subsequent dialog box, you can add custom form letters that appear on the Write menu.

Some Useful Third-Party Products

ACT! has many powerful features for doing merges with template documents. The products I discuss in this section either make ACT! better or do things better than ACT!.

DAZ-zle

When you want to print an envelope or a label, let DAZ-zle do it. DAZ-zle is an envelope and label printing program that makes it easy for you to design and print envelopes, labels, and fliers on any paper size. With just a click of your mouse, you select where you want the return and main addresses to appear. Then you can import graphic images, include messages, and add POSTNET bar codes.

POSTNET bar codes are the ZIP+4 bar codes that identify the destination of the mailing piece: the zip code, delivery point, and carrier route. The presence of the POSTNET bar code is important because your letter will be handled with electronic sorting equipment, which means, you hope, that it will be processed faster and more efficiently.

DAZ-zle can import information directly from ACT!, so you don't even have to play the paste-and-cut game. And if you have the contact's ZIP+4 zip code, DAZ-zle prints POSTNET bar codes.

Oh, you don't have the ZIP+4 zip codes? Not to worry! DAZ-zle has a great feature called Dial-A-Zip. After you've imported an ACT! address — or any other kind of address — into DAZ-zle, Dial-A-Zip dials into a Zip-Station — a remote CD-ROM directory of addresses in the United States. When it makes a connection, DAZ-zle gets the ZIP+4 zip code, adds it to the address on your envelope, and updates the zip code on your contact's contact record. The whole process takes about 20 seconds.

I've been using DAZ-zle to print my envelopes and labels (you can even print single labels) for both individual contacts and lookups. It's just a great product. DAZ-zle is made by Envelope Manager Software, whom you can contact at 247 High Street, Palo Alto, CA 94301; 800-576-3279. Their Web site is www.envelopemanager.com.

Label printers

If you've ever printed labels from your laser printer, you know it's easy to print a whole page of them. But what do you do when you need to print just one label? I hope you're not still using a typewriter or, worse yet, writing them by hand. If you are, I've got a better idea. Use a label printer.

Two very good label printers are Seiko's Smart Label Printer Pro and CoStar's LabelWriter XL Plus for Windows.

These label printers quickly print laser-quality labels on a variety of label sizes, incorporating text, photo-like graphics, special messages, and bar codes. So get rid of your typewriter and use your computer to type all your labels. You'll save yourself hours of time.

For more information contact

- ✔ **CoStar Corporation**, 599 West Putnam Ave., Greenwich CT, 06830; phone 800-4-COSTAR (800-426-7827); Web site www.costar.com.

- ✔ **Seiko Instruments USA, Inc.**, 1130 Ringwood Court, San Jose, CA 95131; phone 800-888-0817; Web site www.seikosmart.com.

FedEx Ship

One of the things that I find very time-consuming is filling out FedEx ship-ping forms. Then I learned about Federal Express's *free* shipping software — FedEx Ship.

FedEx Ship enables you to create and print your FedEx shipping forms with your computer. And best of all, FedEx Ship reads your ACT! database.

To get a copy of FedEx Ship, call 1-800-Go-FedEx. It's free.

Using ACT!'s Word Processor

In the final section of this chapter, I cover how to format your text by using ACT!'s word processor.

Before I begin, I should mention that I don't want you to think that ACT!'s word processor is the greatest word processor that's ever been created, because it isn't. However, ACT!'s word processor can play a very big part in helping you save time and become more efficient because it integrates seamlessly with your ACT! database and it's fast.

When you know how to take advantage of its major strengths, ACT!'s word processor is a huge time-saver.

And you may find that ACT!'s word processor is more convenient to use than WordPerfect and Word for sending routine correspondence, writing form letters, and creating fax cover sheets.

Opening ACT!'s Word Processor

To open an existing word processing document or template from within ACT!, here's what you do:

1. **Select File⇨Open.**

   The Open File dialog box appears.

2. **Select the type of file you want to open from the drop-down menu in the Files of Type field.**

   When you select the type of file you want to open, ACT! automatically changes to the appropriate directory and displays the list of files within that directory. Select ACT! Word Processor Document (*.AWP), and ACT! changes to the Document directory. Select ACT! Word Processor Templates (*.TMP), and ACT! changes to the Template directory.

3. Highlight the name of the file you want to open and click Open.

ACT! opens that document or template within the word processor for further editing.

When you want to create a new document or a form letter template from scratch, select File⇨New, and the New dialog box appears. Highlight either the ACT! Word Processor Document or ACT! Word Processor Template entry and click OK.

Setting your word processing preferences

To set ACT!'s word processing preferences, open the Preferences dialog box by selecting Edit⇨Preferences from the menu bar.

In the Preferences dialog box's General tab, you can specify the measurement units (inches, centimeters, points, or picas) that you want ACT! to use. You can also enable or disable the Tool Tips option. A Tool Tip is the description of a toolbar button that ACT! displays when you pass your cursor over a button.

In the Spelling tab of the Preferences dialog box, you specify which main and custom dictionaries you want to use when spell-checking documents. You can also decide whether you want the Auto Suggest Spelling Changes option enabled. (When the Auto Suggest option is on, ACT!'s spell checker tries to suggest a correct spelling for any word you use that's not in its dictionaries.)

Formatting your documents

The following section explains how to format your ACT! word processing documents.

Working with the Page Setup dialog box

After you've opened a document in ACT!'s word processor, you may want to change the size of the paper for which the document has been designed. To specify a new paper size, select File⇨Page Setup, and the Page Setup dialog box appears. You can change the page orientation, paper size, default margins, and paper source for both new documents or previously created documents.

Setting your page margins

The white space that surrounds the text that's printed on a page is the page's margins. When you're writing your letters or creating form letter templates, you'll often want to change the margins of your text.

To set your page margins for the whole document, select Format⇨ Page Margins, and the Page Margins dialog box appears. The default margins for a new document are 1 inch for both the top and bottom margins and 1.25 inches for the left and right margins. From the Page Margins dialog box, you can select different margins for all sides of your document.

The easiest way to change a paragraph's margins is to place your cursor within a paragraph, or highlight the block of text if you want to change the justification of several paragraphs, and then reposition the margin markers on the ruler bar that's displayed at the top of the word processor screen.

From the ruler bar, you can change the position of the left and right margins for a highlighted block of text or for the entire document. You can also change the distance that the first line in the paragraph is indented from the left margin by moving the inverted-T marker.

To change a paragraph's margin, drag the marker to the left or right with your mouse pointer. When you release your mouse button, the highlighted text lines up with the Margin marker.

From the ruler bar, you can also set the position of your tabs, set your document's line spacing, and set the justification of your text.

If you want to see or hide your page margins — top, bottom, left, right, headers, and footers — on the word processing screen, select View⇨ Page Glides.

Justifying your text

When you justify text, you determine its alignment within a paragraph. In ACT!'s word processor, you have four justification choices: left, center, right, and full.

This is how you justify your text:

1. **Position your cursor within the paragraph whose text you want to justify, or highlight a block of text if you want to change the justification of several paragraphs.**

2. **Click one of the paragraph justification buttons located on the ruler bar.**

   The buttons appear in this order: Justify Left, Justify Center, Justify Right, and Justify Full.

Changing the spacing of your text

In ACT!, you have a number of line spacing choices. You can have single spacing, one-and-a-half-line spacing, double spacing, and spacing at a user-defined measure.

To change line spacing, just position your cursor within the paragraph whose text you want to change the spacing of, or highlight a block of text if you want to change the spacing for several paragraphs, and click the Single Space, One-and-a-Half Space, or Double Space buttons on the ruler bar.

Keeping your paragraphs together

Many times, when you're writing a letter or creating a document, you want to keep specific lines of text or paragraphs together on the same page, thus preventing the automatic insertion of a page break between the lines of text or paragraphs. The following steps show you how to keep your text together:

1. **Highlight the paragraph or block of text that you want to keep together on the same page.**

2. **Open the Paragraph dialog box (Format⇨Paragraph).**

3. **Check the Keep With Next box in the Paragraph dialog box.**

Setting your tabs

In ACT!, you can add, move, and remove tab markers from the ruler bar or from the Tabs dialog box, which you open by selecting Format⇨Tabs from the menu bar. You can also access the Tabs command by right-clicking within a word processor document.

Applying your tab and margin settings to another paragraph

If you want to copy a specific paragraph's setting — margins, tabs, and so on — from one paragraph to another paragraph within the same document without having to redefine the paragraph's settings, use the Copy Ruler command.

To copy your ruler settings, place your mouse pointer anywhere within a paragraph that contains the margin or tab settings that you want to copy. Choose the Copy Ruler command from the Edit menu or the right mouse button menu to copy the ruler settings.

To apply the settings to another paragraph, position your mouse pointer within the paragraph, or highlight a block of text, and choose the Apply Ruler command from the Edit menu or the right mouse button menu.

Inserting things into your document

In ACT!, you can insert headers, footers, page breaks, dates, time, and special characters into a document. The next few pages show you how.

Inserting headers and footers

A *header* is text that appears at the top of every page of a document, and a *footer* is text that appears at the bottom of every page of a document.

If you would like to insert a header or a footer in a document, choose the Header and Footer command from the Format menu, and the Header and Footer dialog box appears.

From this dialog box, choose the Header or Footer option to insert a header or footer. Enter the height of the header or footer in the Inches box. After you've made your selections, click OK.

If you're placing a header or a footer in your document and don't want the header or footer to appear in the document's first page, select the Exclude Header and Footer from First Page option.

To enter header or footer information in your document, move to the top or bottom of the first page of your document, place the cursor in the header or footer box with your mouse, and enter the text. When you've finished, use your mouse to move the cursor to the main body of the document.

To remove a header or footer from your document, open the Header and Footer dialog box and remove the check from the Header or Footer check box.

Inserting a page break

When you want to insert a page break in your document, position the cursor where you want the pages to break and choose Page Break from the Insert menu or press Shift+Enter. A gray bar indicates the start of the new page.

To remove a page break, move your cursor to the top of the new page and press the Backspace key.

Before you insert a page break into your document, place the cursor in front of the first character of the paragraph that you want to appear on the next page. Then choose the Page Break command, and a page break appears at the selected insertion point.

Inserting the current date and time into your document

To insert the current date into an ACT! document, place your cursor where you want the date inserted, select Insert⇨Date, and the Insert Date dialog box appears.

To insert the time into an ACT! document, select Time from the Insert menu, and the Insert Time dialog box appears.

ACT! uses the Windows 95 date and time settings to enter dates and times into a document. To change the date format, open the Windows Tools folder and select Control Panel. Click the Regional Settings icon to open the Regional Settings dialog box. To set the Date format, select the Date tab. To set the Time format, select the Time tab. When you're finished, click OK to save your settings.

Inserting page numbers within your document

When you write a letter, the automatic insertion of page numbers gives your letter a very polished look. To insert a page number in your document, place your cursor where you want the page number positioned and select the Page Number command from the Insert menu. ACT! automatically inserts the page number in your document. Remember, though, that ACT! doesn't offer page numbering options such as Roman numerals.

To remove a page number from your document, highlight the number and delete it.

To number the pages in your document, place the Page Number command in a header or a footer. If you don't want the page number to appear on the first page of your letter or document, you must place the page number in either a header or a footer and then select the Exclude Header and Footer from First Page option in the Header and Footer dialog box.

Chapter 19

Faxing from ACT!

. . . .

In This Chapter

▶ Setting your faxing preferences

▶ Sending Quick Faxes from the Contact window

▶ Sending Quick Faxes from the Contact List window

▶ Sending faxes from your word processor

▶ Additional WinFax PRO sending options

▶ Working with your ACT! database from within WinFax PRO

. . . .

*A*CT! and WinFax PRO (you need version 8.03 or higher) now have complete integration. You can launch and operate WinFax PRO from within ACT!'s Contact window and Contact List window.

You can read and edit your WinFax PRO directory from within ACT!, and you can read your ACT! database from within WinFax PRO.

If you do a lot of faxing from your computer, you need to use WinFax PRO — it makes faxing a breeze. A trial copy of WinFax PRO is included on your ACT! CD-ROM. For more information you can call Symantec Customer Service at 800-441-7234. Symantec's Web site is www.symantec.com.

Setting Your Faxing Preferences

To make ACT! and WinFax PRO work properly, you've got to do two things:

1. Select WinFax PRO as your faxing software.

You do this by selecting Edit⇨Preferences from the menu bar, which opens the Preferences dialog box. On the General tab, you make your faxing selection.

2. Select your WinFax options.

You do this by selecting the WinFax Options tab from within the Preferences dialog box, which is shown in Figure 19-1.

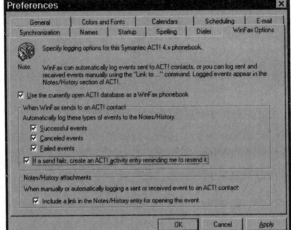

Figure 19-1:
ACT!'s
WinFax
PRO
preferences
settings.

WinFax PRO's faxing options

From the WinFax Options tab you have a number of faxing options to select. You select faxing options by placing, or not placing, a check mark in the check box.

- Do you want to use the currently open ACT! database as a WinFax phone book?

- What information do you want WinFax to log in the contact's Notes/ History tab when a fax is sent to an ACT! contact?

   - **Successful events:** The fax was sent and received.

   - **Canceled events:** The fax transmission was canceled.

   - **Failed events:** The fax wasn't received.

- If a send fails, do you want ACT! to automatically schedule a reminder to resend it?

- Do you want ACT! to automatically attach a fax — either sent or received — to the contact's Notes/History?

Sending Faxes

ACT! enables you to send faxes in a variety of ways. The following sections show you how.

Sending Quick Faxes from the Contact window

ACT!'s Quick Fax command enables you to send a fax to someone directly from the Contact window.

This is what you do:

1. **Click the Quick Fax icon.**

   ACT! launches WinFax PRO. The WinFax PRO Send dialog box opens, which is shown in Figure 19-2.

2. **Click the Phonebook button.**

   The list of contacts in your ACT! database appears.

3. **Select the person you want to send to and click the Add To List button.**

   The person's name is inserted in the Recipient List field.

4. **Enter the fax regarding information in the Subject line.**

5. **Type your message in the Quick Cover Page box and click the Send button.**

   ACT! opens the WinFax PRO Preview window.

6. **Click the Send Fax button from within WinFax PRO.**

   WinFax PRO sends your fax and makes an entry in the contact's Notes/History Tab and logs the fax in WinFax PRO's Send Log folder.

If you want to send the fax to additional recipients, you can choose them from the current lookup, the selected ACT! groups, or the categories listed in the ID/Status field. You make your selection by highlighting the contact(s) and clicking the Add to List buttons.

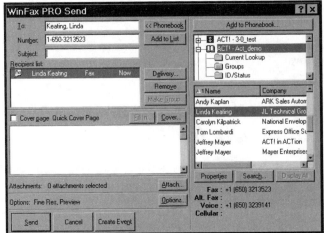

Figure 19-2:
WinFax PRO
Send dialog
box with
phone book
open.

Sending Quick Faxes from the Contact List window

ACT! also gives you the ability to send the same fax to several people. This is how you do it:

1. **Open the Contact List window.**

2. **Select the people to whom you want to send a fax.**

3. **Click the Quick Fax icon.**

    ACT! launches WinFax PRO.

4. **Follow the same steps in the previous section on sending Quick Faxes from the Contact window.**

Sending faxes from your word processor

ACT! also enables you to send faxes from your word processor, which I discuss in Chapter 18.

Working with ACT! and WinFax PRO

From within WinFax PRO, you can send faxes to people who are in your ACT! database, and you can add people to your ACT! database from within WinFax PRO.

Sending faxes to people in your ACT! database from WinFax PRO

From within WinFax PRO, you can send faxes to people who are in your ACT! database. This is how you do it:

1. **Select Send⇨New Fax from the menu bar.**

   The WinFax PRO Send dialog box opens (see Figure 19-2).

2. **Select the person to whom you want to send a fax from the list of ACT! databases.**

   The person's name appears in the To field and their fax number appears in the Number field.

3. **Enter the fax regarding information in the Subject line.**

4. **Click the Add to List button.**

   The person's name is added to the Recipient List.

5. **Type the fax message in the Quick Cover Page field, or select an attachment.**

6. **Click the Send button.**

   The WinFax PRO Preview window opens.

7. **Click the Send Fax button.**

   WinFax PRO sends your fax.

Adding contacts to your ACT! database from within WinFax PRO

From within WinFax PRO, you can add people to your ACT! database by using the WinFax PRO Send dialog box. This is how you do it:

1. **Enter the person's name in the To field and their fax number in the Number field.**

2. **Select the ACT! database you want to add this person to.**

3. **Click the Add To Phone Book button.**

   The Symantec ACT! 4.0 Contact Properties dialog box opens with the person's name and fax number displayed.

4. **Enter the person's other information, such as Company, Phone Number, and Address information.**

5. **Click OK.**

   WinFax PRO adds the person to your ACT! database.

Chapter 20

ACT! and E-Mail

● ●

In This Chapter

▶ Setting your e-mail preferences

▶ Adding an e-mail address to an ACT! contact record

▶ Creating an e-mail message

▶ Using your e-mail Drafts folder

▶ Using your e-mail Inbox

▶ Using your Briefcase

● ●

*W*ith ACT!'s e-mail features, you can perform numerous tasks that will save you time and increase your productivity. Here are some of the other things you can do:

✔ Attach one or more files of any type to an e-mail message.

✔ Attach a single Contact Record, a Lookup, or a Group to an e-mail message. And, you can include the contact's or group's notes, history, and activities.

✔ Attach contact records using the vCard Standard format, making them compatible with Microsoft Outlook.

✔ Send confirmations of scheduled calls, meetings, and to-dos from the Schedule Activity dialog box.

✔ Send documents directly from your word processor.

✔ Create reports and send them as e-mail attachments.

✔ Set your preferences such that when you send an e-mail message, ACT! automatically makes a history record.

And you can do all of this with just a few clicks of your mouse.

ACT!-Supported E-Mail Systems

The following e-mail systems are supported by ACT!:

- ✔ cc:Mail
- ✔ cc:Mail Mobile
- ✔ CompuServe
- ✔ Eudora
- ✔ Internet Mail (With the release of Microsoft Internet Explorer 4.0, this has been renamed Outlook Express.)
- ✔ Lotus Notes
- ✔ MS Exchange or Outlook

Setting Your E-Mail Preferences

Before you begin using ACT! to send and receive e-mail, you need to choose your e-mail system and set up the e-mail default settings. You can access ACT!'s e-mail setup by doing either of the following:

- ✔ Selecting Help⇨QuickStart Wizard
- ✔ Clicking the E-Mail System Setup button on the E-Mail tab inside the Preferences dialog box
- ✔ Clicking the E-Mail System Setup button on the E-Mail Addresses dialog box. You open this dialog box by selecting Contact⇨E-Mail Addresses from the menu bar.

You setup your default e-mail preferences from within the Preferences dialog box, which you open by selecting Edit⇨Preferences then clicking the E-Mail tab.

Why can't I use America Online as my e-mail system?

ACT! users have been asking the question: "Why can't I use AOL as my e-mail system?" for several years. The answer is quite simple. AOL's e-mail system is proprietary. To date they have not allowed Symantec's ACT! programmers access to their e-mail code. Maybe someday they'll lighten up!

ACT!'s E-Mail Preference options are shown in Figure 20-1.

Here's a rundown of your e-mail preferences.

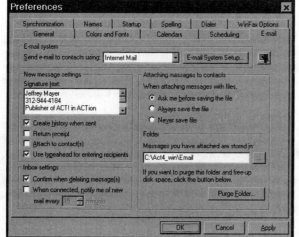

New message settings

In the New Message Settings section of the E-Mail Preferences you can do the following:

- **Signature text:** Here, you create default text to appear as the signature of all your e-mail messages.

- **Create history when sent:** If you want ACT! to automatically create a history item for each e-mail message you send, select this option.

- **Return receipt:** To request a return receipt for each e-mail message you send, select this option.

- **Attach to contact:** To automatically attach this e-mail message to the recipient's contact record, choose this option. If the recipient is not in your ACT! database, the message attaches to the My Record contact record.

- **Use typeahead for entering recipients:** To select e-mail recipients from an address book by typing the first few letters of their name, select this option. Otherwise, you will need to enter the recipients' full name or select them from a list.

Inbox settings

ACT! gives you the option of setting the following in-box default settings:

- ✔ **Confirm when deleting message:** To have ACT! ask you if you *really* want to delete this message, select the Confirm When Deleting Message(s) box.

- ✔ **Notify me of new mail:** Checking the When connected, notify me of new mail every __ minutes check box lets you can set the frequency with which ACT! checks your e-mail system for incoming messages. (This option works only if you are logged on and permanently connected to your e-mail server.)

Attaching messages to contacts

When attaching files to e-mail messages. you've the following choices:

- ✔ **Ask me:** ACT! always asks before saving the file.

- ✔ **Always save:** ACT! always saves the file.

- ✔ **Never save:** ACT! never saves the file.

E-mail messages are stored in ACT!'s Email folder by default. Click the Browse button to select a different folder.

To purge all e-mail messages that are attached to contact records, click the Purge Folder button.

Selecting and setting up your e-mail system

You select your primary e-mail system — the default system for sending all e-mail messages from ACT! — from the Send e-mail to contacts using drop-down menu.

You set up your e-mail system by clicking the E-Mail System Setup button, and ACT!'s E-Mail Setup Wizard appears.

The Wizard walks you through the set-up process for whichever e-mail system(s) you choose. Your choices are: cc:Mail, CompuServe, Eudora, Internet Mail (Outlook Express), Lotus Notes, and MS Exchange.

If you're using Eudora, Internet Mail (Outlook Express), or MS Exchange, you need to know such information as your user name, outgoing SMTP server, and incoming POP3 server. You can find this information inside each program's default settings. Or you may need to contact your Internet service provider.

Selecting a format for attaching ACT! contacts

ACT! now enables you to attach ACT! contacts to e-mail messages in both the ACT! format and the vCard/vCalendar formats. With this enhancement, you can share ACT! contact information with people using ACT! and/or people using Microsoft Outlook. And people who are using Microsoft Outlook can share their contact information with people using ACT!. (vCard/vCalendar is the format used by Microsoft Outlook.)

You make the default selection in the Attaching Contacts/Activities To Messages section of the General Tab of the Preferences dialog box.

You can also make this selection when you're attaching the contact to the e-mail message.

Adding an E-Mail Address to a Contact's Record

To add an e-mail address to an ACT! contact record, just place your cursor in the E-Mail Address field and type in the address.

To edit an existing e-mail address, or add additional addresses to the contact's record, select Contact⇨E-Mail Addresses from the Contact window menu bar, and the E-Mail Addresses dialog box appears.

You can also open the E-Mail Addresses dialog box by placing your cursor in the E-Mail Address field and pressing F2 or clicking the down-arrow and selecting Edit E-Mail Address from the drop-down menu.

From the E-Mail Addresses box you can do the following:

- ✔ Add a new address
- ✔ Edit an existing address
- ✔ Delete an old e-mail address
- ✔ Access the E-Mail Preferences dialog box

Creating an E-Mail Message

You can open the E-Mail Message window, which is shown in Figure 20-2, in any of the following ways:

- ✔ Select Write⇨E-Mail Message from the menu bar in the Contact, Contact List, Group, Calendar, or Task List windows.

- ✔ Click the View E-Mail button to open the E-Mail window, and select the E-Mail⇨Create Message command.

- ✔ Press Ctrl+E in the E-Mail window.

- ✔ Select the Send E-Mail Message To Activity Participants option in the Advanced Options tab of the Schedule Activity dialog box; then click OK.

- ✔ Select Write⇨E-Mail Message from the right mouse button menu in the Contact, Contact List, or Group windows.

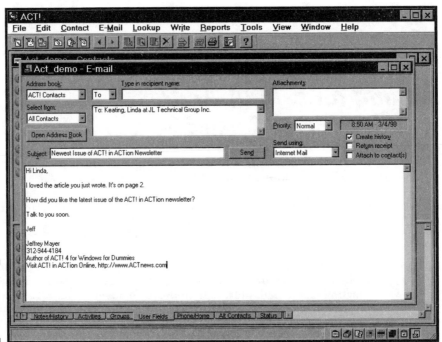

Figure 20-2:
The E-Mail
Message
window.

Addressing your e-mail message

The first thing you have to do when you want to send an e-mail message is select the person to whom it will go. Here's how you do it:

1. **In the E-Mail Message window, select the Open Address Book button.**

   The Address Book dialog box appears, as shown in Figure 20-3.

Figure 20-3:
The Address Book dialog box.

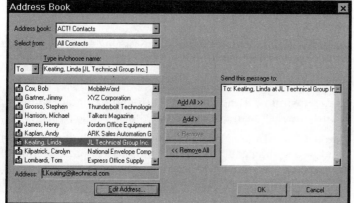

2. **Select an address book from the e-mail system(s) listed in the Address Book drop-down list.**

   The address book opens.

3. **Select** To, cc, **or** bcc **from the drop-down list.**

   You follow the same steps when creating cc (carbon copy) and bcc (blind carbon copy) e-mail addresses. If you send a carbon copy of an e-mail message, the e-mail message includes the list of the people who received a copy. In a blind carbon copy, the e-mail message does not include a list of the people who received a copy.

4. **Highlight a person's name in the Address Book Entries field.**

5. **Click the Add button.**

   ACT! inserts that person's name in the Send This Message To box.

To edit the person's e-mail address, highlight the name and click the Edit Address button.

Using your e-mail address books

When you select your ACT! database as your e-mail address list, you can search for e-mail addresses from within the active lookup or the current directory. You can also send an e-mail message to every member of an ACT! group.

When you select your CompuServe, Eudora, MS Exchange, Lotus Notes, or the cc:Mail address book as your e-mail address list, it enables you to search for e-mail addresses from your address book(s) for that particular service provider or e-mail program.

You can select your e-mail recipients by dragging and dropping their name(s) on the Recipient section of the e-mail message. This is how you do it:

- **Contact window:** Drag the contact from the Contact window and drop it onto the Recipient section of the e-mail message.
- **Contact List window:** Highlight the contact(s) in the Contact List window and drag and drop them onto the Recipient section of the e-mail message.

Entering the subject line

The subject line is the most important part of an e-mail message. You use this line to summarize the content of your message in a very brief but descriptive manner.

If you make your subject line so descriptive that it grabs your readers' attention, they'll probably read your message first. Depending upon which e-mail program you're using, you may have 25 to 35 characters for a subject line, so make the most of them.

Typing your e-mail message

You enter your e-mail message in the Message Body field of the E-Mail Message window.

When writing your e-mail message, write short, easy-to-read sentences and paragraphs. Put the most important information in the first few sentences of the first paragraph. Here are some other e-mail-writing tips:

- Try to keep your e-mail message on one screen. If a message takes more than one screen, shorten it.

- ✔ If you're including a list of items, use a bulleted or numbered list (like this one). It's easier to read.

- ✔ If you must send a long message, attach the file as an enclosure. (Go to the next section to find out how to attach a file to your e-mail message.) Write a brief description of the message in the subject line. The e-mail message itself should contain a description of the enclosed file.

- ✔ If you attach a document to an e-mail message, write a brief but thorough description of the document. Don't forget to include the purpose of the document, detailed instructions regarding what the recipient is supposed to do with the document, and the date you need a response. This item of business should then be added as an ACT! activity.

Attaching a file to your e-mail message

If you want to attach a file — a word processing document, spreadsheet, or report, for example — to your e-mail message, select E-Mail⇨ Attach To Message⇨File from the menu bar of the E-Mail window. The Choose File To Attach dialog box appears, where you can select one or several files to attach to the e-mail message.

Select the file(s) to include, click OK, and ACT! adds the selected file(s) as attachments to your e-mail message. (The file's name and path are inserted in the Attachments field in the E-Mail Message window.)

From Windows Explorer, you can attach a file by dragging and dropping it onto the e-mail message.

Attaching a contact or group record to your e-mail message

To attach an ACT! contact or group record to an e-mail message, select E-Mail⇨Attach To Message⇨(Contact or Group) from the menu bar on the E-Mail window, and the Attach Contact(s) or Group(s) dialog box appears.

From this dialog box, you choose one or many contact records to attach to an e-mail message. This is how you do it:

1. Select All Contacts⇨Current Lookup, or Selected Group.

The list of contacts is displayed.

To sort by name or company, click either the Contact or Company bar. To sort in ascending or descending order, hold down the Shift key while clicking the Contact or Company bar.

2. **Highlight your contact(s) and select the Add button.**

3. **Select the Include Notes/History or Activities boxes if you want to include a contact's notes/history or activities with the e-mail message.**

4. **Select the desired contact format.**

   You can choose the ACT!, vCard (compatible with Microsoft Outlook), or both formats.

5. **Click OK to attach the selected contact(s) to your e-mail message.**

   You can also attach a contact to an e-mail message by dragging and dropping the contact's name using either method following.

   • **Contact window.** Drag the contact from the contact window onto the Attachments section of the e-mail message.

   • **Contact List window.** Select the contact(s) in the Contact List window and drag them onto the Attachments section of the e-mail message.

   To attach a group, from the menu bar of the E-Mail window, select E-Mail⇨Attach To Message⇨Group and the Attach Group(s) dialog box appears, where you can attach one or more groups to your e-mail message. (If you want to include a group's notes, history, or activities with the e-mail message, select the appropriate box.)

   If you change your mind and decide that you don't want to include a specific contact record, group record, or file as an attachment, just select the attachment in the E-Mail Message window and press Delete.

Additional e-mail options

ACT! gives you some additional e-mail options:

✔ **Setting the priority.** In the E-Mail Message window, you can designate your e-mail message as Low, Normal (which is the default), or High priority by selecting one of these three choices on the right side of the dialog box.

✔ **Creating a history.** To create a history for this e-mail message, select the Create History check box.

✔ **Attach to contact(s).** To attach this e-mail message to selected contact(s), select the Attach to Contact(s) check box.

✔ **Getting a receipt.** To receive an acknowledgment that your message was received and opened, select the Receipt check box.

Sending your e-mail message now or later

After you've written your e-mail message, ACT! gives you a choice. You can send your message now or later. To send your e-mail message now, select E-Mail⇨Send Mail Now, or press Ctrl+Enter. If you want ACT! to store your e-mail message in the Drafts folder, to send at a later time, select E-Mail⇨ Send Mail Later command or press Ctrl+Shift+Enter. (ACT!'s Drafts folder is discussed later in this chapter.)

Creating an E-Mail Message with Your Word Processor

You can also send e-mail from within your word processor. Here's how:

1. **Create your document.**

2. **Select File⇨Send⇨E-Mail from the menu bar.**

   The Send E-Mail dialog box appears.

   When sending an e-mail message from your word processor, you choose which parts of the word processing document you want to include in your e-mail message and how you want to include them. You have the following options:

   - Include the entire document as a file attachment.

   - Include the entire document in the message's body.

   - Include selected text in the message's body. (This option is available only if text has been selected.)

3. **Make your choice and click OK.**

   ACT! sends your e-mail message.

Confirming a Scheduled Activity

When you schedule a new activity or modify a previously scheduled activity, you can send an e-mail message from the Schedule Activity dialog box. Select the Advanced Options tab and choose the Send E-Mail Message To The Activity Participants option. Click OK, and ACT! opens the E-Mail Message window, inserts the contents of the Regarding field into the E-Mail Subject field, and enters the activity information in the Message Body area.

Attaching Activities by Dragging and Dropping

You've several ways to attach an activity to an e-mail message by dragging and dropping.

- ✔ **Activities Tab of the Contact Window:** Open the Activities tab and highlight the activity. Then drag the activity onto the Attachments section of the e-mail message.
- ✔ **Task List Window:** Highlight the activity(s) in the Task List window; then drag the activity onto the Attachments section of the e-mail message.

Sending a Report as an E-Mail Message

When you create a report, you can send it as an attachment to an e-mail message without ever printing it out or viewing it on-screen. First, select the type of report to create from either the Reports menu or the Open Report dialog box (choose Reports⇨Other Report). The Run Report dialog box appears. From the Run Report dialog box, select the report's particulars (which contacts, notes/history items, and activities you want included in the report). In the Send Output To section, select E-Mail, click OK, and ACT! compiles the report, opens the E-Mail Message window, and adds the report as an attachment.

To attach a report that's already been created and saved, attach it to your e-mail message as a file. Preparing ACT! reports is discussed in Chapter 21.

Using the Drafts Folder

Use ACT!'s Drafts folder to store your outgoing e-mail messages so that you can send them at a later time. For example, create several e-mail messages before you log onto your e-mail system, and send them all at once, instead of sending each message one at a time. This is a nice feature when you're traveling or working from home. When you're ready to send your messages, select the ones you want to send and select E-Mail⇨Send Mail Now from the menu bar.

Your Drafts folder does not have password protection.

E-mail etiquette

You should be aware of the many informal rules, regulations, and other requirements for writing proper e-mail messages. Here are some of them:

✔ Don't send carbon copies (cc) of messages to people who don't have to see the message.

✔ Don't send out blind copies (bcc) casually; they can imply that you're going behind someone's back.

✔ Don't ask for a receipt unless it's really necessary. You may be insulting the recipients by implying that they don't read their mail.

✔ Beware of crying wolf. Use the "urgent message" notation sparingly. If you use it too often, your future messages may be ignored.

✔ Don't use all capital letters. WHEN YOU TYPE YOUR MESSAGE IN ALL CAPITALS, IT'S KNOWN AS SHOUTING IN THE E-MAIL WORLD, and people don't like to be shouted at. Use upper- and lowercase letters just as you do when you type an old-fashioned letter.

✔ Put addresses in the To, Copies (cc), and Blind Copies (bcc) lines in alphabetical order by the recipients' last names. Doing so keeps you from accidentally insulting people — such as your boss, supervisor, or manager — because you listed them in the wrong place. (If you're going to go out of your way to insult someone, do it on purpose!)

✔ Don't overuse your mailing list. Only send your messages to people who need to receive them. By limiting your list of recipients, you'll build your credibility as an e-mail sender. The fewer messages you send, the greater the attention they receive.

✔ Send only work-related messages when you're at work. Messages such as jokes or invitations to non-work-related events are best handled outside of e-mail.

✔ Type positive messages your readers look forward to receiving. Even when you must communicate a negative message, try your best to say it in a positive way.

✔ If your message is very important, controversial, confidential, or could easily be misunderstood, use the telephone or set up a face-to-face meeting.

ACT! uses icons to indicate whether a message has an attachment and to designate an e-mail message's priority. These icons are positioned to the left of an e-mail message in ACT!'s E-Mail window.

✔ A paper clip appears next to the icon if the message has attachments.

✔ A plain envelope icon appears next to a low-priority message.

✔ A shaded envelope icon appears next to a normal-priority message.

✔ An exclamation point appears next to a high-priority message.

From within the Drafts folder, you can read, print, save, or delete the e-mail messages that you have written but have not yet sent.

- ✔ **Reading your e-mail messages:** To read an e-mail message stored in your Drafts folder, select the message and choose the Read Message command from the E-Mail menu, or double-click on the message itself, and the E-Mail Message window appears. Here, you can edit your message or add attachments. The E-Mail Message window is shown back in Figure 20-2.

- ✔ **Printing your e-mail messages:** Select the message you want to print, and choose File⇨Print from the menu bar. The Print dialog box appears. Click OK to print your e-mail message.

- ✔ **Saving your e-mail messages:** Select the message that you want to save, choose File⇨Save, and the Save dialog box appears. Give the file a name, specify a storage location , and click the Save button.

- ✔ **Deleting your e-mail messages:** Select the message you want to delete and press the delete key.

Using Your E-Mail Inbox

When you receive e-mail messages, they appear in your inbox when you're online. The Folders section of the E-Mail window lists inboxes for the e-mail services you're using.

If you have multiple supported e-mail systems listed in your My Record contact record, a Combined Inbox is available in the E-Mail window. The Combined Inbox contains messages from all of the supported e-mail systems.

To open an e-mail system Inbox, just double-click the Inbox, or select E-Mail⇨ Get/Send Mail. (If you're using CompuServe, you select E-Mail⇨Open Inbox.)

You print, save, and delete messages from the Inbox the same way you do from the Outbox, which is described previously in this chapter.

Connecting to an e-mail system

You can create a new e-mail message without logging onto your e-mail system, but, as you probably know, you eventually need to log on to the system to send and receive your e-mail messages. You use the E-Mail window to log on because it contains the E-Mail menu, which offers all the commands you need to send and receive e-mail messages.

Follow this procedure to log on to an e-mail system:

1. **Choose View⇨E-Mail when you are in the Contact window, or click the E-Mail icon at the bottom of the Contact window.**

   The E-Mail window appears.

2. **Select your e-mail service and choose the Get/Send Mail command from the E-Mail menu.**

   With some e-mail systems, a dialog box appears prompting you to log on to the e-mail system.

3. **If some sort of Logon dialog box appears, enter your name and password and click OK.**

   You are now logged on to your e-mail service, and the Inbox for that e-mail system appears.

Reading your e-mail messages

To read an e-mail message, select the message and choose E-Mail⇨ Read Message from the menu bar, or select the Read Message command from the right mouse button menu, and the e-mail message appears. In addition to reading the e-mail message, you can reply to the message, forward the message to someone else, print the message, save the message, or delete the message — all by clicking the appropriate icons.

You can also do the following:

- ✔ Attach the e-mail message to a contact by selecting E-Mail⇨ Attach E-Mail To Contact.
- ✔ Add the contact to your ACT! database by choosing E-Mail⇨ Create Contact From Sender.

If someone sends you a message with attachments, you can do any of the following:

- ✔ **Open the attachment:** If a contact record or group record is attached to the e-mail message, highlight the attachment and select Open Attachment from the right mouse button menu. (You can also double-click on the attachment.) The Merge Options dialog box opens where you decide how you want the contact or group merged into your ACT! database.

✔ **Save the attachment:** If a file is attached to the e-mail message, high-light the attachment and select Save Attachment from the right mouse button menu. The Save As dialog box opens where you give the attach-ment a name and save it.

✔ **Merge the attachment:** If you receive an e-mail reminder for a sched-uled activity — the activity is attached to the e-mail message — you can merge the activity into your database, and it appears on your calendar.

Replying to an e-mail message

You can reply to an e-mail message from either the Inbox, the message itself, or the Briefcase. To reply to an e-mail message, highlight the message, select E-Mail⇨Reply To Message (Ctrl+Y), and the Reply/Forward Options dialog box appears.

From the Reply/Forward Options dialog box, you can tell ACT! to include the body of the original message in your reply or to include attachments you want to send. If the message was sent to a number of people, not just you, you can reply to all of the recipients (their names are listed on the recipient list) by selecting the Reply To All box.

Forwarding an e-mail message

To forward an e-mail message to someone other than the person who sent it to you, highlight the message, select E-Mail⇨Forward Message (Ctrl+F), and the Reply/Forward Options dialog box appears. (The steps you follow to forward an e-mail message are the same steps you use to reply to an e-mail message.)

Using Your Briefcase When You're Off-line

ACT!'s Briefcase stores your downloaded messages and serves as your Inbox when you are not connected to your e-mail system. Your ACT! Briefcase provides all the options available to you when you're connected to your host system from the Inbox and allows for e-mail-message management when you're not connected to your host system.

To access the Briefcase, which is identical to the Inbox, click on the Brief-case icon in the Folders section of the E-Mail window. (Note that the Brief-case does not have password protection.)

Chapter 21

Working with Reports

● ●

In This Chapter

▶ Generating ACT!'s instant reports

▶ Generating a standard ACT! report

▶ Accessing ACT!'s standard reports

▶ Converting your ACT! 2 report templates to ACT! 4's format

▶ Creating custom reports

▶ Working with graphics

▶ Inserting merge fields into a report template

▶ Making reports look nice

● ●

*A*CT! comes with a set of standard reports that you can use to analyze the results of your daily activities. I explain how to use these reports in this chapter. In the last section of this chapter, I explain how to create custom reports.

But first, I want to talk about reports in general. Your ACT! reports are only as good or as useful as the information you put into your ACT! database. The following list presents stuff you can do to make your ACT! database a much more powerful reporting tool (because you can then review the information in the contact's Notes/History tab):

✔ Always enter activity information in the Regarding field so that when you clear an activity, ACT! can properly record the purpose or nature of that activity as a History item.

✔ Always clear your scheduled activities after you complete them so you have a record of what you've done.

✔ Always record the results of your phone calls — Call Completed, Call Attempted, Call Left Message, or Call Received — in the Record History dialog box so that you know what happened with each and every phone call.

- ✔ If you want to keep track of how much time you spent on a call or activity, use ACT!'s timer.

- ✔ When you send out correspondence — letters, memos, faxes, and e-mail messages — *always* create a History notation so that the correspondence is logged as a History item or Attachment item.

- ✔ Use the Record History dialog box to record what happened during impromptu meetings.

- ✔ Use the Record History dialog box to record the completion of to-dos that weren't on your things-to-do list.

- ✔ Use the Last Results field to summarize the results of your last meeting, phone call, or other contact activity.

- ✔ Use the Insert Notes command to open the Notes/History tab, where you can write detailed notes about what took place at a meeting or what was discussed during a phone conversation. I find the habit of keeping notes of meetings and phone conversations to be an enormous timesaving, productivity-improving tool.

Generating ACT!'s Instant Reports

A brand new ACT! 4 feature is its instant reports. ACT! instant reports enable you to print out a report identical to the information you see on your computer screen.

The following reports can be printed from within the Contact window:

- ✔ **Notes/History report:** Select File⇨Print Notes/History to print the selected contact's notes, history and attachments.

- ✔ **Activities report:** Select File⇨Print Activities to print the selected contact's scheduled activities.

- ✔ **Printing the Group report:** Select File⇨Print Groups to print the list of groups in which the selected contact is a member.

To print a report of all the information — contact information, scheduled activities, and note/history information — in the Contact Record, select Reports⇨Contact Report.

The Contact List and Task List reports print from their respective windows.

- ✔ **Contact List report:** From within the Contact List window, select File⇨Print Contact List.

- ✔ **Task List report:** From within the Task List window, select File⇨Print Task List.

The following instant reports can be printed from within the Group window:

- ✔ **Notes/History report:** Select File⇨Print Notes/History to print the selected contact's notes, history, and attachments.

- ✔ **Activities report:** Select File⇨Print Activities to print the activities scheduled for a selected contact.

- ✔ **Printing the Contact Members report:** Select File⇨Print Contact Members to print the list of the members of the selected group.

Generating a Standard ACT! Report

The process of generating an ACT! report is usually the same for each and every ACT! report. Here's how you do it:

1. Select a report from the Reports menu.

The General tab of the Run Report dialog box appears, as shown in Figure 21-1.

ACT! 4's database structure

A new ACT! 4 feature enables you to convert your ACT! 3 database to an ACT! 4 database format. The only difference between the two database structures is that ACT! 4 includes the Company Name and Company Phone Number as fields that can be displayed in the Task List window.

So when you create the Task List Report and put it in your briefcase, you also have the company's name and phone number. (If you plan to share this database with someone who is still using ACT! 3, you shouldn't make the conversion.)

However, you can always save an ACT! 4 database as an ACT! 3 database by selecting the File⇨Save As command and selecting the Save Copy in ACT! 3.0 Format option in the Save Copy As dialog box.

Tip: If your database is still in the ACT! 3 format and you wish to convert it to the ACT! 4 format, open the Task List and select Add Columns from the right mouse button menu. The Add Columns dialog box opens and the Company and Phone fields will be listed as additional columns. Click the Add button and the Convert Database message box appears. It tells you: In order to add the Company Name or Telephone Number fields to the Task List you must convert this database from ACT! v3.0 format to ACT! v4.0 format. If you share this database with others who use ACT! v3.0, you must not convert it to the v4.0 format. If you want to make the conversion, click the Yes button.

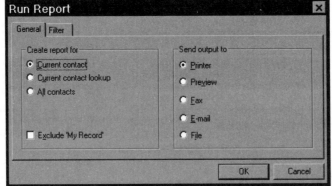

Figure 21-1:
The General
tab of the
Run Report
dialog box.

ACT! offers ten standard reports to choose from. (If you want to create a report that isn't on the list of available reports, select the Reports⇨ Other Report command, and select from the list of available reports in the Report directory.)

2. **In the General tab of the Run Report dialog box, make selections from each of the following options:**

   • **Contacts:** Select the group of contacts — Current contact, Current contact lookup, or All contacts — you want to appear in the report.

   • **My Record:** Include or exclude the My Record information from the report.

   • **Output:** Select where you want the report to go: the Printer, Preview, Fax, E-Mail, or File.

3. **In the Filter tab of the Run Report dialog box, shown in Figure 21-2, specify what data you want to include in the report. You have the following choices:**

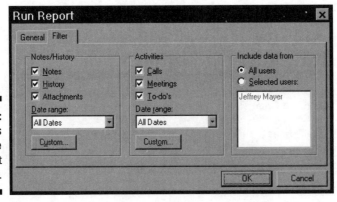

Figure 21-2:
The Filters
tab of the
Run Report
dialog box.

- **Notes/History:** From the Notes/History section, you include or exclude notes, history, or attachments from your report. Then you select the date or range of dates to span.

- **Activities:** From the Activities section, you include or exclude calls, meetings, or to-dos from your report. Then you select what date, or range of dates you want to include.

- **Include Data From:** In this section, you select the users whose data you want to include in the report.

4. **After you've made your selections, click OK.**

   ACT! compiles your report and sends it to the printer, sends it as a fax, sends it as an e-mail message, or saves it to file. You can also preview the report before printing it.

Here are some ACT! reporting tips:

✔ Depending upon the type of report you are running, some of the options in the Filter dialog box may or may not be available.

✔ You can create ACT! reports by selecting File⇨Print or by pressing Ctrl+P to bring up the Print dialog box. Choose Reports as your Print-out Type and select from the list of files. Scroll through the list of available reports, and when you find the report you want, highlight it and click OK, and the report generation process begins. From the Print dialog box, you can also print your address book, Day calendar, Week calendar, and Month calendar, envelopes, and labels.

✔ For reports you run frequently, record a macro to run your report. This speeds up the report-compiling time. (I cover macros in Chapter 24.)

✔ If you run certain reports frequently, add them to your Report menu. This feature is discussed later in this chapter.

✔ You can speed up the report-compiling time by compressing and re-indexing your ACT! database. (I discuss database maintenance in Chapter 25.)

✔ Creating an ACT! report can be a tedious and time-consuming process, especially if you haven't done it before. Therefore, you may want to hire an ACT! Certified Consultant to help you design your reports. To learn more about how an ACT! Certified Consultant can help you get more out of ACT!, read Chapter 27. For an up-to-date list of ACT! Certified Consultants, visit Symantec's ACT! Web site at `www.symantec.com/act`.

Accessing ACT! Standard Report Templates

ACT! comes with a number of standard report templates you can use to view and print information about your contacts. You can also modify these report templates to create your own custom reports. All these reports — except the Group List and Group Report — appear in the Reports menu. To choose the Group List or Group Report, choose Other Report from the Reports menu and then select the report you want to use. A summary description of ACT!'s standard reports appears in Table 21-1.

Table 21-1	ACT!'s Standard Reports
Report Title	*Description*
Contact Report (CONTACT.REP)	Displays all contact information, including the history, activities, and notes, for the selected contacts.
Contact Directory Report (DIRECTORY.REP)	Displays the primary address and home address for each contact.
Phone List Report (PHONELST.REP)	Lists the company, contact, primary phone number, including extensions, of a selected group of contacts in a spreadsheet format.
Task List Report (TASKLIST.REP)	Displays the calls, meetings, and to-dos scheduled with all the contacts in your ACT! database for the specified range of dates.
Notes/History Report (NOTEHIST.REP)	Displays the contact's notes and history items for a specified date range.
History Summary Report (HISTORY.REP)	Displays the number of attempted calls, completed calls, meetings held, and letters sent for an individual contact or group of contacts over a selected range of dates.
Activities/Time Spent Report (ACTIVITY.REP)	Displays a list of the activities scheduled and time spent with each contact during a specified date range.

Report Title	Description
Contact Status Report (STATUS.REP)	Displays the information in the ID/Status field and the Last Results field, as well as to-do information for the selected group of contacts.
Source of Referral Report (REFERRAL.REP)	Displays referred by information for each contact.
Group Membership Report (GRPMEMBR.REP)	Displays a list of all ACT! groups and all contacts in each group.

Converting Your ACT! 2 Report Templates to ACT! 4's Format

If you're an ACT! 2 for Windows user, you probably have some ACT! report templates that you would like to convert to ACT! 4's format. If so, follow these steps:

1. **Select ACT! as your word processor (if it isn't already).**

   You do this in the General tab of the Preferences dialog box. Open the Preferences dialog box by selecting Edit⇨Preferences from the menu bar. Close the Preferences dialog box when you are done.

2. **Select File⇨New from the menu bar in the Contact window.**

   The New dialog box appears.

3. **Select ACT! Word Processing Document as your File Type and click OK.**

   ACT! opens the word processor.

4. **Choose File⇨Open from the menu bar.**

   The Open dialog box appears.

5. **From the File Of Types drop-down list, select All Files.**

6. **Browse to the location of the report template you wish to convert, which is *probably* in your actwin2\reports directory.**

   When you install ACT! 4 it copies all your reports from the actwin2\reports directory to ACT! 4's Oldrep directory. So look for your reports in either of these directories.

7. **Highlight the file from the list of files and click Open.**

   ACT! opens the template in the word processor.

8. **Select File⇨Save As to save the file in the ACT! 4 format.**

   The Save As dialog box appears.

9. **Locate the directory in which you want to save this report template, which is probably the ACT! 4 Report directory.**

10. **Select ACT! Report Template (it has an .REP extension) in the Save As Type list if it's not already selected.**

11. **Give the file a new name, if desired, and click Save.**

   ACT! saves your template in the ACT! 4 format.

After you convert an ACT! 2 report into the ACT! 4 format, you need to edit the converted report. At a minimum you have to adjust field sizes and line spacing.

Creating Custom Reports

Earlier in this chapter, I discussed how to create ACT! reports using the standard report templates that came with ACT!. However, you can do a lot more with ACT!'s reporting capabilities by creating your own custom reports, and that's what I cover here.

You can create an ACT! custom report in two ways: You can create a report from scratch, or you can modify an existing ACT! report template.

 ✔ To create an ACT! report from scratch, select File⇨New or press Ctrl+N, and the New dialog box appears. Choose Report Template, and ACT! opens a blank report template in ACT!'s Report Designer.

 ✔ To modify an existing ACT! report template, select Reports⇨Edit Report Template, and the Open dialog box appears. Highlight the report you want to modify, click Open, and the report appears within ACT!'s Report Designer. For illustrative purposes, the Task List report template is shown in Figure 21-3.

Here are some ACT! reporting tips:

 ✔ When you create a new ACT! report template by modifying an existing ACT! report template, always save the template with a new name (use the File⇨Save As command) before you start making changes to it. Doing so ensures that should you make a mistake, you can always go back to the original template and start over again.

 ✔ If you accidentally make changes to an original ACT! report, you can reinstall it by performing a custom ACT! installation from your original ACT! CD-ROM.

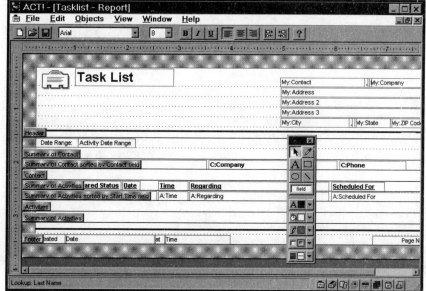

Figure 21-3:
The Task
List report
template.

✔ To learn more about how ACT! reports work, print all the standard ACT! reports for the active contact and study the corresponding report templates on your computer's monitor. Put the two of them side-by-side to study the layout of the merge codes in the template. In the upcoming section, you see how the contact information is merged into the actual report.

Setting up the Report Designer

Before you start designing your report, you need to consider several options:

✔ To choose the paper size you want your report printed on, select File⇨Page Setup from the menu bar, and the Page dialog box appears. Here you select the paper size, the orientation (portrait or landscape), the margin sizes, and your printer.

✔ To configure your ruler settings (the rulers display on the top and left sides of the Report Designer screen), open the Ruler Settings dialog box by selecting View⇨Ruler Settings from the menu bar. In the Ruler Settings dialog box, you select your units of measurement and the number of division markers you want displayed. (The default is 16 division markers.)

For more reporting power, try Crystal Reports

If ACT!'s report-generating capabilities aren't powerful enough for you, or if you're spending too much time trying to create custom ACT! reports, get yourself a copy of Crystal Reports. Crystal Reports is a powerful, yet easy-to-use program designed to create custom reports with graphs, lists, and labels, using data from your ACT! database.

Crystal Reports establishes a connection with one or more of your databases and then draws the information from the ACT! database fields and uses that information in the report. You can use your ACT! database information in its original form or as part of a formula that generates even more information.

Crystal Reports works with all kinds of data: numbers, currency, text, dates, and Boolean fields. It has a wide range of built-in tools you can use to analyze your database information to fit your needs. Crystal Reports is made by Crystal Services, 1050 West Pender Street, Suite 2200, Vancouver, B.C., Canada V6E 3S7; phone 800-877-2340 (U.S.); Web site www.seagatesoftware.com/crystalinfo.

✔ To show or hide your rulers, select View⇨Show/Hide Ruler from the menu bar.

✔ To show or hide the grid lines, select View⇨Show/Hide Grid from the menu bar. The number of dots on the grid line correspond to the number of division markers you selected in the ruler settings.

✔ If you want your objects to snap (stick to) to the grid, select the Snap To Grid option from the View menu.

✔ To show or hide the report's section titles, select the Show/Hide Section Titles command from the View menu.

Understanding the sections of an ACT! report

The most important concept to understand when you're working with report templates is that ACT! report templates contain different sections of information, and every report *must* have at least one section. The various report sections are labeled on-screen.

For example, a very simple report may have just three sections: header, contact, and footer. You add, modify, or delete ACT! report sections from the Define Sections dialog box. Defining the sections of an ACT! report is covered in the next section, but here I give you a brief explanation of each of the sections you can include in an ACT! report template:

Slice & dice your ACT! reports

Lon Orenstean, who is a very good friend of mine, is president of Computer Support Network (CSN). Lon was a beta user of ACT! 1.0 back in 1986 and has remained closely involved with ACT! ever since.

Lon has written several ACT! Sales Force Automation Add-on's — *ForecastManager!, RepManager!, ReportManager!* — all based upon *Crystal Reports*. With his off-the-shelf reporting software, you can turn ACT! into a sophisticated training, reporting, and forecasting system.

Using Lon's programs, you can create reports from ACT! that can slice & dice, multiply & divide, and even include charts and graphs that display your data in whatever format you desire.

Symantec even recognizes CSN's expertise: Their corporate sales force uses *Forecast Manager!* to track their business.

You can reach Lon at Computer Support Network, 3883 Turtle Creek, Suite 606, Dallas, TX 75219; phone 800-238-0560; e-mail sales@support4u.com; Web site www.support4u.com.

✔ **Header:** A header appears at the top of every page, unless you add a separate title header, which is placed above the header on the first page of the report.

Use a header for any information or graphic object you want to appear on every page, such as the current date, column headings, or a company logo.

✔ **Footer:** A footer appears at the bottom of every page.

Use a footer for information that you want on every page, such as the page number, date, or time.

✔ **Title header:** The title header appears only on the first page of a report, above the header.

✔ **Title footer:** The title footer appears only on the first page of a report, just above the footer.

✔ **Contact section:** The Contact section contains information from the fields in a contact's record. The information in the Contact section appears for each contact you include when you run the report. The Contact section of the Phone List report, for example, contains information from the Company Name, Contact Name, Phone, Phone Extension, and Car Phone fields.

A report can contain only one Contact section or one Group section. It cannot contain both. A Contact section can, however, contain a Group subsection, and vice versa.

- ✔ **Group subsection:** The Group subsection of the Contact section contains information from fields in the Groups tab of a Contact record. For this reason, you can only include a Group subsection if you have a Contact section in the report template.

- ✔ **Group section:** Here you find information from fields in your Group records. The information in the Group section appears for each group that you include when you run the report. The Group section of the Group report, for example, contains the group name and address, the group's description, the name of the primary contact, his or her phone number, and much more.

- ✔ **Contact subsection:** The Contact subsection of the Group section contains information from fields in the Contact's tab of a group record. For this reason, you can only include a Contact subsection if you have a Group section in the report template.

- ✔ **Notes/History section:** This section contains information from fields in the Notes/History tab of a Contact or Group record. Therefore, you can include a Notes/History section below either a Contact section or a Group section, as long as you have a Contact or Group section in your report template.

- ✔ **Activities section:** The Activities section contains information from fields in the Activities tab of a Contact or Group record. So, you can include an Activities section below either a Contact section or a Group section if you have the corresponding section in your report template.

- ✔ **Summary section:** Summaries can be totals, averages, counts, and minimum or maximum values. A Summary section can contain one or more summary fields. You can place the Summary section above or below the section it summarizes.

- ✔ **Summary Sorted By section:** The Summary Sorted By section contains a summary of the values sorted by a specific field. For example, the History Summary report includes a Summary Sorted By section that displays total counts of the notes and histories sorted by type. You can also use a Summary Sorted By section just to sort a section without putting in any summary fields.

Adding, changing, and deleting sections

You add, change, and delete sections of an ACT! report by opening the Define Sections dialog box, which you access by choosing Edit⇨Define Sections from the menu bar. The Define Sections dialog box for a Task List report is shown in Figure 21-4. The Define Sections dialog box always displays the sections currently included in the report template.

By default, every report template has a header, Contact section, and footer.

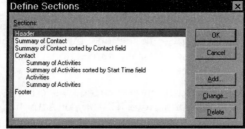

Figure 21-4:
The Define
Sections
dialog box
for a Task
List report.

Adding Sections to an ACT! Report

You add a section to an ACT! report template from the Define Sections dialog box. Here's how:

1. Click the Add button.

The Add Section dialog box appears, as shown in Figure 21-5.

The available sections appear in the Sections box. If a section name is dimmed, you cannot add it to the currently selected section. For example, if you select the Contact section, the Group section is dimmed because you cannot add a Group section to a Contact section. You can, however, add a Group subsection to a Contact section.

The Add Section dialog box and Change Section dialog boxes do the same things; they just have different names.

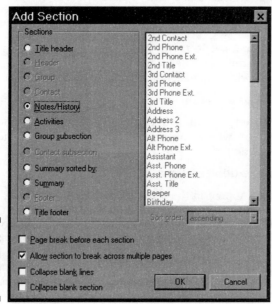

Figure 21-5:
The Add
Section
dialog box.

2. **Select the section(s) you want to add.**

   A basic report contains a header, footer, and a Contact or Group section. Under the Contact or Group section, you can add Notes/History, Activities, and Contact or Group subsections. Under the subsection, you can add notes/history items and activities.

   You can place a Summary and Summary Sorted By section above or below a selected Contact, Group, Notes/History, or Activities section.

   When you select the Summary Sorted By section, the Field list on the right side of the dialog box and the Sort Order drop-down list become available. Select the field by which you want to sort the data, and select Ascending or Descending order from the Sort Order drop-down list. Click OK and place the section either above or below the selected section.

3. **Specify how you want the information in the selected section to display and print.**

   You have the following options:

   • **Page break before each section:** This option starts a new page at the beginning of the selected section.

   • **Allow section to break across multiple pages:** This option displays and prints all the information in a section, even if it doesn't fit on a single page. If you turn this option off, a page break inserts before the section if the section can't fit in the remaining space on the current page.

   • **Collapse blank lines:** This option eliminates lines in the selected section that contain fields with no data or fields that are duplicated. Any graphic objects whose upper-left corners fall within the line are also eliminated.

   • **Collapse blank section:** This option eliminates sections in the report that contain no data. Any graphic objects whose upper-left corners fall within the section are also eliminated.

4. **Click OK to add your section settings to the ACT! report.**

   ACT! closes the Add Section dialog box and returns you to the Define Sections dialog box, where you can add, change, or delete another section or subsection.

5. **When you finish editing sections, click OK.**

   The new sections appear in the report template.

Now that you've created the sections of your ACT! report, you probably want to add fields to your report. Adding fields is covered in the "Inserting merge fields into a report template" section of this chapter.

Changing sections of an ACT! report

To change a section in an ACT! report, highlight the section in the Sections box, click the Change button, and the Change Settings dialog box appears, which is identical to the Add Settings dialog box. Make your changes, click OK, and you return to the Define Settings dialog box.

Deleting sections from an ACT! report

To delete a section from an ACT! report, highlight the section in the Sections box of the Define Sections dialog box and click the Delete button. If the section contains any fields, graphic objects, text objects, or subsections, a message appears asking, `Are you sure that you want to delete the report section, the objects it contains, and related sections?` If you are sure, click Yes, and the section along with its objects are deleted from the report template.

Changing the size of a reports section

To change the size of a report's section within the Report Designer, click on the section's title and move it up to enlarge the report section or down to reduce the section. If the section titles aren't displayed, select View⇨Show Section Titles from the menu bar to show the section titles.

Working with graphic objects

Items you place on an ACT! report template — fields, field labels, text, rectangles, ellipses, and lines — are referred to as *graphic objects*. You place graphic objects on a report template from the Tool Palette.

You use the tools on the Tool Palette, shown in Figure 21-6, to design and edit your report templates. From the Tool Palette, you can do the following:

- Insert graphic objects. A graphic object includes ACT! fields and field labels, text, rectangles, ellipses, and lines.
- Change the object's background color.
- Change the object's fill pattern.
- Change the object's frame style.
- Change the object's frame color.
- Change the object's frame width.
- Change the color of the object's font.

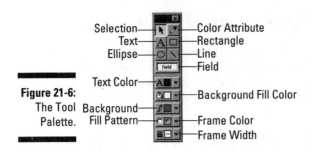

Selection
Text
Ellipse

Color Attribute
Rectangle
Line
Field

Text Color

Background
Fill Pattern

Background Fill Color

Frame Color
Frame Width

Figure 21-6:
The Tool
Palette.

Because the Report Designer works exactly like the Layout Designer (which is covered in Chapter 23), the way you insert and manipulate graphics is exactly the same for both. And because most ACT! users are more likely to use the Layout Designer than the Report Designer, I decided to cover the features of the Tool Palette in Chapter 23.

Here's a list of the tasks you can perform in the Report Designer:

- ✔ Inserting graphic objects
- ✔ Moving graphic objects
- ✔ Moving objects from front to back and vice versa
- ✔ Making objects the same size
- ✔ Getting objects to line up
- ✔ Aligning your objects to the grid

All of these tasks are covered in detail in Chapter 23. If you're not familiar with the Tool Palette, I'm sorry to make you jump to another section, but I'd much rather use a cross-reference than repeat the same information.

Inserting merge fields into a report template

A Merge Field command instructs ACT! to pull information from a specific ACT! field and insert it into an ACT! report. You insert merge fields into an ACT! report from the Field List dialog box, which is shown in Figure 21-7.

This is how you open the Field List dialog box:

1. **Click on the Tool Palette's Field tool, and the cursor becomes a large cross-hair.**

   If the Tool Palette is hidden, select the Show Tool Palette command from the View menu.

Figure 21-7:
The Field
List
dialog box.

2. **Place the cursor in the section of the report in which you want to insert the field, hold down the mouse button, and drag the cursor right or left until the field is the desired width; then release the mouse button.**

   The Field List dialog box appears.

The Field List dialog box has five tabs: Contact, Group, Notes/History, Activities, and System. ACT! automatically selects the tab that corresponds to the section of the report that you want to insert a field into.

ACT! has two types of merge fields: a Detail field and a Summary field.

✔ A Detail field is any ACT! field that contains contact information. This includes any field in the Contact or Group layouts and any column available for viewing in the Notes/History tab or the Activities tab.

✔ A Summary field contains information from any field designated as a numeric, currency, date, or time field.

Both of these types of fields are discussed on the following pages.

Inserting Detail fields into an ACT! report template

The following options are available to you when you select the Detail field as the field type:

✔ Selecting the Contact tab displays every Contact field in the database in the Available fields box.

✔ Selecting the Group tab displays all the Group fields in the database in the Available fields box.

✔ Selecting the Notes/History tab shows every available column from the Notes/History tab in the Contact window.

✔ Selecting the Activities tab shows you every column available in the Activities tab in the Contact window.

✔ Selecting the System tab enables you to insert the page number, date, time, activity date range, or notes/history date range into your report template.

Place the page number, date, or time in the report's header or footer.

To insert a Detail field into an ACT! report template from the Field List dialog box, follow these steps:

1. **Select one of the five tabs — Contact, Group, Notes/History, Activities, or System — if one is not already selected.**

2. **Select Detail Field in the Field Type Section if it's not already selected.**

3. **Select the field you want to insert from the list of available fields in the Available Fields box.**

4. **Select the Add Field Label option if you want a label to appear with the field you are adding.**

5. **Select the Use My Record option if you want to insert a merge command that pulls contact information from the My Record contact record.**

   The Use My Record option is only available on the Contact tab.

   The information from the My Record contact record is usually placed in the header of a report. It includes such information as your name, company name, address, and so on.

6. **Click the Add button to insert the selected field into the ACT! report template.**

   When you've added the fields that you want in your report template, click Close to close the Field List dialog box. You can then position the fields in the appropriate places on the template.

Inserting a Summary field into your ACT! report template

A Summary field is one containing information from more than one contact record. For example, if you want ACT! to count the number of records with information in a selected field, you select Count as the Summary Type for that field.

To give you another example, say you made the User 1 field an Amount of Last Sale field, and made it a Numeric or Currency field, where you can only insert numbers. When you select Total as the field's summary type, ACT!

gives you a total of all of your last sales. If you select Average as the field's summary type, ACT! gives you the average size of all of your last sales.

If you make a field a Numeric, Currency, Date, or Time field and select Minimum or Maximum as the summary type, ACT! can find the lowest or highest number and the earliest or latest date or time.

Only fields you designate as Numeric, Currency, Date, or Time fields in the Define Fields dialog box appear in the Available fields list when you select Total, Average, Minimum, or Maximum as the summary type.

You insert a Summary field into an ACT! report template by taking the following steps:

1. **Select Summary Field in the Field type section of the Field List dialog box.**

2. **Select a summary type — Count, Total, Average, Minimum, or Maximum — in the Summary type section.**

3. **Select a field from the list of fields in the Available Fields box.**

4. **Enter a field label name for the Summary Type field you're creating in the Summary Field label field.**

5. **Click the Add button to insert the selected field into the ACT! report template.**

When you've added the fields that you want in your report template, click Close to close the Field List dialog box. You can then position the fields in the appropriate places on the template.

Changing ACT!s merge field properties

After you've placed all of your merge fields (*objects* in ACT!-speak) onto a report template, you may want to change a field's properties: the field's style, font, field type, and format. You do this from the Object Properties dialog box.

You access the Object Properties dialog box by double-clicking the selected object or by selecting the Properties command from the menu that appears when you right-click an object.

To change the properties of several merge fields at the same time, hold down the Shift key and click the desired merge fields.

Changing a merge fields style

From the Style tab, which is shown in Figure 21-8, you can make the following changes to the selected merge field:

- ✔ Change the background fill color
- ✔ Change the background fill pattern
- ✔ Change the frame style
- ✔ Change the frame color
- ✔ Change the frame width

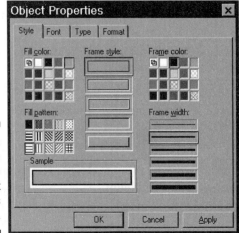

Figure 21-8:
The Style
tab of the
Object
Properties
dialog box.

Changing a merge fields font

From the Font tab, you can change the font's appearance within the merge field. You have the following options:

- ✔ Change the font
- ✔ Change the font style (italic, bold, bold italic, and so on)
- ✔ Change the font size
- ✔ Choose strikeout
- ✔ Choose underline
- ✔ Choose a color

Confirming a fields type

In the Type tab, ACT! displays the basic information about the field, which includes the following:

✔ The field name

✔ The field type (Detail, Summary, System)

✔ Summary options, if the field is a Summary Type field

✔ Use My Record: If the merge field is a My Record, the Use My Record box is checked

Selecting a fields format

From the Format tab, ACT! enables you to set the merge field's format. You have these options:

✔ **Don't Print If Duplicated:** Choose this option if you don't want ACT! to print the selected field if more than one of them is in the template. If you are creating a report that includes a company's name, for example, choose this option if you *don't* want the name inserted with each contact.

✔ **Wrap Text:** If you want text in the selected field to wrap at the end of a line, choose this option.

✔ **Close Up Blank Space:** Select this option if you do not want any blank space between the text and the right-hand edge of the field.

✔ **Field Name:** This field displays the merge field's name.

✔ **Data Type:** The Data type field displays the merge field's data type: Detail, Summary, Date, Time, Numeric, and so on.

✔ **Appearance:** In the Appearance box, you can select how a Numeric, Date, or Time field appears. For a Numeric field, you can also select how negative numbers display and how many decimal places appear.

Only the options that apply to the specific field type appear in the Format tab.

Changing a merge fields appearance from the Toolbar

You can also change a selected merge field's appearance by clicking buttons on the Toolbar, as shown in Figure 21-9. From left to right, you can access these options: font, font size, bold, italic, underline, left justification, centered, and right justification.

You customize your toolbar by right-clicking on a blank portion of the toolbar and selecting the Customize command. The Customize ACT! dialog box opens, where you choose options to customize the toolbar, the menus, and the keyboard. Customizing ACT! commands is covered in Chapter 24.

Figure 21-9:
The Report
Designer's
Toolbar.

Enhancing the appearance of your report

To improve the appearance of your report, you may want to create fancy and elaborate report titles or section headings by adding rectangles, ellipses, lines, and text to your report. You can then position these objects in front or behind each other to create the look you want.

Adding rectangles, ellipses, and lines

To add a rectangle, ellipse, or line to your ACT! report, select the appropriate tool from the Tool Palette, place the cross-hair pointer where you want the object to start, and drag it up, down, left, or right until your graphic is the desired size.

To make a square, circle, or straight line, hold down the Shift key while you create the object with the Rectangle, Ellipse, or Line tools.

To change a rectangle, ellipse, or line's style, select the rectangle, ellipse, or line with the Selection tool, double-click on the object, and the Style tab of the Object Properties dialog box appears. The Object Properties box is discussed earlier in this chapter. You can also change the rectangle, ellipse, or line's style using the Tool Palette's appearance tools.

Adding Text

To add text to your ACT! report, select the text tool from the Tool Palette, place the cross-hair pointer where you want the line of text to start, drag the pointer left or right until it is the desired size, release the mouse button, and begin typing your text.

To change the text's style, select the text object with the Selection tool, double-click, and the Object Properties dialog box appears. You can select from the features of the Style, Font, and Format tabs, which were discussed earlier in this chapter. You can also change the text's style by using the Tool Palette's appearance tools or the text appearance icons that are on the Toolbar, both of which were discussed earlier in this chapter.

Selecting Default Settings for Reports

After you've laid out the merge fields of your report, ACT! gives you the capability to select the *default* settings that you want to have applied to this report. You create these default settings from the Define Filters dialog box.

The Define Filters General tab is identical to the General tab of the Run Report dialog box, which is shown way back in Figure 21-1. The Define Filters Filter tab looks just like the Filter tab of the Run Report dialog box, which is shown back in Figure 21-2. You open the Define Filters dialog box by selecting Edit➪Define Filters from the menu bar.

Here are a few examples of how you can use your filtering defaults:

✔ To create a report giving you information about your activities, including any notes or history entries during the last quarter, set the filtering options to display this information for the last quarter only.

✔ You can create a report that displays your scheduled activities for the next week, month, or quarter, making it easy to answer your boss's question: "What do you have lined up for the next month?"

You use the General tab to specify which contacts to make the report for, where to output the report, and whether or not to include the My Record contact record.

Use the Filter tab to specify what data to include in your report. In the Notes/History section, you can include or exclude notes, history, or attachments from the report for a specific date or range of dates. In the Activities section, you include or exclude calls, meetings, or to-dos for a selected date or range of dates. You can include data from all users or selected users in the report in the Users section.

Testing Your Report

After you've created your report, you'll probably want to test it to see if it comes out the way you want it to. Here's how you run a report directly from the Report Designer:

1. **Select File➪Run from the menu bar or press Ctrl+R.**

   The Filters dialog box appears.

2. **Make your filtering choices in the General and Filter tabs and click OK.**

   ACT! runs the report.

If the report comes out the way you wanted it to, congratulations for a job well done. If it doesn't, you have to do a bit more work. (Sorry about that!)

Modifying Your Report Menu

After you've created a custom report, ACT! makes it easy for you to use it. You can add the report template as an additional option that's available from the Report menu. To add your report template to the Report menu, select Reports⇨Modify Menu, and the Modify Menu dialog box appears. Here, you can add items to the Report menu.

Part VI
Advanced ACT! Stuff

The 5th Wave   By Rich Tennant

"For my finale, Rollo here will flawlessly activate my voice recognition system while I empty this bag of marbles into my mouth."

In this part . . .

If I weren't so great at explaining things, the material in this part would be a little hard to follow. (Somebody smack me.) Sure, customizing contact layouts and windows, creating macros, and managing databases are all complex topics, but I know that you can do this stuff. Just give it try.

Chapter 22

ACT! and the Internet

· ·

In This Chapter

▶ Logging onto a contact's Web site

▶ Asking for driving directions

▶ Getting information about the company

▶ Finding people over the Internet

▶ Forging additional Internet links

▶ Linking to Symantec's ACT! Web site

▶ Adding new sites

· ·

*T*he use of the Internet has exploded, and ACT! correspondingly expanded its Internet functionality. With the click of a button, you can log on to selected Web sites, find people using Internet searches and add them to your ACT! database, and log on to selected Web sites directly from the ACT! menu bar.

Logging on to a Contact's Web Site

Let's say that you had an appointment scheduled with one of your clients or prospects and wanted to get the latest information about their company as you planned for the meeting. The first thing you would probably want to do is visit the company's Web site and review or download the latest financial information.

ACT! has already designated a field on the Alt Contacts tab as a URL field.

This is how you make an ACT! User Field a URL field:

1. Select Edit⇨Define Fields.

The Define Fields dialog box opens.

2. **Select the User Field you want to make a URL field.**

3. **Select URL Address as the field type from the drop-down list in the Types box.**

4. **Change the field's name in the Field Name box, if desired.**

5. **Click OK to save your settings.**

6. **Enter the URL address in the selected field and press the Enter key.**

   ACT! enters the URL address.

To log on to the Web site just double-click on the Web site address. ACT! launches your Web browser and logs on to the selected site.

Getting Directions

Before you walk out the door you may want driving directions from where you are to where your client is located. This is how you get them:

1. **Select Tools⇨Internet Links⇨Yahoo! Driving Directions. The Yahoo! Driving Directions dialog box appears, as shown in Figure 22-1.**

2. **Select the Origin location from the drop-down list of contacts.**

3. **Select the Destination location from the drop-down list of contacts.**

4. **Click the Drive It! button.**

   ACT! logs onto Yahoo! Maps and displays both a map and detailed driving instructions.

You can then print out the directions or save them to your computer and attach them to the contact's Notes/History Tab.

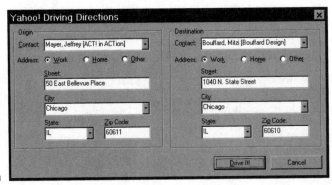

Figure 22-1:
The Yahoo!
Driving
Directions
dialog box.

Getting Information about a Company

If you would like detailed business and financial information about a company, you can select from any of the following Internet links. Once you're connected to Yahoo!, just enter the company's stock symbol in the Get Quotes field.

- ✔ **Yahoo! Corporate News:** Here you can view recent articles about the selected company or use any of the available search engines, including Alta Vista, WebCrawler, HotBot, Lycos, Infoseek, Excite, and more.

- ✔ **Yahoo! Stock Quote:** Here you can view the price of the last trade, the change in price from the previous day in both a dollar amount and a percentage, the day's volume, and lots more.

- ✔ **Yahoo! Ticker Symbol Lookup:** Here you can view the price of the last trade, the day's range, its 52-week range, and lots more.

Finding People on the Net

To find people over the Internet, you can use Yahoo! Person search. With this search, Yahoo! searches for everybody who has the first and last name of the currently displayed contact.

To perform a lookup from one of the Internet directories — Bigfoot, WhoWhere, or Yahoo! — select Lookup⇨Internet Directories from the menu bar, and the Internet Lookup dialog box opens. In this dialog box, you enter a person's name, select which directory you want to use, and click the Search button.

A list of people who match your search criteria comes up. You can then add the person to your ACT! database, send an e-mail message, or both!

Using the Internet Directory is discussed in Chapter 10, where I cover ACT! Lookups.

Forging Additional Internet Links

Here are some additional Internet links:

- ✔ **Yahoo! Weather:** To find out the weather just select Yahoo! Weather, and Yahoo! displays the weather forecast for the city of the currently displayed contact.

- **Yahoo! Yellow Pages:** If you need to buy something, just select Yahoo! Yellow Pages and you can search a local business located in the city of the currently displayed contact record.

- **Bigfoot E-Mail Services:** To subscribe to Bigfoot's e-mail service — and have your e-mail address for life — select this Internet link.

- **Inquisit Contact Watcher:** Inquisit is a subscription-based personal intelligence service that lets you track customers, competitors, markets, technologies — or almost anything that impacts your job or business — and delivers it to you via e-mail, pager, or cell phone. The service lets you create your own personal agents, which monitor more than 600 Inquisit content sources and search for breaking information. Once located, the information is delivered immediately, or on your pre-defined days and times. Free trial subscriptions are available.

Linking to Symantec's Web Site

When you need ACT! information, one of the quickest ways to get it is to go directly to Symantec's ACT! Web site. ACT! gives you six direct links. You access them by selecting Tools⇨Internet Links⇨Symantec, and then select the desired Web site from the Symantec sub-menu.

- **ACT!:** The ACT! site gives you direct links to ACT! Product Information, News Releases, ACT! Certified Consultants, Symantec Authorized Training Centers, Publications and Training Materials, ACT! Add-On Catalog, Free Downloads, Technical Support, and lots, lots more.

- **Small Business Resource Center:** This site has information and tips on how to run your business more efficiently. The Center lists some of the best places on the Internet to get "inside information" and cutting-edge technology.

- **Mobile Resources:** At this Symantec site, you find useful information about cities you may visit for trade shows, conferences, or other business reasons. For each city, you find links to several modem-friendly hotels, local access numbers for AOL and CompuServe, names of restaurants for quiet business meetings, links to Visitor Information Centers, and links to street maps.

- **Technical Support:** At Symantec's Online Technical Support page you can download files, search Symantec's knowledge base, ask questions of ACT! technical support, join ACT! online discussion groups, and lots, lots more.

- **Try It Before You Buy It:** From this site, you can try any of Symantec's products before you decide to make a purchase. Just select the product you want to try and download a trial version.

✔ **Symantec's Web site:** This site gives you links to all of Symantec's products, including ACT!, Norton AntiVirus, CrashGuard Deluxe, Uninstall Deluxe, Norton Utilities, pcANYWHERE, Visual Café for Java, WinFax, and other products. You also have links to Symantec technical support and lots, lots more.

Adding New Sites to Your List

Now I know you'll certainly like the sites that are pre-installed for you, but I'm sure you'll want to add your own sites to the list.

Unfortunately, this can't be done from inside ACT!, but it can be done from the Windows 95 Explorer. This is how you do it:

1. Open Explorer.

2. Go to your ACT! 4 directory.

If you don't know where this, open the Preferences dialog box by selecting Edit⇨Preferences, and look for the directory displayed in the Default Location section of the General Tab.

3. Click the ACT! 4 subdirectory named NetLinks.

The list of files displays in the right-hand pane. The NetLinks folder is shown in Figure 22-2.

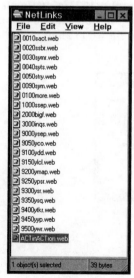

Figure 22-2:
The files
of the
NetLinks
folder.

4. Open the first file named `0010SACT.web`.

This is the link to the Symantec ACT! Web page. The code looks like this: `[&Symantec|&ACT!]http://www.symantec.com/act/index.html`.

- The text inside the brackets, `[&Symantec|&ACT!]` is the information displayed on the menu bar under Tools⇨Internet Links.

- The ampersand (&) in front of the "S" in Symantec and the "A" in ACT! places the underline under the "S" and the "A" and makes them appear as Symantec, and ACT! on the menu. This turns those letters into hot keys. Press the Alt+T+I+S+A keys and you log on to the ACT! Web page.

- The Symantec sub-menu is created by placing the bar (|) between the "c" in Symantec and the ampersand "&A".

5. Save this file with a new name, by using File⇨SaveAs.

The file must have the .web extension.

6. Make the changes to the Web site's description within the brackets, and enter the new Web address.

7. Save your file by selecting File⇨Save or by selecting File⇨Exit.

If a message box appears asking if you want to save this file as a Word Document, Rich Text Document, or Text Document, select Text Document.

Put a direct link to my ACT! in ACTion Online Web site onto your menu bar. On this site, you have access to articles from the *ACT! in ACTion* newsletter, links to products and services that will save you time and help you make more money, and lots, lots more. The link is shown in Figure 22-3.

Figure 22-3:
ACT! in
ACTion
Online's
Internet
Link.

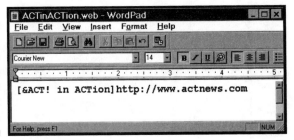

Chapter 23

Designing Layouts

● ●

In This Chapter

▶ Getting a handle on the design basics

▶ Adding graphic objects

▶ Inserting fields into a layout

▶ Making your layout look better

● ●

ACT! comes with a number of contact and group layouts. But as you use more of ACT!'s features, you'll find that you want to reposition fields, change the size of fields, and even place new fields on your layouts.

With ACT!'s Layout Designer, you can create new layouts or modify existing layouts. You can add or remove fields from layouts, and you can change the appearance of the layouts by using colors and graphic elements.

Using the Layout Designer can become a huge time waster. Unless you're familiar with working with graphic objects, you may find it much more time- and cost-effective to hire an ACT! Certified Consultant to come in and design your layout for you. Chapter 27 tells you about some of the things ACT! Certified Consultants do.

When you're modifying a layout, always work from a copy of the layout by saving it with the File⇨Save As command. This way, if you make a mistake, you can just delete the layout and start over again with the original.

Doing the Basics

To open ACT!'s Layout Designer, select Tools⇨Design Layouts from the menu bar. Figure 23-1 shows the contact layout in the Layout Designer.

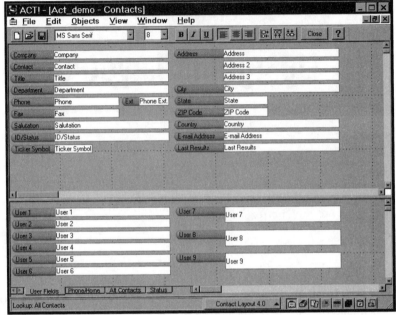

Figure 23-1:
The contact
layout in the
Layout
Designer.

Opening an ACT! layout

To open a layout, first open either the Contact or Group window and then select Tools⇨Design Layouts from the menu bar, and the Layout Designer opens the Contact or Group layout.

Changing layouts

To change from one ACT! layout to another, click the Layout button at the bottom of the Layout Designer window and select a layout from the available list.

To change an ACT! layout from the menu bar, select File⇨Open, and the Open dialog box appears. Select your layout and click Open.

If you're editing a contact layout, only contact layouts are listed in the Open dialog box, and if you're editing a group layout, only group layouts are listed. (Contact layouts have the .CLY extension, and group layouts have the .GLY extension.)

Creating a new layout

To create a new layout, select File⇨New. ACT! responds with a blank layout for you to work with. Here, you can design a layout that fills up the entire window.

Closing the Layout Designer

To close the Layout Designer, click the Close button on the toolbar or select View⇨Records from the menu bar.

Naming and saving your layouts

After creating a new contact or group layout, you will certainly want the new layout to be available in the layout drop-down menu at the bottom of the Contact or Groups window. (That sure makes sense. Why go to the trouble of creating a custom layout if you can't use it?)

In order to have your layout appear in this menu, you need to save the layout and assign a file description to it. To save your layout, use File⇨Save or File⇨Save As.

To give your a layout a description after you save it, do the following:

1. **Position your pointer over a blank area in the layout.**

2. **Click your right mouse button and select the File Description command from the menu that appears.**

   The File Description dialog box appears.

3. **Give the layout a new description and click OK.**

   Your description appears on the Layout button.

Setting Up the Layout Designer

Before you start designing your layout, you need to consider two issues.

Setting up the rulers

To show or hide your rulers, which appear on the top and left sides of the Layout Designer, select View⇨Show/Hide Ruler from the menu bar.

To change your ruler settings, open the Ruler Settings dialog box by selecting View⇨Ruler Settings from the menu bar. In the Ruler Settings dialog box, you can select the unit of measurement (inches, centimeters, or points) and the number of division markers that you want displayed. (The default is 16 division markers.)

Working with the grid line

To show or hide the grid lines, select View⇨Show/Hide Grid from the menu bar. The number of dots on the grid line corresponds to the number of division markers that are selected in the Ruler Settings dialog box.

If you want your objects to snap to the grid, select the Snap To Grid option from the View menu.

Changing the Tabs on Your Layout

To change the tabs that appear on your layout (that is, the User Field tab, Phone/Home tab, the Alt Contacts tab, and so on), open the Define Layout Tabs dialog box by selecting the Edit⇨Tabs command. From this dialog box, you can do the following:

- ✔ **Add a layout tab:** To add a tab, click the Add button, and the Add Tab Layout dialog box appears, where you can give the tab a name.

- ✔ **Rename a layout tab:** To rename a tab, click the Rename button, and the Rename Tab Layout dialog box appears, where you can change the tab's name.

- ✔ **Delete a layout tab:** To delete a tab, click the Delete button.

- ✔ **Position a layout tab:** To change a tab's position, highlight the tab and click the Move Up or Move Down button. Moving a tab's name up or down on the list moves it left or right when it appears in the layout.

Working with Graphic Objects

Items in an ACT! layout — fields, field labels, text, rectangles, ellipses, and lines — are referred to as *graphic objects*. You place graphic objects on a layout by using the Tool Palette, which is shown in Figure 23-2.

Assigning a shortcut key to your tabs

A shortcut key enables you to open a contact's tab by pressing the Alt+the shortcut key. This is how you assign a shortcut key to a tab:

1. **Select Edit⇨Tabs.**

    The Define Tab Layout dialog box opens.

2. **Select either the Add or Rename buttons.**

    The Add Tab Layout or Edit Tab dialog box appears. (Both boxes are the same.)

3. **Give the tab a name, if it doesn't already have one.**

4. **Select a letter from the drop-down menu in the Shortcut Key field.**

    You can select a letter from the list of letters in the tab's name.

5. **Click OK.**

    Your shortcut key is assigned.

The following is a list of default shortcut keys for tabs.

Tab	Default Shortcut Keys
Activities Tab	Alt+A
Notes/History Tab	Alt+N
Groups Tab	Alt+G
User Fields Tab	Alt+U
Phone/Home Tab	Alt+P
Alt Contacts Tab	Alt+O
Status Tab	Alt+S

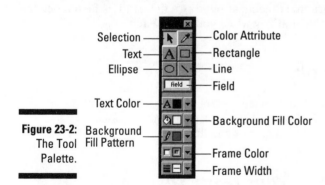

Figure 23-2: The Tool Palette.

With the tools on the Tool Palette, you can design your own layouts by doing these tasks:

✔ Insert graphic objects. (A graphic object includes ACT! fields and field labels, text, rectangles, ellipses, and lines.)

✔ Change an object's background color.

✔ Change an object's fill pattern.

✔ Change an object's frame style.

> ✔ Change an object's frame color.
> ✔ Change an object's frame width.
> ✔ Change the color of an object's font.

Inserting graphic objects

To insert a graphic object in a layout, select the type of object you want to insert from the Tool Palette, and the cursor turns into a cross-hair. Place the cursor where you want the object to start. Drag the object left, right, up, or down until it's the desired size, and release your mouse button.

Inserting fields is covered in the "Inserting, Moving, and Removing Fields" section of this chapter, and inserting text, rectangles, ellipses, or lines is covered in the "Making Your Layout Look Better" section.

Moving graphic objects

To move a graphic object from one position in a layout to another, click the object with the Selection tool and drag it to another position in the layout.

To move two or more graphic objects at once — a field and its field label, for example — hold down the Shift key while you select each object.

Changing an object's size

To change the size of an object, place the Selection tool on one of the object's handles. The Selection tool changes into a Sizing tool. Move the Sizing tool to make the object larger or smaller.

Moving objects from front to back and vice versa

If you place one object on top of another object, also called *layering,* you need to be able to move a selected object forward or backward in relation to another object (for example, you have a black box and place white type over it).

Use the Selection tool to select the object that you want to move and then select the Move To Front or Move To Back commands that are available from the Objects menu and the right mouse button menu. If you have three or more objects that are layered on top each another, to rearrange the objects, use the Move Forward or Move Backward commands that are available from the Objects menu and the right mouse button menu.

To access the Move To Front, Move To Back, Move Forward, and Move Backward commands from the right mouse button menu, you must place the cursor on the object you want to move when you click the right mouse button.

Making objects the same size

When you're designing your layout, you may want selected fields to be the same size. Instead of trying to make them the same size one at a time, you can use the Make Same Height and Make Same Width commands from the Objects menu. This is how you do it:

1. **Select the objects you want to be the same size by holding down the Shift key while you select each object with the Selection tool.**

2. **Select either the Make Same Height or Make Same Width option from the Objects menu.**

   Now that was easy.

Getting objects to line up

When you're laying out the fields in an ACT! layout, you certainly want your fields to line up properly — both left to right and top to bottom. To line up objects, you must first select the objects that you want to align by holding down the Shift key while you select the objects with the Selection tool. You then align your objects by selecting the Align command from the Objects menu, which opens the Align dialog box, as shown in Figure 23-3.

You have the following left and right alignment selections: None, Align left edges, Align centers, and Align right edges.

You have the following up and down alignment selections: None, Align top edges, Align centers, and Align bottom edges.

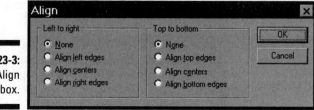

Figure 23-3:
The Align
dialog box.

Aligning your objects to the grid

If you want your objects aligned to the grid, the grid must first be displayed. (To display the grid, select View⇨Show Grid from the menu bar.) Select the objects you want to align to the grid and select the Align To Grid command from the Objects menu.

Inserting, Moving, and Removing Fields

You insert fields onto a layout from the Fields dialog box, which is shown in Figure 23-4. This is how you open the Fields dialog box:

Figure 23-4:
The Fields
dialog box.

1. **Click the Tool Palette's Field tool.**

   The cursor becomes a large cross-hair.

   If the Tool Palette is hidden, select the Show Tool Palette command from the View menu.

2. **Place the cursor in the section of the layout in which you want to insert the field, hold down the mouse button, drag it until it's the desired size, and release the mouse button.**

   The Fields dialog box appears.

   The only fields that appear in the Fields dialog box are fields that have *not* been placed on the ACT! layout.

3. **Select the field you want to insert from the list of available fields in the Fields dialog box.**

4. **Select the Add Label option if you want a label to appear with the field you are adding.**

5. **Click the Add button.**

After you add the fields that you want in your layout, click Close to close the Fields dialog box. You can then position the fields in the appropriate places on the layout. Moving ACT! fields and other objects is covered in the previous section, "Working with Graphic Objects."

To remove a field from your layout, highlight the field with the Selection tool and press the Delete key. (If you're deleting a field, you probably want to delete the field's label also.)

If you change your mind and want to restore a just-removed field, select Edit➪Undo or press Ctrl+Z.

Changing the order of field entry

You can use the Tab key to move through the fields in the default contact and group layouts. Press the Tab key moves the cursor down the left column, and when you reach the last field in the column, the cursor moves to the top of the right column.

You can also use the Enter key to move to the Group Stop fields, which helps you move quickly through the fields and tabs in a layout. By default, the Group Stop fields in the Contact Layout are Company, Phone, Address, and User 1.

You can change the order in which you tab through the fields, and you can add or remove Group Stops in fields.

Do the following to change the order of your Tab Stops:

1. **Select Edit➪Field Entry Order➪Show from the menu bar to display the Tab and Group Stops within the layout.**

   The layout appears with numbers on the right side of each field. If a field is set as a Group Stop, a red stop sign appears just to the left of the number.

2. **Click the number on the fields whose tab order you want to change, and the number disappears.**

   If you double-click either the Tab Stop number or the Group Stop sign, the Object Properties dialog box appears. Click Cancel to make it go away.

3. **Click the fields in the *new* order in which you want the cursor to move when you press the Tab key.**

   ACT! inserts a new number.

Adding and removing Group Stops is just as simple. To add a Group Stop, just click the Group Stop button, and the red stop sign appears. To remove a Group Stop, just click the Group Stop button, and the red stop sign disappears.

Here are some additional things you can do with Tab and Group Stops:

- ✔ **Clear your Tab and Group Stops:** Select Edit➪Field Entry Order➪Clear. Then click the fields in the order in which you want the cursor to move when you press the Tab or Enter keys.

- ✔ **Reset your Tab and Group Stops:** Select Edit➪Field Entry Order➪Reset.

- ✔ **Hide your Tab and Group Stops:** After you set your Tab and Group Stops, you can make them disappear by selecting Edit➪Field Entry Order➪Hide.

Changing field properties

After you've placed all of your objects (fields and field labels) onto a layout, you may want to change their properties. For such a task, you need the Object Properties dialog box. You access the Object Properties dialog box by double-clicking the selected object.

Changing a field's style

From the Style tab of the Object Properties dialog box, you can make the following changes to the selected field: Change the background fill color, change the background fill pattern, change the frame style, change the frame color, or change the frame width.

Changing a field's font

From the Font tab of the Object Properties dialog box, you can change the font's appearance within a field. You have the following options: change the font, change the font style (regular, italic, bold, or bold italic), change the font size, choose strikeout, choose underline, or choose a color.

Confirming a field's format

In the Format tab of the Object Properties dialog box, ACT! displays the basic information about a field:

- ✔ The field's name (Company, Contact, Phone, and so on).
- ✔ The data type (Character, Phone, Date, and so on).
- ✔ In the Appearance box (this box only appears for Numeric, Date, and Time fields), you can select how you want a Numeric, Date, or Time field to appear. For example, in a Numeric field, you can select how you want negative numbers to appear and how many decimal places a field can contain.

Changing a field's appearance

You can also change a selected field's appearance by clicking icons on the toolbar, which is shown way back in Figure 23-1. From left to right, here are the buttons on the toolbar: Font List, Font Size, Bold, Italics, Underline, Left Justification, Center Justification, and Right Justification.

Making Your Layout Look Better

To improve the appearance of your layout, you may want to create fancy and elaborate layout titles or section headings by adding rectangles, ellipses, lines, and text to your layout. You can then position these objects in front or behind each other to create the look you want. (Moving objects forward and backward is discussed earlier in this chapter.)

Adding rectangles, ellipses, and lines

To add a rectangle, ellipse, or a line to your ACT! layout, select the appropriate tool from the Tool Palette (the features of the Tool Palette are discussed earlier in the chapter), place the cross-hair pointer where you want the object to start, and drag it up, down, left, or right until it's the desired size.

To make a square, circle, or straight line, hold down the Shift key while you create the object with the Rectangle, Ellipse, or Line tools.

To change a rectangle, ellipse, or line's style, select the rectangle, ellipse, or line with the Selection tool, double-click the object, and the Style tab of the Object Properties dialog box appears, which is discussed earlier in this chapter. You can also change the rectangle, ellipse, or line's style by using the Tool Palette's appearance tools.

Adding text

To add text to your ACT! layout, select the Text tool from the Tool Palette, place the cross-hair pointer where you want the line of text to start, and drag the pointer left or right until the line is the desired size, release the mouse button, and begin typing your text.

To change the text's style, select the text object with the Selection tool, double-click, and the Object Properties dialog box appears. You can select from the features of the Style, Font, and Format tabs, which are discussed earlier in this chapter.

Changing your background

Now that you've designed your layout (you've positioned your fields and field labels; you've changed their fonts, font styles, and colors; and you've added circles, squares, lines, and text), you have only one thing left to do: Change your background. Just follow these steps:

1. **Place your pointer over a blank area of the layout.**

2. **Double-click with your left mouse button.**

   The Background Properties dialog box appears.

   You have the following options: Change the background fill color, change the background fill pattern, choose a bitmap to use as the background, or choose the Tile option to display the bitmap repeatedly until it covers the entire background area.

3. **Make your selections in the Background Properties dialog box and click OK.**

Chapter 24

Customizing ACT!

· ·

In This Chapter

▶ Customizing the toolbar

▶ Customizing menu commands

▶ Customizing keyboard commands

▶ Creating customized commands for macros and other programs

▶ Automating repetitive tasks with macros

▶ Customizing windows and tabs

· ·

*I*n ACT!, you can customize the commands that appear as icons on the toolbar, menu items that appear on the pull-down menus, and the short-cut key combinations that execute ACT! commands from the keyboard. You can also create your own custom commands (macros) that enable you to automate a series of ACT! commands and launch other programs.

Customizing the Toolbar

You can customize the toolbars in each of ACT!'s 14 different windows. The 14 windows are: the Startup window, Contact window, Group window, Calendar window, Task List window, Contact List window, Query window, Replace Fields window, Layout Design window, E-Mail window, Report window, Envelope window, Label window, and Browser window. To customize a specific toolbar, you must first open the window where the toolbar you want to adjust resides.

The look and feel of the ACT! toolbar can be customized and modified. The following are some of the options you can adjust from within an ACT! window.

Changing the toolbar position

To change the position of the toolbar, click on a blank portion of the toolbar (don't click on an icon) and drag the entire toolbar to another position on the window. If you want the toolbar to float as a palette, just leave it positioned anywhere within the window.

Changing icon size

To change the size of the icons — make them larger or smaller, with or without text, or text only — right-click on a blank portion of the toolbar and make your selection from the menu that appears.

Showing Tool Tips

If you don't remember what an icon does, just place and rest your cursor over it, and a brief description of what the icon does appears. The description is called a Tool Tip. To enable the Tool Tips option, click the right mouse button on an empty spot on the toolbar and select Toolbars from the shortcut menu; then select the Tool Tips option.

Customizing commands on the toolbar

To customize toolbar commands, as well as menus, shortcut keys, and commands, select Tools⇨Customize from the menu bar. The Customize ACT! dialog box appears. The Toolbars tab of the Customize ACT! dialog box is shown in Figure 24-1.

Another way to open the Customize ACT! dialog box is to right-click on the Toolbar and select Customize from the menu that appears.

From within the Toolbars tab you can do the following:

Changing an icon's position
To change an icon's position on the toolbar, select the icon you want to move by clicking it and then dragging it left or right. You can also use the Move Left or Move Right buttons shown on Figure 24-1.

Adding space between icons
To add a space between icons, select the icon and click the Insert Space button.

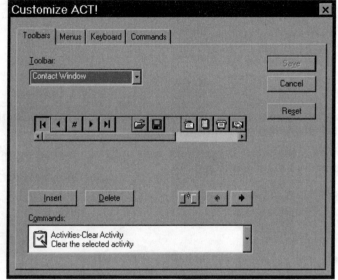

Figure 24-1:
The
Toolbars
tab for the
Contact
window
in the
Customize
ACT! dialog
box.

Deleting an icon

To delete an icon, select it and click the Delete button.

Adding an icon

To add a new icon to the toolbar, try these steps:

1. **Select the icon on the toolbar that you want to place the new icon next to.**

   The new icon is placed to the left of the selected icon.

2. **Select the command that you want to correspond with the new icon from the list of commands in the Commands box.**

3. **Click the Insert button, and the icon is added to the toolbar.**

   • **Add a custom command.** If you have created a custom command (creating custom commands is discussed later in this chapter), select the Toolbars tab, and the custom command appears in the Commands box. Click the Insert button, and the icon is added to the toolbar.

   • **Reset your icons.** To reset your the icons on your toolbar to their default settings, click the Reset button.

Customizing ACT!'s Menu Commands

To customize the commands on ACT! menus, click the Menus tab of the Customize ACT! dialog box. From the Menus tab, you can add, delete, and reorganize the commands on your ACT! menus. To alter the commands, do the following:

1. **Select the menu you want to customize from the list of available drop-down menus in the Menus field.**

2. **Scroll through the list of commands until you find the position of the command you want to modify.**

After locating the command you want, you can make any (or all) of the following changes.

Change a command's position

To change the position of a command, select it and use the Up and Down buttons to move the command upward or downward. You can also drag-and-drop the command to a new position with your mouse.

Change a command's description

To change the description of a command, double-click the command you want to re-describe and edit the description. Note the position of the ampersand in the description.

An ampersand (&) placed in front of a letter indicates that the letter is underlined when the command appears on the menu. This procedure enables you to execute shortcut commands by pressing the Alt key plus the underlined letter. To open ACT!'s Preferences dialog box, for example, all you have to do is press Alt+E+E (the command is Edit⇨Preferences).

For ACT! 2 users: Some of the familiar mnemonic commands from ACT! 2 have been changed. You can use this ACT! customization feature to regain the familiar feel of ACT! 2.

Some ACT! commands appear on the right-click menu that do not appear on the drop-down menus. If you're recording a macro that needs to execute one of these commands, you've got a problem. With the Menu Customization feature, you can add such commands to the menu bar and then record your macro.

Add a new command

To add a new command, take these steps:

1. **Select the position where you want the new command inserted.**

2. **Select the command you want to insert from the list in the Commands box.**

3. **Click the Insert button, and the command is added to the Menu.**

Add a menu or submenu heading

To add a menu or submenu heading to an ACT! menu, do the following:

1. **Select the command under which you want this new menu or submenu inserted.**

2. **Select the Insert Custom Menu button.**

   ACT! inserts a new menu or submenu command beneath it.

3. **Give the command a name.**

4. **Add any additional submenu or sub-submenu commands beneath this command as desired.**

You can also alter your ACT! menus in the following ways:

- ✔ **Insert a line:** To add a line between menu commands, select the command under which you want the line inserted, click the Insert Line button, and ACT! inserts a line.

- ✔ **Delete a command:** To delete a menu command or a line, highlight the command and click the Delete button.

- ✔ **Reset your menus:** To reset your menus to their default settings, click the Reset button.

Customizing Keyboard Shortcuts

To customize ACT!'s keyboard shortcuts, click the Keyboard tab. From the Keyboard tab you can add, delete, and modify the shortcut keys that activate ACT! commands.

After selecting the window whose keyboard shortcuts you want to customize, you can do the following.

Change a keystroke combination

To change the keystroke combination for a keyboard shortcut, follow these steps:

1. **Double-click a command, and its current keyboard shortcut appears in the Shortcut-key field.**

2. **Press the keys you want the new keystroke combination to be, then click the Insert button.**

You can select the Ctrl, Shift, and Alt keys (including all three keys) in combination with any other key.

If you're selecting a keystroke combination that is already assigned as the keyboard shortcut for another command, the Insert button becomes the Replace button. Click Replace, and a message box appears, warning you that you're about to replace an existing keyboard shortcut. If that is your intention, click Yes and ACT! assigns the new keystroke combination as the keyboard shortcut for the selected command.

Add a new keyboard shortcut

This is how you add a new keyboard shortcut to your keyboard:

1. **Select a command from the list of commands in the Commands box.**

2. **Press the keys on the keyboard to select a new keystroke combination.**

3. **Click the Insert button.**

   If the keystroke combination has already been assigned, the Replace button appears; then you have to select another keystroke combination.

Delete a keyboard shortcut

To delete a keyboard shortcut, highlight the command and click the Delete button.

Reset your keyboard shortcuts

To reset your keyboard shortcuts to their default settings, click the Reset button.

Creating Commands to Run Macros or Launch Other Applications

You can create custom commands to perform actions outside of ACT!. For example, you can launch another program or open a file in another application. You can also record an ACT! macro and add it as a custom command.

After you create a custom command, it's added to the list of commands displayed in the Command drop-down menu in the Toolbars, Menus, and Keyboard tabs. You can then add your new custom command to any toolbar, any menu, or to your keyboard.

To create a custom ACT! command, select the Commands tab in the Customize ACT! dialog box.

Creating a custom command

To create a custom ACT! command, do the following:

1. **Click the New button.**

   ACT! inserts Generic Custom Command in the Commands window.

   If Generic Custom Command is already displayed, you don't need to click the New button.

2. **Click the Browse button, which opens the Open dialog box.**

3. **Locate the executable file of the program you want to launch and click Open.**

   ACT! does the following:

   • Inserts the program's name in the Command name field.

   • Inserts the program's path in the Command line field.

4. **In the Start in field, enter the name of the file, if any, you want ACT! to open when it launches the program you have chosen.**

   If you don't want ACT! to open a specific file, leave this field blank.

5. **In the Description field, enter the description you want displayed when this command appears in the Commands drop-down list in the Toolbars, Menus, or Keyboard tabs.**

6. **In the Button/Tooltip Text field, enter the description you want to represent this command after it is added to the toolbar.**

7. **In the Menu Text field, enter the description you want displayed when this command is added to the menu.**

8. **Select Normal, Minimized, or Maximized in the Run drop-down list.**

9. **Click Save to save your custom command.**

Making a macro a custom ACT! command

After you've recorded an ACT! macro (which is discussed in the next section of this chapter), follow the same steps that are described in the preceding section to turn the macro into a custom ACT! command.

ACT! macros are stored in ACT! 4's Macro directory. ACT! macros all have the .MPR extension.

Other custom command features

In addition to creating a new ACT! command, you can copy it by selecting the command and choosing the Copy button.

If you don't need a custom command, select the command and choose the Delete button to remove it.

Automating Repetitive Tasks with Macros

ACT! macros can save you time and make you much more productive. So if you find yourself repeating the same series of keystrokes over and over again, record them in a macro and let ACT! execute those commands — in the same order you record them — for you.

What is a *macro?* It's sort of like the redial feature on your phone. A macro enables you to record a series of commands (keystrokes or mouse actions) so you can replay those commands without having to enter those same keystrokes or mouse actions over and over again.

Macros save me lots of time

I find ACT! macros to be huge time-savers and big productivity boosters. Let me tell you about a few of the macros I've created.

✔ **Dialing the phone:** I'm on the phone all day long, calling many different people, so I wrote an ACT! macro that dials the phone for me.

✔ **Clearing my calls:** Because I spend so much time on the phone, I recorded a macro that clears my calls.

✔ **Opening a new database:** I have several databases that I use, and I found it quite time-consuming to move from one database to another and back again, so I recorded a macro that opens each of my databases.

✔ **Transferring contacts from one database to another:** I frequently move contacts from one database to another, so I wrote a macro that transfers the current contact to a different database.

Recording a macro

To record an ACT! macro, follow these steps:

1. Select Tools⇨Record Macro or press Alt+F5.

The Record Macro dialog box appears.

2. Give the macro a name.

Enter the name you want to give the macro in the Name Macro To Record field.

3. Write a description.

In the Description field, write a brief description about what this macro does. Always write a description; otherwise, you may not remember what this macro is supposed to do.

4. Pick a recording option.

In the Recording Events field, ACT! gives you three options for recording your keystrokes or mouse actions:

- **Record Clicks and Drags (mouse events):** This option records all your mouse actions and ignores any keystrokes and commands you execute from the keyboard.

- **Record Everything:** This selection records both the ACT! commands you execute with your mouse and the keystrokes you execute from the keyboard.

• **Record Everything Except Mouse Events:** This option tells ACT! to record any keystrokes you execute from the keyboard and to ignore any commands you execute with the mouse.

My suggestion is that you execute all of your ACT! commands from the keyboard and ignore the mouse. When you execute your commands from the keyboard, you are forced to be precise as to which commands you want ACT! to perform. You can use the mouse to execute commands that you don't want recorded in your ACT! macro (the actual compiling of a report, for example), or to stop the macro itself.

Some ACT! commands are only available from the menu that appears when you right-click. If you need to use one of those commands in your macro, add the command to either the menu bar or a keyboard short-cut. Then record your macro. (Adding commands to the menu bar and keyboard is discussed earlier in this chapter.)

To bring up the right mouse button menu, press Shift+F10. To select an item from the menu, just press the key that matches the underlined letter.

5. **Click the Record button.**

The Record Macro dialog box disappears, and you return to the ACT! window.

6. **Record your macro.**

Execute the series of keystrokes and/or mouse actions you want to record in your macro in the precise order you want ACT! to play them back.

7. **Stop the recording of your macro.**

After completing all the keystrokes or mouse actions of your macro, press Alt+F5 to stop the recording of your macro. You can also select Tools⇔Stop Recording Macro.

To stop the recording of an ACT! macro from almost anywhere within ACT!, press Alt+F5. For example, you can activate a pull-down menu and stop the macro while the menu is still displayed. And you can bring up an ACT! dialog box and stop the macro so that you can make your selection manually from the dialog box. (You cannot pause an ACT! macro and then continue recording the macro.)

After you start recording an ACT! macro, ACT! does not have any sort of indicator to remind you that you are in the process of recording a macro. (I hope that Symantec adds such a feature in the future.) The only way you can be sure that the macro recorder is off is to press Alt+F5. If the Record Macro dialog box appears, then you aren't recording a macro.

The secret of the Tab key, the space bar, and the OK button

In many of the ACT! dialog boxes, you must click an OK button to tell ACT! that you've made your selections and you want ACT! to continue doing something. An example would be the Run Report dialog box, where you need to click OK before ACT! can create a report.

The following steps show you how to record a macro involving an ACT! dialog box.

1. **Make your dialog box selections by using the Alt+underlined letter keys.**

2. **After you've made your selections, use the Tab key to move the cursor to the OK button.**

   You know the OK button is highlighted when the letters OK are surrounded by a dotted box.

3. **Press the space bar (not the Enter key).**

   This, in effect, selects the OK button and ACT! continues doing whatever it's supposed to do.

If you press Enter instead of using the Tab key to tab over to the OK button, the macro may stop. (I don't know why this happens, so I can't explain it to you.)

When you run your macro, ACT! opens the dialog box, makes the selections that you chose with the Alt+underlined letter keys, tabs over to the OK button, and continues along to the next macro command.

Practice your keystrokes. ACT! macros can't be edited, so you are best off thinking through exactly what you want your macro to do. Before you record your macro, walk yourself through each step of the macro so that you can identify every command you want the macro to execute. You may even want to write these steps down.

Once you begin recording a macro, every action you make is recorded, including the mistakes you make — and their corrections — until you stop recording the macro.

Running your macros

The easiest way to run an ACT! macro is to assign the macro to an icon, a menu item, or a keyboard shortcut.

You can also assign macros to field triggers, so that when you enter or exit an ACT! field, ACT! runs the a specific macro. Turning a field into a Trigger field is discussed in Chapter 6.

Troubleshooting macros

If your macro isn't running properly, you can run it at the recorded speed, not the playback speed, to troubleshoot it. The following steps show you how.

1. **Select Tools⇨Run Macro.**

   The Run Macro dialog box appears.

2. **Scroll through the list of macros displayed in the Macros field.**

   Each macro's description is shown in the Description field.

3. **Select the macro you want to run.**

4. **Select the Run at Recorded Speed option to play your macro at the same speed you used to record it.**

   If your macro isn't working properly, this selection enables you to see exactly what went wrong.

5. **Click OK.**

Customizing ACT!s Windows and Tabs

As you use ACT!, you may find you want to customize its look. In each window and tab, you can change the color, size, and style of the font, as well as the color of the window's or tab's background. You make these changes in the Colors and Fonts tab of the Preference dialog box. Open the Preferences dialog box by selecting the Preferences command from the Edit menu.

From the Colors and Fonts tab you can do the following to an ACT! window or tab:

✔ Change the font, style, size, and color.

✔ Change the background color.

✔ Display or hide the grid lines for the Contact List and Task List windows, the Notes/History tab, the Activities tab, the Group tab in the Contact window, and the Contacts tab in the Group window.

Chapter 25
Database File Management

Doing Routine Database Management

This section deals with the basic day-to-day stuff that you do with an ACT! database.

Opening a database

To open an ACT! database, select File⇨Open or press Ctrl+O, and the Open File dialog box appears. Highlight the database file you want to open, click OK, and ACT! opens the new database.

Closing a database

To close an ACT! database, select File⇨Close, press Ctrl+W, or Alt+F4, and ACT! closes your database.

If you have an automatic backup system, closing your ACT! database before the backup begins is a good idea. The backup program may not be able to open and copy your ACT! database files if the database is open.

Deleting a database

To delete a database from your computer, select File➪Administration➪ Delete Database, highlight the database you want to delete, and an ACT! message box asks you, Are you sure you want to delete this database? Click Yes, and ACT! deletes the database. Click No, and ACT! cancels the deletion. (If the database has a password, you must enter the password before ACT! deletes the database.)

Deleting a database deletes all the contacts within your ACT! database. After a database is deleted, all of its contact information is gone.

Creating a new database

ACT! offers you two ways to create a new database. You can select the File➪New command, or you can use the File➪Save Copy As command.

Using the New command

When you want to create a brand-new ACT! database, this is how you do it:

1. **Select File➪New or press Ctrl+N.**

   The New dialog box appears.

2. **Select the ACT! Database option and click OK.**

   The New Database dialog box appears.

3. **Give your new database a name and click Save.**

   ACT! begins to create the new database, and the Enter "My Record" Information dialog box opens.

4. **Make any changes to the My Record information and click OK.**

   ACT! creates the new database.

ACT! takes the My Record information (name, address, phone, and so on) from the database that is open at the time the new database is created. The My Record contact record contains information about the user of the database. (In a shared database, the My Record contact record belongs to the currently logged on user.) The name and address information in My Record appears in letters, memos, faxes, and reports, identifying the creator of these documents.

If you want to assign a password to a database, open the Set Password dialog box by selecting File➪Administration➪Set Password.

Using the Save Copy As command

When you want to make a copy of your ACT! database, use the Save Copy As command in the File menu. With this command, you can make a copy of your entire database or create an empty database.

After you choose the Save Copy As command, a message box appears that asks whether you want to copy the entire database or create an empty copy.

You're also given the choice of saving this database in the ACT! 3 or ACT! 4 format.

If you're sharing this database with an ACT! 3 user, you don't select the Save Copy in ACT! 4 Format option. The only difference between the two formats is that you can add the company and telephone number as columns in the Task List in the ACT! 4 format.

Select the Copy Database command and click OK. The Save As dialog box appears. Here, you give the database a name and tell ACT! in which directory you want to save it.

Click Save and ACT! makes a copy of all the files that make up the database.

The Save Copy As command can be useful when you want to back up your database to another directory or onto a different disk or hard drive.

You use the Create Empty Copy option to copy all your custom ACT! field settings so that you (or another ACT! user) can use them in another database. (Of course, you have to import or key in the contact records into this new database.)

Exporting contact and group records to a new database

When you want to take a group of ACT! contacts that are in one database and copy the contact records into a new ACT! database, follow these steps:

1. **Select File➪Data Exchange➪Export.**

   The Export Wizard appears.

2. **From the Export Wizard, select ACT! (*4.0.dbf) as the file type.**

3. **Click the Filename and Location Browse button, which opens the Save As dialog box.**

4. **Give the new database a name and click Save.**

   You return to the Export Wizard.

5. Click the Next button.

The Wizard asks, `What kind of records do you want to export?`
You have the following choices:

- Contact Records Only

- Group Records Only

- Contact and Group Record

6. Make your choice and click the Next button.

The Wizard asks, `Which contact or group records do you want to export?`

If you selected the Contact Records Only option, you can choose from the Current Contact, the Current Lookup, or All Records.

If you selected Group Records Only or Contact and Group Records, your only choice is All Records.

7. Click the Next button.

The Import Wizard's Contact Map appears (see Figure 25-1). The Contact Map is only available if you selected Contact Records Only or Contact and Group Records in Step 5.

Figure 25-1:
The Import
Wizard's
Contact
Map.

8. Map the contact fields of the database that is being imported with the database that is open.

Mapping ACT! fields is discussed later in this chapter.

9. Click the Next button.

The Import Wizard's Group Map appears. (The Group Map is only available if you selected Group Records Only or Contact and Group Records in Step 5.)

10. Map the group fields of the database that is being imported with the database that is open.

11. Click the Finish button to create your new ACT! database.

Saving a database as a delimited (.TXT) file

If you want to copy your ACT! database for use in another program, you can save it as a delimited file. A *delimited file* is a word processing file that has special codes, called *delimiters,* that separate the individual fields. There are two types of delimited files: tab and comma.

✔ **Tab delimited:** A tab stop indicates the beginning of a new field; that is, the fields are laid out in spreadsheet form.

✔ **Comma delimited:** All the fields are enclosed in quotation marks and separated by a comma.

This is how you create a delimited file:

1. **Select File⇨Data Exchange⇨Export.**

   The Export Wizard appears.

2. **From the Export Wizard, select Text - Delimited as the file type.**

3. **Click the Filename and Location Browse button, which opens the Save As dialog box.**

4. **Give the new database a name (and path, if desired) and click Save.**

   You return to the Wizard, and ACT! inserts the file's path in the Wizard's Filename and Location box.

   Note that the file must have a .TXT extension.

5. **Click the Next button.**

   The Wizard asks: What kind of records do you want to export? You can choose one of these:

   • Contact Records Only

   • Group Records Only

6. **Click the Options button to view additional export options.**

   The Export Options dialog box appears in which you select your field separators — comma or tab — and whether you want to export the database's field names.

7. **Make your export option selections and click OK.**

   You return to the Export Wizard.

8. Click the Next button.

The Wizard asks, `Which contact or group records do you want to export?`

If you selected the Contact Records Only option, you can choose from the Current Contact, the Current Lookup, or All Records.

If you selected Group Records Only, your only choice is All Records.

9. Click the Finish button to create your delimited (.TXT) file.

Merging Databases

When you want to import the contacts from one database (the *source*) with the contacts in the currently open database (the *destination*), use ACT!'s Import command. Here's how:

1. Select File⇨Data Exchange⇨Import.

The Import Wizard appears.

2. Select ACT! 3.0 or 4.0 (.dbf) as the type of file you want to import.

3. Click the Filename and Location Browse button.

The Open dialog box appears.

4. Select the ACT! database you want to import into the currently open database and click Open.

You return to the Import Wizard.

5. Click the Next button.

The Wizard asks: `What kind of records do you want to import?` You can choose

- Contact Records Only

- Group Records Only

- Contact and Group Records

6. Click the Options button to access additional options.

The Merge Options dialog box appears (see Figure 25-2), in which you tell ACT! what you want it to do when it finds contact records that do, or do not, match during the merge process. (ACT!'s merge options are discussed in the following section.)

7. Make your selections and click OK.

You return to the Import Wizard.

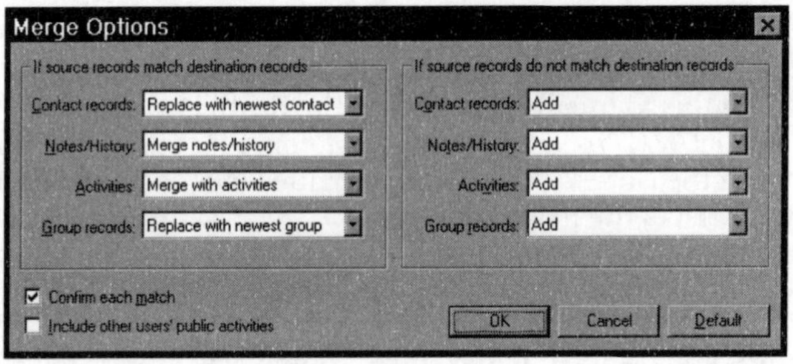

Figure 25-2:
The Merge
Options
dialog box.

8. **Click the Next button.**

   The Import Wizard's Contact Map appears (refer to Figure 25-1). (The Contact Map is only available if you selected Contact Records Only or Contact and Group Records in Step 5.)

9. **Map the contact fields of the database being imported with the open database.**

   Mapping ACT! fields is discussed after the section on merge options.

10. **Click the Next button.**

    The Import Wizard's Group Map appears. (The Group Map is only available if you selected Group Records Only or Contact and Group Records in Step 5.)

11. **Map the group fields of the database being imported with the database that is open.**

12. **Click the Finish button.**

    ACT! merges the source database into the destination database.

Setting merge options

From ACT!'s Merge Options dialog box you tell ACT! what to do when it finds contact records that match or do not match during the merge process. The Merge Options dialog box is shown in Figure 25-2.

Dealing with unique IDs

In the Merge Options dialog box, you select the data you want to merge from the source database with the destination database. Contacts are always merged on the basis of their unique IDs. The *unique ID* is an invisible ID number that ACT! stamps on each contact record. ACT! assigns this number when you create or import a contact from one database to another database.

Using the default settings

The default settings should work just fine for the majority of your database merges. When the source records match the destination records, the default settings instruct ACT! to select the newest contact record, and it merges the information in the Notes/History and Activities files together. If the groups match, ACT! selects the newest group.

If the two sets of contact criteria do not match, ACT! adds the contact as a new contact record to the destination database, along with the contact's notes/history items and activities. If ACT! finds new groups, ACT! adds them to the destination database. Here are some things to keep in mind:

✔ Because merging has the potential to overwrite contact data, you should back up your destination database before choosing the Merge command. During the merge process, you can only alter the destination database. Backing up the source database is not necessary.

✔ Before you merge an ACT! database, compress and reindex both databases so that all the deleted contacts have been swapped out. This way, you have the newest and freshest indexes available, and you'll complete your merge in half the time.

✔ If you want to clean up an ACT! database that has a number of duplicate records in it, create a new database and merge the old database into the new one. The first time ACT! encounters a contact record, ACT! enters the contact record into the new database. The second time ACT! encounters a contact record with the same secondary-match criteria, it merges the two contact records together.

ACT! uses primary and secondary merge criteria to determine when contact records match. The default merge criteria for Contact records are Company, Contact, and Phone. The default merge criteria for Group records are Group Name and Record Creator. You can change your merge criteria by selecting the Advanced tab in the Define Fields dialog box and changing the duplicate matching fields. (You open the Define Fields dialog box by selecting Edit⇨Define Fields.) Checking your ACT! database for duplicate records is covered in Chapter 26.

✔ The date that you merge a contact record into an ACT! database is recorded in the Merge Date field on the Status tab.

Doing custom merges

When you perform a custom merge, the merge options you select in the fields of the Merge Options dialog box determine what ACT! will do when it finds contact records from the source database that match those in the destination database.

Matching contact records

When the contact records in the source database match those of the destination database, you have the following choices regarding what ACT! will do with the information in the contact's record:

✔ **Replace with newest contact:** ACT! compares the Edit Dates of each contact record in the source and destination database to determine the newest contact record. If the contact record in the source database is newer, ACT! uses that contact information.

✔ **Replace with source contact:** ACT! replaces the contact information in the destination database with the contact information from the source database, regardless of which contact record is the newest.

✔ **Do not change:** ACT! makes no changes to the information contact fields of the destination database.

Matching Notes/History files

If the contact records in the source database match those in the destination database, you have the following choices for notes/history items:

✔ **Merge Notes/History:** ACT! adds new notes/history items to the contact's Notes/History file in the destination database and updates matching entries with the latest information.

✔ **Replace with source notes/history:** ACT! replaces the contact's notes/history items that are in the destination database with those that are in the source database.

✔ **Do not change:** ACT! makes no changes to the notes/history items that are in the destination database.

Matching schedules

When the contact records in the source database match those of the destination database, you have the following choices regarding the contact's scheduled activities:

✔ **Merge activities:** ACT! adds new activities to the destination database's contact record. (You can also reconcile cleared activities, provided that you select the Merge History option.)

✔ **Replace with source activities:** ACT! replaces the contact's scheduled activities in the destination database with the contact's scheduled activities that are in the source database.

 ✔ **Do not change:** ACT! makes no changes to the contact's scheduled activities in the destination database.

Matching Group Records

If the Group Records in the source database match those of the destination database, you have the following choices:

 ✔ **Replace with newest group:** ACT! compares the Edit Date of the Group Records in the source and destination databases. If the Group Record in the source database is newer, ACT! uses that group information.

 ✔ **Replace with source group:** ACT! replaces the Group Record in the destination database with the Group Record from the source database, regardless of which group record is the newest.

 ✔ **Do not change:** ACT! makes no changes to the Group Records of the destination database.

Dealing with non-matching contact records

When you perform a custom merge, the merge options that you select in the fields of the Merge Options dialog box determines what ACT! will do when it finds contact records from the source database that do not match those in the destination database.

If a contact record in the source database does not match any of the contact records in the destination database — this means that it's a new record — you have to decide what ACT! will do with the contact records, notes/history, activities, and group records. You can have ACT! add them to the destination database, or you can have ACT! not add them to the destination database.

Confirming each match

If you want ACT! to confirm each match, select the Confirm Each Match box. When ACT! finds a match, the Confirm Merge dialog box appears, and you can look at the contact's basic information. If you want to accept the merge, click the Merge button. If you don't, click the Skip button, and ACT! moves on to the next current record; otherwise, ACT! makes the changes automatically.

Including public activities

If you want to include all public activities, select the Include Other User's Public Activities option.

Mapping your Contact and Group fields

When you import one ACT! database into another, you want to make sure that everything ends up in the right place, so you use the Import Wizard's Contact Map and Group Map. The process that I'm describing is identical for both the Contact Map and the Group Map. (The Contact Map is shown in Figure 25-1.)

Mapping, in this instance, is the process of matching the fields of the source database with those of the destination database, which ensures that everything ends up in the right place.

You can map any field in the source database to any field in the destination database. You can also exclude any field you want from the merge process.

The Contact Map dialog box displays the contents of each field of the source database, and it enables you to map, or match, each of those fields to the appropriate field in the destination database.

To map the imported fields with the appropriate ACT! fields, choose a field in the Map This Field column and then select the field that you want to map it to from the drop-down list in the To This Field column. You then work your way through the list of fields that you're importing into ACT!, one field at a time, and determine which field you want to map the imported field to. If you don't want to import a particular field into ACT!, you can exclude that field by choosing the Do Not Map selection from the drop-down menu, which leaves the field blank.

Viewing the contacts information

After mapping the fields of your first contact, click the View Next Record button to view the contact information of the next contact in the source database. Viewing the records of several contacts helps you determine how the imported fields should be mapped to the destination database's corresponding fields. To view the previous contact's information, click the View Previous Record button.

Continue this process until all the fields from the source database have been mapped to the correct fields in the destination database (or have been excluded from the importing process).

If the data in a source database's field is larger or longer than the field in the destination database you are mapping it to, ACT! truncates the data.

Saving your map settings

After you've mapped your data, you can save your map settings by clicking the Contact Map's Save Map button. Saving your map settings enables you to use the settings again if you need to merge information from the same source into one of your ACT! databases.

Using your map settings

When you want to apply one of your previously saved map settings, click the Contact Map's Load Map button and select the setting that you want to use from the list that appears in the Open dialog box. Then click OK.

Sharing Information through Data Synchronization

If you are frequently away from your office, you can easily share contact information with your coworkers. ACT! 4 includes a data synchronization feature that enables you to exchange information with other ACT! 4 users so that the contacts in your database match the contacts in the other user's database. This is what database synchronization does:

- ✔ Database synchronization consolidates the changes you make to your database and creates a file containing these changes. The update file is then attached to an e-mail message and is either sent to a shared folder or directly synchronized with another database.

- ✔ Synchronization enables you to receive updates that have been sent to you from another user.

- ✔ Synchronization works on a field-by-field basis, with the latest change taking effect. It merges contact data and compares the fields to determine which data is the most recent.

- ✔ Synchronization merges a contact's notes/history items and activities.

Synchronization ensures that you and your colleagues have the most up-to-date information about all your contacts and groups of contacts, including their notes, histories, and activities. And even if you don't need to share data with other ACT! users, you may need to synchronize data between a laptop and a desktop computer.

Data synchronization is a very powerful feature. It is, however, beyond the scope of this book. (In fact, an entire ...*For Dummies* book could be written about how to perform database synchronization.) I suggest that you contact an ACT! Certified Consultant (ACC) and have him or her help you set up and design a synchronization program. See Chapter 27 for information on finding an ACT! Certified Consultant.

You can also get information about ACT! Certified Consultants on Symantec's ACT! Web site at www.symantec.com/act.

Backing Up Your ACT! Database

ACT! has two ways for you to back up your database:

- ✔ Zipping up your database, or
- ✔ Using Connected Online Backup

Zipping up your ACT! database

ACT! makes it easy to back up your database to a floppy disk or another directory on your hard drive or your network. This is how you do it:

1. **Select File⇨Backup⇨Standard from the menu bar.**

   The Backup dialog box opens.

2. **Select the directory in which you want to save the database.**

3. **Click the Options tab to select which additional files you want to include with this backup.**

4. **Click Start to start the backup process.**

Using Connected Online Backup

Connected Online Backup is a third-party product that enables you to back up your files over the Internet. The backup software is included on the ACT! 4 CD-ROM. To access Connected Online Backup from within ACT!, select File⇨Backup⇨Using Connected Online Backup. After you install your software on your computer, you must register with Connected Online Backup. After a free-trial period you pay a charge for this backup service.

Restoring your ACT! database

This is how you restore a database you've backed up:

1. **Select File➪Restore➪Standard from the menu bar.**

   The Restore dialog box opens.

2. **Select the file you want to restore and the folder in which you want to restore it.**

3. **Click the Start button.**

   ACT! restores your files and places the database, envelopes, labels, layouts, and reports in the appropriate file.

Part VII
The Part of Tens

The 5th Wave   By Rich Tennant

ANAGRAM
COMMUNICATIONS

O HELL...

In this part . . .

Every *...For Dummies* book ends with lists of ten items. It's tradition. (According to my publisher, it's the law.) Well, I still want to present you with meaty information that you can use rather than a bunch of lists. True, the next few chapters each have at least ten tidbits of information in them, but some of the chapters aren't arranged as easy-to-read lists. I prefer to use my own hard-to-follow prose.

Chapter 26

At Least Ten Database Maintenance Tips

In This Chapter

▶ Working with the Database Maintenance dialog box

▶ Deleting duplicates

▶ Administering a multi-user database (the bare minimum)

Keeping Your Databases in Tip-Top Shape

You must maintain — compress and reindex — your ACT! databases if you want them to work properly. I can give you two reasons:

✔ Whenever you delete a contact from your database, the disk space holding that deleted contact is not usable; it becomes fragmented. When you compress your database, you remove the wasted space that's inside your database. If you've deleted a substantial number of contacts, you have a great deal of wasted space inside your database, which causes ACT! to slow down.

✔ You want to make sure that ACT!'s indexes are working properly; otherwise, ACT! may begin to have some difficulty locating contact records. The process of fixing ACT!'s indexes is called reindexing.

To perform maintenance on your database, choose File⇨Administration⇨ Database Maintenance. The Database Maintenance dialog box appears. From the Maintenance dialog box, ACT! gives you a number of reindexing options:

✔ **Do not reindex:** When you choose this option, ACT! doesn't reindex or compress the database. When you select this option, you can still purge information from your notes, history, attachments, transaction logs, or cleared activities.

✔ **Reindex database:** When you choose the Reindex Database option, ACT! reindexes the database. When you reindex a database, the Reindexing Databases progress gauge appears to keep you apprised of the status.

✔ **Compress and reindex database:** When you select this option, ACT! both compresses and reindexes your database. After the process begins, a series of progress messages appears. Depending on the size of the database, compressing can take several minutes. I suggest that you compress your database at least once per week.

✔ **Purge Notes, Histories, Attachments:** While you're performing your database maintenance, you can remove part or all your notes, history, or attachments. When you select any of the Purge Notes, Purge Histories, or Purge Attachments check boxes and click OK, a calendar appears. Choose a date or range of dates, click OK, and ACT! deletes from the database the selected items for the active lookup for the specified range of dates.

✔ **Purge Transaction log:** The Purge Transaction Log option enables you to delete synchronization transaction log entries that were created prior to a specific date. Database synchronization is covered briefly in Chapter 25.

✔ **Purge Cleared activities:** The Purge Cleared Activities option enables you to delete activities that you cleared prior to a specific date.

After you make your choices in the Database Maintenance dialog box, click OK, and a series of progress messages about compressing the database or reindexing the database appears.

Never interrupt ACT! while it is compressing or reindexing your database because you can cause considerable damage to your database.

Every once in a while, you may find that the index within one of your databases has become so damaged that you're unable to open the database. (A message appears telling you that you need to reindex your database.) If this happens, you can reindex a damaged database from an empty ACT! screen. Close all your ACT! databases and then select File⊅Administration⊅ Database Maintenance. The Open dialog box appears. Select the database that you want to reindex, click Open, and the Database Maintenance dialog box appears where you make your selections.

If you're unable to open ACT! because the database that you're having trouble with is the database that ACT! opens when you launch ACT!, try this: Use the File Manager or Windows Explorer to move the database to another directory. (Remember that an ACT! database has more than 17 files.)

Clean up database problems with TroubleSpotter

A good friend of mine, Linda Keating, who is an ACT! Certified Consultant in Palo Alto, California, found that many of her clients were having reindexing problems. So she developed a product called TroubleSpotter.

TroubleSpotter searches your ACT! database for all sorts of nasty stuff: characters in date fields, invalid pointers to note formatting records, duplicate Unique IDs, missing links in note records, and much, much more. TroubleSpotter can identify an offending record and can usually purge it from the database.

For more information on TroubleSpotter, you can call Linda at 415-323-9141. You can download a demo copy from Linda's Web site at www.jltechnical.com.

Launch ACT!. When the Startup window opens, select File⇔Administration⇔ Database Maintenance and reindex the database.

Only the database administrator can compress or reindex a shared ACT! database. The Database Maintenance command is active only when the database administrator is the only user of the database. All other users must be logged off.

An unexpected interruption of power while using an ACT! database is often the cause of database corruption. If you're not protecting your computer with a quality surge protector, you need to go out and purchase one this very moment.

What is an index?

Each time you enter contact information into ACT!, ACT! updates lists of all the contact's first names, last names, company names, phone numbers, addresses, and so on. (The fields listed on the Lookup menu are all indexed.)

When you perform a lookup, ACT! searches its lists, or indexes, for the lookup criteria, which is much faster than searching the entire database. ACT! stores these indexes in separate files in ACT!'s database directory. The following are some of ACT!'s index files:

- Activity database (.ADX extension)
- Contacts database: (.MDX extension)
- E-mail database: (.EDX extension)
- Groups database: (.GDX extension)
- History/Notes/Activities database: (.HDX extension)

Back up your ACT! database! The more you use ACT!, the more important backing up your database on a regular basis becomes. Losing data or other files can be disastrous. And the easiest way to back up your hard drives and your ACT! databases is to use an automatic backup system. (Check out Chapter 25 for more on backing up your databases.)

Getting Rid of Duplicates

When you have many contact records in your database, you may find that you have accidentally entered the same contact more than once. Now you have two or more records for the same person. With ACT!'s Scan for Duplicates command, you can scan your database for duplicate contact or group records. When ACT! finds duplicates, you decide which of the contact records to keep.

If you have useful information in a duplicate record, use the Copy and Paste commands to transfer the information to the record that you plan on keeping. You can also use the Copy and Paste commands to move notes, histories, and attachments from one contact record to another.

Setting your criteria

To set your duplicate search criteria, you must open the Advanced tab in ACT!'s Define Fields dialog box. Select Edit➪Define Fields, click the Advanced tab, and select Contact or Group as your Record Type.

The default search criteria for finding duplicate contact records are Company, Contact, and Phone. The default search criteria for finding duplicate Group records are Group Name and Record Creator. (If duplicate groups were created by two different people, the Record Creator is different, and ACT! can't locate the duplicate records.)

You can use any criteria, including the contact's first or last name.

Enabling duplicate checking for contact and group records

To enable duplicate checking, you must first select either Contact or Group as your Record type and then select the Enable Duplicate Checking option.

Scanning for duplicates

To scan your database for duplicates, select the Tools⇨Scan For Duplicates command, and ACT! creates a lookup of all the contacts that meet the selected criteria.

The Bare Minimum on Administering a Multi-User Database

You can share your ACT! database with other users, even if you're using ACT! on a stand-alone computer. You, as the administrator, can add new users to your ACT! database. You can also remove a user from your shared ACT! database. To do these tasks, select File⇨Administration⇨Define Users, and the Define Users dialog box appears. From the Users dialog box, you can add a new user or remove an existing user.

That's really all I ought to say about this topic, as anything more would be beyond the scope of this ...*For Dummies* book. I'm assuming that the typical ACT! user isn't the administrator of a shared database.

However, here are some additional sources for database administration information:

✔ **ACT! Administrators Guide:** The ACT! Administrators Guide includes information that helps you set up, administer, and maintain ACT! databases for multiple users on a network. It also contains information about sharing and synchronizing data.

   The guide is included as part of the ACT! 4 CD-ROM. Its name is ACTADMIN.PDF, and it's located in the ACTDOCS folder.

✔ **ACT! Users Guide:** The ACT! Users Guide, which is also on the ACT! 4 CD-ROM has a whole chapter on Database Administration. Its name is ACT40.PDF, and it's located in the ACTDOCS folder.

✔ **The Knowledge Base on ACT!'s Web site:** On the ACT! home page, www.symantec.com/act, you can find a great deal of information about database administration by visiting the Knowledge Base, a collection of written articles that can answer your technical questions.

Chapter 27

More Than Ten Technical Resources

● ●

In This Chapter

▶ ACT! telephone support

▶ ACT! Certified Consultants

▶ ACT! user groups

● ●

*1*f you have a technical problem, contact ACT! technical support.

If you want to have someone help you set up your ACT! database, or show you how to administer it, or just help you discover how to get the most out of ACT!, then you need to call an ACT! Certified Consultant. They're trained to solve ACT! problems.

ACT! user groups meet on a regular basis and offer tips, tricks, and advice on how to work with ACT! to save time and make more money.

ACT! Telephone Support

Symantec offers a number of different telephone support packages. For more information about these different support packages, and their costs, you can call Symantec customer service at 800-984-2475 or visit the ACT! Web page at www.symantec.com/act and select the Technical Support link. On the ACT! Technical Support page, select the Telephone Support link, which takes you to the ACT! Telephone Support page.

The following is a brief description of the different types of ACT! technical support that is available.

Standard Care

Standard Care support, available by calling 541-465-8645, is free for all registered users for 90 days from the date of their first call.

Priority Care

Priority Care offers two access options that guarantee faster service:

- ✔ **Per Incident Fee:** If you have an in-depth problem, this is a good option for receiving technical support. The phone number for this service is 800-927-3989.
- ✔ **Per Minute Fee:** If you have a quick question, use this technical support service. The phone number for this service is 900-646-0001.

Gold Care Support

Gold Care is a membership program offering ongoing priority support for you or your small company.

Gold Care provides cost-effective support programs for customers who need ongoing technical support. You can select the level of Gold Care that meets your needs and receive priority support on a toll-free 800 number with a minimal hold time.

Call Customer Service at 800-441-7234 to become a member and receive these benefits:

- ✔ Priority support on a toll-free 800 number
- ✔ Average hold times of three minutes or less
- ✔ Support hours from 6:00 a.m. to 5:00 p.m. Pacific Time; 9:00 a.m. to 8:00 p.m. Eastern Time

Platinum Support

Platinum Care is the corporate solution. Platinum Care customers receive unlimited use of a toll-free 800 number and access to the Platinum Web site.

Platinum Support gives corporate customers all the features they need to be successful: unlimited toll-free calls, extended hours of operation, and access to the most senior technical analysts. In addition, you receive quarterly updates of your software, detailed "inside information," and much more.

ACT! Certified Consultants

ACT! Certified Consultants (ACCs) are trained individuals who set up and design ACT! databases to meet the specific needs of ACT! users. They offer a variety of services:

- **Training:** Many ACCs offer individual and group training. Classes range from introductory to advanced. Some ACCs can customize their courseware to meet your needs.

- **Network installation and configuration:** Setting up ACT! on a network can be an involved task. You need to explore different user options and to take into account your organization's objectives. An ACC can provide a needs analysis before proceeding with this implementation.

- **Data conversion:** Often times, data needs to be converted and manipulated before being brought into ACT!. ACCs have a great deal of experience in a variety of data conversion situations.

- **Consulting:** An ACC consulting service can offer you a great deal of information, depending upon your needs and requirements.

In addition, Symantec provides ACT! Certified Consultants with the latest information regarding Symantec's products and keeps them informed about other software products that integrate with ACT!.

Unfortunately, I can't provide you with a list of all the ACCs. Their ranks are constantly growing and changing. But I can point you in the right direction. For an up-to-date list of all the ACT! Certified Consultants worldwide, visit Symantec's Web site at www.symantec.com/act.

You can also call Symantec Customer Service at 800-441-7234 (United States and Canada). Finally, you can obtain the current list of ACCs from Symantec's Fax on Demand service, whose 24-hour number is 541-984-2475.

I would like to thank Rich Spitz, an ACT! Certified Consultant in Mamaroneck, New York, for his help in explaining all the things that an ACT! Certified Consultant does. If you need a good ACT! Certified Consultant, you can reach Rich at 914-698-7410.

If you need to reach ACT! Technical Support, call 541-465-8645.

ACT! User Groups

Table 27-1 lists ACT! user groups that ACT! enthusiasts or ACT! Certified Consultants support. These ACT! user groups exist for the benefit of ACT! users of all types who attend the meetings: small business owners, ACT! users who work in large organizations, and resellers of computer- or software-related products.

Most user groups meet monthly and attract anywhere from 25 to 75 ACT! users who come to exchange tips and tricks, see new products, and find out how to use ACT! better. Some groups sponsor special event meetings once or twice per year in which they can attract 200 to 250 ACT! users who come to see new versions of ACT! or hear ACT! insiders talk about where ACT! is going in the future.

The best way to get more out of using ACT! is to share your experiences with other users. If you can't find an ACT! user group in your community. Why not think about starting one yourself?

Table 27-1	ACT! User Groups	
City	*Contact*	*Phone No.*
Boston, MA	Stephen Del Grosso	888-848-2658
Charlotte, NC	Andy Kaplan	704-593-1997
Chicago, IL	Alan Lee	847-619-2000
Houston, TX	Robert Malone	713-461-3096
Indianapolis, IN	Art Russ	317-843-0186
Miami, FL	Nathan Schor	305-895-6417
Minneapolis, MN	David Sunnarborg	612-789-7053
San Francisco, CA	Linda Keating	650-323-9141
Stamford, CT	Andy Kaplan	203-328-3720

Index

(continued)

(continued)